The Economics of Heritage

The Economics of Heritage

A Study in the Political Economy of Culture in Sicily

Edited by

Ilde Rizzo

University of Catania, Italy

and

Ruth Towse

Erasmus University, Rotterdam, The Netherlands

Edward Elgar
Cheltenham, UK • Northampton, MA, USA

Published by
Edward Elgar Publishing Limited
Glensanda House
Montpellier Parade
Cheltenham
Glos GL50 1UA
UK

Edward Elgar Publishing, Inc.
136 West Street
Suite 202
Northampton
Massachusetts 01060
USA

A catalogue record for this book
is available from the British Library

Library of Congress Cataloguing in Publication Data

The economics of heritage : a study in the political economy of culture in Sicily / edited by Ilde Rizzo and Ruth Towse.
   p . c m
Includes index.
   1. Cultural property—Economic aspects—Italy—Sicily. 2. Culture—Economic aspects—Italy—Sicily. 3. Culture—Political aspects—Italy—Sicily. 4. Sicily (Italy)—Cultural policy. 5. Politics and culture—Italy—Sicily. I. Title: Study in the political economy of culture in Sicily. II. Rizzo, Ilde. III. Towse, Ruth, 1943-

DG865.6 .E36 2002   2002021259

ISBN 1 84376 041 X
Printed and bound in Great Britain by MPG Books Ltd, Bodmin, Cornwall

Contents

PART III DEMAND FOR HERITAGE

PART IV COMPARATIVE PERSPECTIVES

Figures

Tables

Contributors

Françoise Benhamou: Professor of Economics, Rouen University and MATISSE, Paris I, University.

Maurizio Caserta: Associate Professor of Economics, University of Catania.

Annalisa Cicerchia: Researcher, Institute of Applied Economics (ISAE), Rome.

Salvo Creaco: Associate Professor of Environmental Economics, University of Catania.

Tiziana Cuccia: Lecturer in Cultural Economics, University of Catania.

(Sir) Gerald Elliot: Retired industrialist, former chairman of the Scottish Arts Council and board member of museum and heritage bodies.

Isidoro Mazza: Associate Professor of Public Economics, University of Catania.

Anna Mignosa: Junior Researcher, University of Catania, Erasmus University, Rotterdam.

Giovanni Montemagno: Associate Professor of Regional Economics, University of Catania.

Maria Musumeci: Associate Professor of Economics, University of Catania.

Giacomo Pignataro: Associate Professor of Industrial Economics, University of Catania.

Ilde Rizzo: Professor of Public Economics, University of Catania.

Giovanni Signorello: Associate Professor of Resource Valuation and Environmental Economics, University of Catania.

Ruth Towse: Senior Lecturer in Cultural Industries, Erasmus University, Rotterdam.

Glossary of Italian Terms

- Ministero per i Beni e le Attività Culturali = Ministry of Heritage and Culture.
- Assessorato Regionale dei Beni Culturali Ambientali e della Pubblica Istruzione (plural: Assessorati) = Sicilian Regional Office for Culture and Education.
- Assessore dei Beni Culturali = Regional Officer for Culture.
- Assessorato Regionale Bilancio e Finanze = Sicilian Regional Finance Office.
- Soprintendenza (plural: Soprintendenze) = Provincial Boards for Culture.
- Soprintendente (plural: Soprintendenti) = Provincial Director for Culture.

Preface

This book is part of the research programme of cultural economics which is being carried out by a group of scholars within the Department of Economics and Quantitative Methods of the University of Catania. The department is a member of the University's Research Centre on the Causes of Decay and the Enhancement of Cultural and Monumental Goods.

So far, there have been a number of research and educational projects in the subject, in collaboration with many national and international academic institutions. Among them, are two innovative research projects that are being undertaken with Italian research institutions. The first, with the National Research Council, is 'Theoretical and organisational aspects of cultural goods conservation' and the second one, funded by the Ministry of Scientific and Technological Research, is 'Organisational analysis and training on conservation, management and use of architectural heritage'. Both are co-ordinated by Ilde Rizzo and are included in a wider research project entitled: 'The enhancement of architectural heritage in East Sicily: the architectural urban emergency and rural development. Knowledge, interventions and training', which was initiated by the Research Centre on the Causes of Decay and the Enhancement of Cultural and Monumental Goods at the University of Catania.

The chapters in this book were first presented at a workshop held in Catania, Sicily from 11 to 13 November 1999. The conference was made possible by the University of Catania. We are grateful to *Domenico Sanfilippo Editore* who kindly gave permission to reproduce the old map on the cover. We acknowledge the Italian Research Council for its financial support (nos 96.03896.CT15, 97.04684.CT15 and 98.03435.PS15). Most of the technical preparation has been done by Leonardo Mercatanti and Giuseppina Santagati, Catania. Language-editing was done by Mairi-Claire Hamill, Palermo.

ILDE RIZZO
RUTH TOWSE

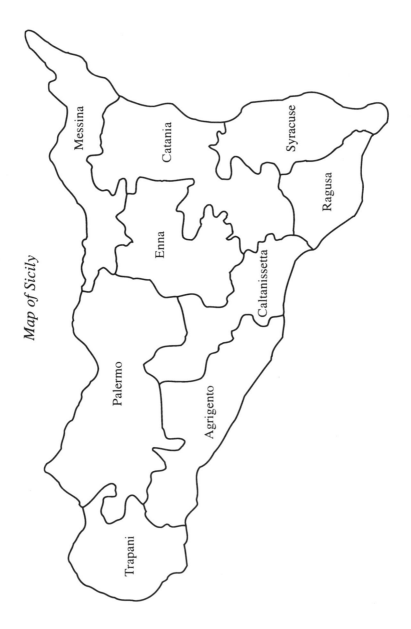

Map of Sicily

Messina

Catania

Syracuse

Ragusa

Enna

Caltanissetta

Palermo

Agrigento

Trapani

PART I

Institutions

1. The Cultural Economy of Heritage

Ruth Towse

1. INTRODUCTION

The economics of heritage is by now a well-established area of investigation in cultural economics with a literature on the economics of museums, on markets for art and collectibles and on the economic aspects of the built heritage. The term 'built heritage' is used in a general sense to include all manmade structures, ranging from archaeological remains to individual buildings and cities of historical and artistic significance. This book concentrates on two features of heritage in Sicily – the built heritage and museums. Sicily has a rich heritage of both: a wealth of archaeological sites and buildings from Ancient Greek, Roman and Norman times, as well as perfectly intact Baroque towns; and museums, which range from those containing finds from the archaeological sites to ones that reflect local interests and identities.

But this book is not only a study of the cultural economics of heritage: it is also a compilation of various approaches that economists trained in different branches of economics have brought to bear on this subject. It is a political economy of heritage policy seen from several points of view: as part of cultural economics, it is a study of the economic problems of defining and valuing cultural resources; it is an application of the theory of property rights; as a case study in the economics of regulation, it analyses incentives and principal–agent problems of heritage policy; the public choice view of fiscal federalism is applied to the devolved administration of heritage policy in Sicily as a case in point; as an exercise in microeconomics, the efficiency of museums is assessed; and the cultural heritage is also viewed as a tourist asset and analysed as part of the economics of tourism but, at the same time, it is recognised that tourism can have a negative effect on cultural value. The book is therefore a sort of Cook's Tour of applied economics.

A particular feature of heritage that has been pointed out by Peacock (1997) is that it has not intentionally been produced as a good or collection of goods but is an accretion of items produced for various purposes that have come down to us as having a deeper significance. What comes to be seen as heritage is a social and cultural construction, created and monitored by experts such as art historians, archaeologists and museum directors. This construction changes over time and with societal perceptions of what is culturally interesting and valuable. Sociologists such as Pierre Bourdieu express this as the creation of cultural symbols by 'consecration'. In the case of heritage, this is largely achieved through regulations controlled by, or at least heavily reliant upon, expert opinion. In Sicily, the heritage authorities are responsible for all aspects of heritage regulation, policy, administration and expenditure (see Chapter 2).

A seemingly inevitable result of this designation of heritage by expert regulators is that the stock of heritage items, whether built heritage or museum collections, forever increases; Benhamou gives some revealing figures on the built heritage in France (Chapter 12). The stock of heritage items can be increased by sleight of hand, for example, by designating all items over a certain age or of a certain type as part of heritage or increasing the scope of designation, say, by including new categories.[1] But although the stock of heritage is subject to regulatory control, there are also economic choices to be made on how much to invest in adding value by conservation and display; access to the stock has a supply price and so economic decisions are part and parcel with art historical ones. Allocation decisions with respect to the built heritage are further complicated by the fact that sites are geographically fixed and cannot be relocated in response to relative prices. This creates problems for visitor services and influences both the quality and quantity of services offered; no visitors or too many both present economic problems for the heritage authorities.

Heritage has strong externality and public goods characteristics and these strengthen the tendency to state finance and management. The value of heritage is therefore very difficult to measure and this presents problems for the economic evaluation of heritage policies (Throsby, 2001). Financial values are elusive. We cannot sensibly think of a market price for a Greek temple, for example, and cultural value is not expressed only in prices. But whatever the true value is, it is not infinite and there are limits to the expenditure of current resources for preserving heritage and providing associated services. There is clearly no economic or historical rule that endows rich countries with a wealth of heritage items and, indeed, the converse is often the case, with poorer countries struggling to maintain a huge cultural inheritance which may be of worldwide importance (examples are UNESCO World Heritage Sites). Sicily is the location of one of the most notable concentrations of heritage items in Europe while being historically one of its less wealthy regions. There is inevitably a relative shortage of funds from all sources (regional, national and the European Union: EU) for heritage measures and this exacerbates universal economic problems of heritage policy and management, making Sicily a particularly interesting case study.

2. REGULATION AND SUPPLIER-INDUCED DEMAND FOR HERITAGE

One of the peculiar characteristics of heritage is that it is strongly dependent upon regulation for the determination of supply. Information problems are so strong as to prevent the market from being a reliable institution for allocating resources to satisfy present and future consumption. In this respect, heritage shares the features of many other goods and services for which information about quality and standards must perforce rely on expert opinion rather than on consumers' preferences expressed via the market. Heritage is therefore a case of supplier-induced demand; as with education, health and the arts, information problems are solved by regulation, which, instead of informing consumers directly, controls the supply so that it conforms to expert-designated standards. A generous interpretation of this tendency is that it thereby informs ordinary people through their experience of the good; consumers acquire tastes through a quality-controlled experience. A less generous interpretation is that experts (art historians, architects and archaeologists in the case of heritage, doctors in the case of health and teachers in the field of education) seize control not only of the supply but also of taste formation. By so doing, experts are able to create professional enclaves, which ensure that they capture economic reward and psychic rents throughout their careers. Regulators thus have their own preference functions, which they impose on the public. This is a typical public choice issue. We see this in the case of Sicily, where experts are firmly in control of heritage policy and administration.

In accordance with the notion of supplier-induced demand, heritage regulators control the stock of heritage items and also influence demand for them (see Chapter 6). A standard means of controlling heritage supply is by legal rules that restrict the use of buildings, sites and artefacts. Heritage regulation includes a range of measures: limitation on the freedom of individual owners to exercise ordinary property rights, zoning laws (planning permission) and specific heritage measures, such as controls on appearance and repairs. Freedom to use property rights is restricted in many everyday ways (compulsory purchase of land, rights of way, compulsory licences and so on); ownership and rights are not the same thing as Benhamou (Chapter 12) points out in her application of the theory of property rights to heritage issues.

The economic analysis of property rights has alerted economists to the many rights that are typically bundled together in a specific piece of property. For example, the owner of a dwelling house has rights to the land, the building, access from the street, rights to light, to name a few. Rights often also imply duties – not to block access of others, maintenance of sidewalks and paths. Heritage regulations that restrict the right to alter a private house in one way or another may also be seen as a duty to maintain quality.[2]

One question that follows from this approach is whether regulation of heritage must be done by direct control: could it be done instead by imposing standards that owners have a duty to meet? In Sicily, the heritage authorities not only designate the stock of heritage, they also set standards of repair and maintenance services to owners of designated heritage items; this is the case in France as well. Another question concerns the level of government that is appropriate for heritage policy and administration: is heritage a national or local issue? Regulation of heritage in Sicily has been devolved by the Italian national government to the Sicilian regional government; Mignosa (Chapter 2), Rizzo (Chapter 3), Mazza (Chapter 4) and Cicerchia (Chapter 14) all consider the political economy aspects of this particular devolution and Elliot (Chapter 13) considers the similar case of Scotland, where political devolution has transferred competence for the arts and the heritage to the Scottish Parliament.

Whatever the political and administrative organisation of regulation, it seems that some regulation is necessary as a means of solving information problems. Because of public goods and externality elements and because heritage is also perceived as a merit good, public authorities inevitably will be involved in heritage designation and quality control one way or another. It is therefore worth questioning what form this intervention should take – who should do it and how.

3.   POLITICAL ECONOMY OF HERITAGE

Cultural economics has traditionally had its primary focus on market failure arguments justifying subsidies to the arts and heritage and there has been much discussion of the relative merits of direct subsidy in the form of grants to cultural organisations and indirect subsidy by tax breaks and the like.

Regulation has been discussed in cultural economics in connection with rules and laws, such as export controls on works of art and heritage items but it has not yet received the full attention it deserves as a central determining feature of heritage (see, however, Giardina and Rizzo, 1994;

also O'Hagan, 1998a). But while the natural tendency of economists is to think of otherwise 'free' markets in which freedom to transact is inhibited by regulation, in the heritage field we more typically face a situation of a planned economy that is state owned, state managed and regulated. That is not to say that there is no private ownership of heritage items: much of the built heritage is in private hands, being used for housing and offices and many works of art, such as pictures, sculptures and craft items are also privately owned. But when they are subject to heritage regulations, freedom to use these properties is limited by regulators acting like managers in a planned economy.

In most European countries the state owns outright the land, buildings and contents of the major museums, art galleries, archaeological sites and buildings of historical interest (from battlefields to palaces), all government buildings, national and local public monuments, statues, old battleships, parks and gardens (not to mention archives and libraries), that is, the whole of heritage. These heritage facilities are managed by the state (national and local government) and the organisations that run them are mostly staffed by civil servants. Privatisation may have made some dents in this pattern – museums in some countries (for example, the UK and the Netherlands) are managed by parastatal organisations employing their own staff rather than civil servants – but by and large the planned economy model rules. Even those people who favour encouragement of private finance do not advocate selling off the Crown jewels and apart from marginal sales of items from collections, no country to my knowledge has privatised whole collections or state buildings.

An implication of the above is that we need to take more account of theories of public choice and bureaucracy in order to understand the heritage economy. This is a central focus of Chapters 3 and 4 by Rizzo and Mazza, respectively.

4.   FINANCE OF HERITAGE

The mixed economy nature of heritage, with its public and private goods characteristics, regulation, direct government provision and subsidies, inevitably requires a mix of public and private finance from national and local taxes and private sources.

Finance of heritage can be analysed from various points of view:

1. incentive effects to the different participants – levels of government, specialist heritage authorities, taxpayers and consumers;
2. distributional effects on citizens, taxpayers and consumers who pay for

heritage; and
3. crowding-out of one type of finance by another.

I shall discuss these in turn.

4.1 Incentive Effects

Rizzo and Mazza (Chapters 3 and 4) consider the incentives to regulators (heritage authorities) of different sources of funds, such as the incentive to exercise powers of regulation at a lower level while using finance from a higher level; such a situation reduces accountability.

Regulators may or may not have spending competence and there are clearly different levels of accountability – to superiors within a bureaucracy, to politicians and policy-makers and to the public. Rizzo discusses the question of the impact of devolution on incentives and accountability and concludes that in the case of Sicily, devolution has made little difference to incentives and to responsiveness to local voter preferences. Elliot (Chapter 13) discusses the devolution of responsibility for the arts and heritage to the recently formed Scottish Parliament, placing emphasis rather on the opportunity it could open up for increasing finance from private sources – non-profit organisations, sponsorship and consumers – and he looks to the creation of incentives to encourage that shift.

A source of dispute between cultural economists and heritage authorities is how much visitors should be asked to pay (O'Hagan, 1998b). Entry prices can clearly be used to raise revenues but the effect on access is controversial.

Typically, when entry prices are raised visitor numbers fall in the short run but recover in the long run. Heritage authorities may well worry, however, about the interim impact on voters and face a shortfall of funds. Entry fees have been a political football in the UK for over 30 years and experience there has shown that visitor numbers do eventually rise with the introduction of prices (for a long time museums in the UK were free and some still are) but that political will is needed to encourage all providers to adopt the policy and charge similar entrance fees (Museums and Galleries Commission, 1997).

4.2 Distributional Effects

Direct provision and subsidy by governments are visible sources of finance, even though there are problems in many countries in finding out exactly how much money is involved (see Mignosa, Chapter 2. She also found gaps in financial data for Scotland; see Appendix to Chapter 13). Regulation, however, may impose costs on citizens – heritage property owners, car-users in heritage cities – that are invisible and are not taken into account by policy-makers. This insight is one of the chief contributions of Benhamou (Benhamou, 1996 and Chapter 12), who applies it in particular to controls on private owners (often of their homes). Heritage regulators have the incentive to increase the scope and extent of regulation without financial accountability, even though this may well increase heritage expenditures from both private and public sources. Owners have the incentive to improve their property if values increase and also have the incentive to spend taxpayers' money in the form of grants for heritage maintenance.

Depending on the relative values of these items, there will be a redistribution of financial liability between taxpayers and the owners of heritage-designated property. As both Rizzo (Chapter 3) and Benhamou (Chapter 12) point out, part of the cost of complying with heritage regulations is borne in various ways by private owners and the extent of this depends upon the stipulations and scope of heritage regulations and upon the way the property and art markets respond to them, that is whether prices discount the risk of future liability for maintenance as a negative factor or rise because of the perceived increase in utility and value.

4.3 Crowding-out

Crowding-out of private expenditure by public expenditure is well understood by economists in all areas of the economy. Public expenditure reduces the incentives to private sources of finance and increases incentives to free ride.

Some external benefits from heritage could be appropriated by private organisations if there were the right incentives and regulatory framework. For example, in economic impact surveys, firms often express the value of the presence of the arts and heritage for their image and for employee utility. That suggests they would be willing to pay for these local benefits through sponsorship and donations. Tax breaks and the like may also encourage them to contribute over and above these benefits. However, many countries do not have such tax incentives.

Rizzo (Chapter 3) adds another angle to this question: the disincentive effect to private owners of heritage buildings by uncertainty about regulators' behaviour. Under Italian law, responsibility for failure to properly identify and preserve archaeological historical and aesthetically important heritage features falls on the shoulders of the heritage authorities, and fear of failure causes them to be overcautious and to monitor the renovation of buildings at every stage. The discovery during renovation of, say, a Norman feature previously hidden by a Baroque façade would cause work to be stopped by the heritage authorities and the owner would then incur considerable extra costs of conservation and delays. This is tantamount to the belief that there is no opportunity cost to any discovery and that its value is almost infinite. Rizzo argues that this kind of uncertainty caused by non-stop regulatory intervention crowds out private willingness to finance heritage conservation. It is interesting to ask why markets do not discount this intervention through property prices: the answer probably lies in the uncertainty (rather than risk) element.

In Sicily, the strength and reach of regulators therefore militates against private finance of heritage protection. Private owners of heritage buildings may have to pay for renovations that are more expensive because of the requirement to meet specified standards. Many countries have similar types of regulation that apply to private owners; Benhamou (Chapter 12) shows that France combines regulation with public finance of heritage conservation of listed properties in private hands; however grants are large enough not only to compensate owners but also to stimulate 'new entrants' with the result that there is an ever-expanding list of heritage buildings and calls on the public budget to restore them. She questions the public benefit to be had from this policy unless owners are forced to comply with requirements to give access to members of the public wishing to see the subsidised items.

5.   MULTIPLE OUTPUTS OF HERITAGE

A feature of heritage that makes it a complex economic good is that it supplies jointly produced, multiple outputs. Museums are viewed by cultural economists as multiproduct firms (Johnson and Thomas, 1998); they offer services of display and education to visitors, preservation and conservation services, specialised storage facilities and research services, only some of which may directly benefit the present generation of visitors; this is also true of built heritage. Multiple outputs in joint production exacerbate the difficulties of applying marketplace criteria to the production of heritage services discussed above; even if all these services could be regarded as providing private benefits and priced accordingly, it would be difficult to assign prices for each use (though ancillary services, such as cafeterias and shops, can be run as separate concessions on a for-profit basis). The multiple outputs of heritage providers give rise to problems in evaluating the performance of heritage authorities; Pignataro (Chapter 5) discusses this in detail (see below).

Heritage tourism is another 'output', which, however, is almost never directly under the control of heritage authorities or of heritage site managers. It is a spin-off from heritage provision that may be difficult for heritage providers to appropriate. Montemagno (Chapter 6) and Musumeci

(Chapter 8), demonstrate the economic importance of tourism to Sicily and its connection with Sicilian heritage. Local property taxation of hotels, restaurants and other enterprises that benefit from tourism is certainly feasible but unless there is the power to levy such taxes, external effects of heritage tourism cannot be captured by the heritage organisations or the region in which they are located.

The problem of charging users for multiple outputs is exacerbated by the public goods element. This is a problem in the case of the urban built heritage where buildings may be freely viewed from public places. Private owners could charge for entry to the interiors of buildings and the outsides could be thought of as an externality of consumption. However, a historic city centre (sometimes rather infelicitously called 'city of art') is closer to a pure public good because the whole entity is greater than the sum of the parts – the individual buildings, monuments, parks and squares that make up the city. The benefits of the totality could not be appropriated even if each individual item were private. Such cities, therefore, are common property and, according to the 'tragedy of the commons' are liable to overuse. To overcome free-riding associated with these public goods, some communal authority must manage these heritage cities and control the effect of visitor use, such as congestion of people and cars, in order to maintain quality.

The finance and regulation of the use of heritage public goods and externalities could in principle be administered by local city authorities alongside zoning and traffic control and paid for out of local taxation. However, historic cities are considered to provide national, even international, benefits and local authorities may not be able to appropriate communal benefits through local taxation or offer conservation services of a high enough standard.

6.   DEMAND FOR HERITAGE SERVICES

The multiple outputs of heritage identified above suggest that heritage providers supply different services to segmented 'customers', only one group being the visiting public.[3] Consumer demand for heritage is viewed by cultural economists as consisting of demand by visitors for access to heritage items (museum collections, sites, buildings and so on), for heritage services directly linked to them (display, guides, education) and for ancillary services; all these can, at least in principle and subject to the difficulties outlined earlier, be charged for. However, there is also demand by non-users – for the 'option' to visit or the existence of heritage (and other cultural goods) – which, though present in the form of willingness to pay, cannot be expressed through entrance fees. These sources of demand can only be measured by surveys and willingness to pay channelled through taxation or other forms of collective finance. A further source of demand is that of future generations, who are unable to express willingness to pay either through prices or tax contributions in the present. The present generation may derive utility from knowing that heritage goods are preserved for their successors and be willing to pay for it but that is a different matter. Thus option, existence and future generations' demand call for the finance of heritage by public authorities, either through direct provision (as in state ownership of heritage) or through subsidy to private or non-governmental providers. It should be noted that these types of demand are conceptually different from the demand for public goods and for subsidy to finance externalities. In addition, governments may treat heritage as a merit good and allocate tax revenues to ensure future provision on paternalistic grounds without regard to demand.

The presence of all these features on the demand side means that there is market failure in the provision of heritage services and this calls for estimates of the demand for heritage as a public good. These are increasingly done through contingent valuation studies (Cuccia and Signorello, Chapters 9 and 10). The problem that contingent valuation and other such methods of estimating willingness to pay (also reviewed in Chapter 10 by Cuccia and Signorello) seek to solve is the size of subsidies or the amount of public expenditure from taxes that should be spent on heritage items to achieve social efficiency, defined in terms of Pigovian welfare economics as the output consistent with the equation of marginal social benefit with marginal social cost. (However, heritage authorities may well be indifferent to any notion of economic efficiency.)

One further feature of demand deserves a mention here and that is that demand for heritage items is both 'lumpy' and seasonal. The lumpiness is often due to organised tourism, such as when a busload of visitors arrives at a site (or several simultaneously) which places pressure on heritage services, requiring, for example, more guards, guides or toilet facilities for short periods during the day than are needed at other quieter times. Seasonal tourism occurs in specific holiday periods and necessitates peak provision of services to ensure the quality of visits and the safety of heritage items, which are unnecessary at other times of the year. In principle, such problems could be solved by discriminatory peak pricing but in practice this rarely happens,[4] partly due, no doubt, to management inertia and problems with labour contracts. Even if there were flexibility of hours, however, it would be hard to respond to lumpy demand at isolated sites that are far from places where workers live.

7.   THE SUPPLY OF HERITAGE SERVICES

As indicated earlier, the stock of heritage items is largely determined by regulatory designation and accretion; an active regulatory regime may easily increase the stock simply by administrative fiat. But the supply of heritage services is a different matter. Heritage services range from the simple matter of opening hours of heritage sites and museums to much more complex questions, such as the use of modern technologies offering services that may be complements or even substitutes for location-based services (see Musumeci, Chapter 8 for a detailed account of the technological possibilities). While the stock of heritage is largely a sunk cost, the supply of services requires ongoing expenditure on labour and capital and costs vary according to the number of users. The quantity and quality of services depends upon the responsiveness of the heritage authorities to consumer preferences; with state-owned and -managed heritage sites, little or no notice may be taken of consumers' wants, even when there is some vehicle for expressing willingness to pay and voter preferences (Rizzo, Chapter 3; Cuccia and Signorello, Chapter 10). Bureaucratic inertia and restrictive practices or rigid labour agreements may inhibit extension of opening hours and provision of ancillary facilities, such as shops and cafeterias.

Apart from visitor services, another issue in museum supply is access to the total collection. As is well known, most museums display well under 100 per cent of their items (10 per cent is the figure for the Prado in Madrid, according to Peacock, 1997). This 'Prado Disease' is the result of what has been called the 'magpie tendency' of museologists (and, one might add, of authorities in charge of built heritage) to collect more and more items that do not see the light of day. In museums, this is usually blamed on insufficient resources for preservation and display. However, the economist's solution of deaccessioning, the sale of items in order to raise funds to finance visitor access and services, is staunchly resisted by museums (among other reasons because of legal considerations surrounding the gift of objects by private donors). Cultural economists largely view this as indifference on the part of heritage suppliers to consumer preferences combined with the lack of incentives that would elicit such a response (Montias, 1975; Grampp, 1989). This latter point is often due to the financial management and accounting practices of public sector ownership, whereby any revenues from entrance fees and ancillary facilities are transferred from the managers of the site or museum to the public heritage body or the state (Frey, 2000). Thus, even where pricing policies for heritage services exist that are capable of reflecting consumer preferences for them, revenues do not provide effective incentives or signals to managers. The supply of heritage services is therefore for practical purposes exogenously determined, that is, outside the purview of economic considerations.

In the absence of economic incentives through price signalling, how else might managers respond to the demand for heritage services? As already mentioned, contingent valuation methods may be used. Caserta (Chapter 11) discusses museum societies as another vehicle for the expression of consumer willingness to pay. These enquiries are, however, those of economists rather than of heritage authorities seeking information from their clients. In some countries, museums and other heritage providers conduct detailed surveys of the socio-economic characteristics of their visitors (Dickenson, 1997) but they do not generally seek information about the visitors' preferences. In Sicily, however, there is a marked absence of data of all kinds, not only about visitor preferences, but also about their numbers and even financial data are hard to obtain. The heritage authorities there do not place much weight on the provision of visitor services.

8.   MEASURING THE EFFICIENCY OF HERITAGE PROVIDERS

As we have seen, the combination of multiple outputs and complex demand and supply characteristics means that public intervention by means of direct government-financed provision is typically to be found in the heritage sector.

Any measure of efficiency therefore must be evaluated in relation to the achievement of public policy objectives and social efficiency (Towse, 1994). Private efficiency rules – say, marginal cost pricing of entry tickets – cannot solve the problem of non-user demand and public good free-riding. In addition, policy objectives may be fuzzy and even conflicting. For example, the provision of high-quality labelling of displayed items can be offputting for less well-informed visitors, the objective of education conflicting with simple enjoyment.

Further problems exist because of the difficulties of valuing cultural capital in heritage, for example the choice of the social discount rate at which to calculate the present value of heritage items in order to determine how much to invest for future generations. This is a controversial area because taste cannot be predicted and, furthermore, future generations will be wealthier than the present generation. In consequence, there is an intertemporal redistribution of income, which is essentially inequitable whether we like it or not (Peacock, 1997).

On a more mundane level, there is the practical problem for efficiency measurement of the lack of data on inputs and output (however measured) and of the quality of either. Even simple performance indicators such as visitor numbers do not exist where entry is free. None of this bodes well for evaluating heritage administration. The purpose of performance indicators is to simulate market measures of efficiency in non-market situations. Heroic assumptions must therefore be made in order to undertake even a restricted analysis of management efficiency of a heritage facility. In Chapter 5, Pignataro uses Data Envelopment Analysis to evaluate the efficiency of museums in Sicily. This technique essentially identifies the production function of the best-performing item of the set analysed and compares the rest against that. Best available practice allows the researcher to estimate possible economies of scale, which could be used for policy purposes. This type of measurement of efficiency is an important contribution of economics to any policy debate but it has limitations. The performance indicators used are measures only of technical not economic efficiency and do not take account of economic factors such as relative prices. Although it is technically possible, as Musumeci shows (Chapter 8), to substitute capital for labour, capital-intensive techniques may not be economically feasible. If wage rates are relatively low, capital substitution makes no economic sense.

Moreover, cultural economists are particularly aware of the cultural significance of the arts and heritage in creating values like national pride and cultural identity that cannot be measured; if policy-makers place great emphasis on these values, no amount of measurement of opportunity costs will convince them of the case for policy changes to achieve greater technical or economic efficiency. The cultural importance of a heritage facility in a remote area of the country, for example, may outweigh all economic considerations if its significance is great. These matters can only be resolved by policy-makers and are necessarily politically determined. None of this means, however, that cultural economists should give up. Efficiency measures, even if inevitably crude, provide important information so that policy-makers can decide if a policy is 'worth it'; measuring the opportunity cost of a course of action allows policy-makers to choose between alternative policy measures that would achieve similar outcomes enabling them to choose, say, between maintaining a football stadium and a museum. Having information must always improve political choices for voters as well as administrators and that is why efficiency measures as well as contingent valuation and other techniques for obtaining economic data about heritage are an important part of cultural economics.

9. THE ROLE OF NON-PROFIT ORGANISATIONS

Non-profit organisations have developed into a significant alternative to public and to private provision of a range of goods and services, usually those with a strong public good element or where there are information problems. They occupy what is now often called the 'third sphere' of the mixed economy.[5] In the UK and the USA, many arts and heritage providers are non-profit organisations and this entitles them to tax breaks and encourages private giving especially, in the case of the heritage, through bequests.

Creaco (Chapter 7) reports the findings of a major worldwide study of the size and scope of the non-profit sector in a number of countries. He shows that Italy comes low in the international league table and argues that a reason for this is a consequence of the way non-profits were defined for the purposes of the study, excluding the Italian banking foundations – which are active in the heritage field.

One of the most notable examples of non-profit organisations is the National Trust in the UK with its 'sister' organisation, the National Trust for Scotland (Elliot, Chapter 13; see also Peacock, 1997). The National Trust owns, restores, maintains and manages a large number of what are called stately homes and their gardens (an ignored heritage item in most countries but one of the most popular in the UK) as well as many hectares of areas of outstanding natural beauty, coastline and so on. The National Trust acquires much of its property through gifts in lieu of taxation (mostly death duties, a form of inheritance tax), thus receiving indirect public finance. It is a membership organisation, giving free entry to members and charging quite substantial entrance fees to non-members; it also earns significant revenue from rentals, shops, merchandise and catering. Like many non-profit organisations, it benefits from a considerable body of volunteer workers, which reduces its operating costs. The value of voluntary working should be taken into account in heritage finance but it rarely is and, of course, is difficult to calculate (Colonna, 1995).

Non-profit organisations therefore can be significant providers of heritage services but need the incentive of tax breaks and proper legal status to flourish. These do not exist in all countries; where they do, however, non-profit organisations play a role that private for-profit firms and also governmental organisations fail to fulfil. For certain purposes, they gain the trust of the public to provide high-quality services and information in preference to both public and private providers. Where on the one hand private organisations are seen as motivated solely by the profit motive and as having the incentive to cheat on quality when consumers are not well informed and, on the other hand, government is seen as dominated by bureaucratic and political opportunism, non-profit organisations are perceived as altruistic and reliable, having, as it were, no axe to grind. They therefore overcome problems of supplier-induced demand.

10. CONCLUSION

This chapter has demonstrated the economic complexities of heritage and the range of economic tools and concepts that have been employed in the successive chapters to analyse it. Sicily has provided the backdrop for these enquiries and that is because it presents particular problems.

Sicily is particularly rich in its cultural heritage, is politically responsible for it but does not have a full range of fiscal measures available to finance public intervention. The economic problem is therefore particularly difficult in Sicily and policies for what is already a complex economic problem, preserving the heritage, are therefore more difficult.

There is an additional benefit to studying Sicily, however: it is not often that Anglo-Saxon cultural economists have the opportunity to get to grips with law-making and administrative procedures in the civil code tradition. As will be seen in the next chapter, administration processes which, say, in the UK, would be an executive matter for the civil service of central government or for local authorities at the regional or city level, in Sicily are subject to very different legal and fiscal procedures. Because of language problems, economists rarely have the opportunity to understand how institutions work outside their own country and, as English is the chief language of economics, trade is one-way only. Because this book about Sicily is written in English, it opens up the possibility of grasping how things work there. The result is not only interesting; it also makes the general point very forcefully that without understanding institutions, economists cannot make satisfactory policy prescriptions.

Cultural economics is an international subject (one, however, with a strong European bias) and the economics of heritage is a particularly important topic in European countries. If we wish our subject to develop, we must do thorough international comparisons and bite the bullet of learning how each other's institutions and legal procedures impinge on economic analysis and policies.

NOTES

1. Regulatory controls may be crude blanket measures (in Sicily, for example, all buildings over 50 years of age may be designated as heritage items) or they may be fine-tuned to specific aspects by requiring owners to comply with particular standards, for example, to use a designated material such as stone or a matching style of window to maintain heritage quality.
2. Zoning laws may well have the same inhibitory effects, though they may not

overlap with heritage prescriptions.
3.   Although museums can and do charge for expert services such as specialised research and conservation, I am not aware of any studies by cultural economists of the costs or revenues of these services.
4.   Some museums now sell 'timed' tickets for blockbuster exhibitions and the Royal Academy in London stayed open all night to accommodate visitor demand for its blockbuster Monet exhibition; nevertheless, the prices remained the same.
5.   See Klamer and Zuidhof (1998) for a radical application of this concept to heritage.

REFERENCES

Benhamou, F. (1996), 'Is Increased Public Spending for the Preservation of Historic Monuments Inevitable?', *Journal of Cultural Economics*, **20** (2), 115–32.

Colonna, C. (1995), 'The Economic Contribution of Volunteerism Toward the Value of our Cultural Inventory', *Journal of Cultural Economics*, **19** (4), 341–50.

Dickenson, V. (1997), 'Museum Visitor Surveys – An Overview, 1930–1990', in R. Towse (ed.), *Cultural Economics*, Cheltenham, UK and Lyme, USA: Edward Elgar, pp. 272–81.

Frey, B. (2000), *Arts and Economics*, Heidelberg: Springer.

Giardina, E. and Rizzo, I. (1994), 'Regulation in the Cultural Sector', in A. Peacock and I. Rizzo (eds), *Cultural Economics and Cultural Policies*, Dordrecht: Kluwer, pp. 125–42.

Grampp, W. (1989), *Pricing the Priceless. Art, Artists and Economics*, New York: Basic Books.

Johnson, P. and Thomas, B. (1998), 'Introduction to Special Issue on Museums', *Journal of Cultural Economics*, **22**, 75–207.

Klamer, A. and Zuidhof, P.W. (1998), 'The Values of Cultural Heritage: Merging Economic and Cultural Appraisals', in *Economics and Heritage Conservation*, Report of a Meeting Organised by the Getty Conservation Institute, Los Angeles, Getty Center, December 1998.

Montias, J.M. (1975), 'Are Museums Betraying the Public's Trust?', reprinted (1995), *Journal of Cultural Economics*, **19** (1), 71–80.

Museums and Galleries Commission (1997), 'Museums and Galleries Admission Charges Study', Report Commissioned to the Glasgow Caledonian University, UK.

O'Hagan, J. (1998a), *The State and the Arts: An Analysis of Key Economic Policy Issues in Europe and the United States*, Cheltenham,UK and Northampton, MA, USA: Edward Elgar.

O'Hagan, J. (1998b), 'Art Museums: Collections, Deaccessioning and Donations', *Journal of Cultural Economics*, **22** (2–3), 197–207.

Peacock, A. (1997), 'A Future for the Past: the Political Economy of Heritage', in R. Towse (ed.), op. cit., pp. 387–424.

Throsby, D. (2001), *Economics and Culture*, Cambridge: Cambridge University Press.

Towse, R. (1994), 'Achieving Public Policy Objectives in the Arts and Heritage', in A. Peacock and I. Rizzo (eds), op. cit., pp. 143–65.

2. The Organisation and Finance of Cultural Heritage in Sicily[*]

Anna Mignosa

1. INTRODUCTION

The administration of arts and heritage in Italy is strongly centralised. The Heritage Ministry is responsible for the formulation and supervision of national cultural policy, despite recent reforms aimed at decentralisation.[1] Sicily is the only exception within this framework since the national government devolved full authority on cultural matters to the Sicilian regional government. Thus, the administration of arts and heritage in Sicily constitutes an interesting case of devolution within Italy.

This chapter focuses on the administration of heritage in Sicily. One question to be considered is whether the devolved organisation of the Sicilian institutions responsible for heritage allows for a better safeguard of heritage in the region. The conclusions are based on the analysis of regional legislation that has introduced the present system and on interviews conducted with officials responsible for heritage maintenance in Sicily.[2] The first part of the chapter (section 2), describes the organisation of the institutions responsible for heritage in Sicily, pointing out the main differences with those on the mainland. In the second part (sections 3–6), the focus shifts to the funding of cultural heritage in Sicily. In particular, section 3 summarises the amount of financial resources used by the Sicilian regional government for cultural purposes. The following section reports on the distribution of financial resources to the nine *Soprintendenze*, the peripheral institutions responsible for culture and heritage in Sicily, while section 5 illustrates the differences in the amount of funds devoted to each *Soprintendenza*. Section 6 looks at the ability of Sicilian central and local institutions to spend the resources available on culture. The analysis of expenditure on heritage maintenance in Sicily is intended to furnish an example of the concrete working methods of the institutions responsible for heritage and of their interrelations. It also allows for certain conclusions to be drawn on the efficiency of the administration of arts and heritage in Sicily (section 7).

2. THE ADMINISTRATION OF HERITAGE IN SICILY

The regional laws, which introduced the present system that administers the arts and heritage in Sicily, were inspired by decentralisation. Decentralisation was intended to ensure a better administration of the regional patrimony because it allows for a closer connection between the institution responsible for a heritage item and its location. Consequently, the Sicilian organisation has been divided into several levels corresponding to the subdivision of the region into provinces and towns. The main institutions which make up the regional administration of arts and culture are:

1. the *Assessorato Regionale dei Beni Culturali Ambientali e della Pubblica Istruzione*;[3]
2. the nine *Soprintendenze*; and
3. the regional museums and galleries.

Figure 2.1 Organisation of the administration of cultural heritage in Sicily

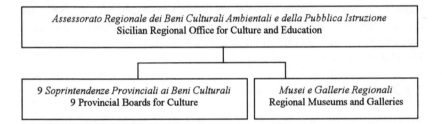

2.1 **The Regional Office for Culture**

At the top of the Sicilian administration responsible for the arts and culture is the *Assessorato Regionale dei Beni Culturali e Ambientali* which exerts an authority comparable to that of the Heritage Ministry in the rest of Italy. The Sicilian *Assessorato* formulates regional cultural policies, controls all the peripheral institutions which manage the arts and heritage and decides on the distribution of funds between them. The Sicilian model of administration of the arts and heritage therefore replicates the Italian one, being highly centralised and dominated by the role of the *Assessorato Regionale dei Beni Culturali e Ambientali* despite the fact that the Sicilian regional law introducing the present organisation was intended to devise a decentralised system.   It can be argued that decentralisation is only theoretical and has not been put into practice. This observation is confirmed in the following sections.

2.2 The *Soprintendenze*

The organisation of the nine Sicilian *Soprintendenze*[4] is completely different from that found on the mainland.   The differences lie both in their distribution within the region and in their internal organisation.   In mainland Italy, these institutions are specialised so that each is responsible for a particular aspect (archaeology, architecture, and so on) of the arts and heritage administration within an entire region or a large portion of it, with possible co-ordination problems.[5]   In Sicily, on the other hand, there are nine *Soprintendenze*, one for every province in the region.   Each of them is made up of seven technical-scientific divisions which cover every aspect of arts and heritage administration.   The Sicilian *Soprintendenze* have been conceived as linking institutions between the *Assessorato Regionale dei Beni Culturali e Ambientali* and the different provinces in the region.   To ensure the connection with local needs and requests, the regional law also foresaw the creation of local councils. However, this never happened and in November 1999 a decree from the *Assessore* abolished them. This example illustrates one of the main problems of Sicilian regional laws regulating the administration of the arts and heritage.   In theory, they have conceived a well-organised and decentralised structure that in practice has never been completely realised.[6]

2.3 The Regional Museums and Galleries

Every Sicilian regional museum and gallery is an independent institution with its own budget and internal organisation though, of course, subordinate to the *Assessorato Regionale dei Beni Culturali e Ambientali*.   The attributions and powers of the regional museums and galleries are comparable to those of the provincial *Soprintendenze*: the internal organisation is practically the same with museums being also made up of technical-scientific divisions; the employees of both institutions are civil servants; the same rules apply for appointing the museum or gallery directors and heads of the *Soprintendenze*. On mainland Italy, there are only six museums which have the same sort of independence, being directly subordinate to the Heritage Ministry; all the other national museums and galleries, such as the Uffizi Gallery in Florence, are answerable to a *Soprintendenza*.

Legally, museums and *Soprintendenze* are responsible for the actions necessary to safeguard heritage under their jurisdiction. However, during interviews with museum directors and *Soprintendenti*,[7] they underlined that the rules in force mainly gave (and give) them the power to make proposals, while final decisions were (and still are) taken by the central office. This confirms the centralisation of the Sicilian organisation responsible for heritage and the impression that it is dominated by the role and power of the *Assessorato* with all the peripheral institutions subordinate to it.

3. EXPENDITURE ON CULTURE

This section looks at the financial arrangements in force in Sicily; in particular, it investigates the distribution of resources to the institutions responsible for heritage maintenance. The allocation of funds takes place by means of a three-stage bureaucratic procedure that is normally quite long and complicated. The regional government distributes its funds between the various *Assessorati* which, in turn, allocate the resources to the various lower-level institutions. For the purpose of this analysis, we concentrate on the allocation of funds from the regional government to the Sicilian *Assessorato Regionale dei Beni Culturali e Ambientali*,[8] and on the subsequent redistribution of resources to the *Soprintendenze*.

Table 2.1 Sicilian regional government and Assessorato Regionale dei Beni Culturali e Ambientali: *allocations and expenditures, 1990–98 (billion lire)*

					Total allocation				
	1990	1991	1992	1993	1994	1995	1996	1997	1998
Assessorato	1,028	1,089	1,113	1,200	1,018	934	887	973	1,001
Sicilian regional government	21,949	22,759	23,380	21,771	21,82	19,940	20,736	21,221	22,210
					Total expenditure				
	1990	1991	1992	1993	1994	1995	1996	1997	1998
Assessorato	484	580	585	589	578	617	591	629	973
Sicilian regional government	13,897	14,628	15,473	13,162	16,32	14,567	15,851	16,203	15,643

Note: 1 euro = 1,936.27 Italian lire.

Sources: Sicilian Regional Government, *Annual Budget,* 1990–98.

The data collected refer to the 1990–98 period. Table 2.1 shows the total amount of funds used by the regional government and the Sicilian *Assessorato Regionale dei Beni Culturali e Ambientali*. Two different groups of figures are recorded: 'funds allocated' and 'expenditure'. These amounts do not coincide with each other as not all the funds awarded by the Exchequer are spent in the financial year. The trend of both allocations and expenditure of the Sicilian regional government and the Sicilian *Assessorato Regionale dei Beni Culturali e Ambientali* is almost the same, increasing from 1990 to 1993, then falling slowly.

Comparing the amount awarded to the *Assessorato* with the total funds allocated to and spent by the Sicilian regional government, it is possible to deduce the share of financial resources that the latter designates to culture. During the period 1990-98 the allocations to the Sicilian *Assessorato dei Beni Culturali e Ambientali* were, on average, approximately 5 per cent of the total allocations of the regional government, and expenditure, 4 per cent of the total regional expenditure. These percentages remained constant during the whole period.

4. PUBLIC EXPENDITURE ON HERITAGE MAINTENANCE IN SICILY

The funds awarded to the *Assessorato Regionale dei Beni Culturali e Ambientali* are meant to cover all kinds of expenditure linked to arts. To identify the part of these resources devoted to heritage maintenance, it is necessary to focus on the distribution of funds from the *Assessorato* to the *Soprintendenze*, as the latter are the institutions which handle heritage in the areas under their jurisdiction. Figures for allocations and expenditure of the *Soprintendenze*, for the 1990–98 period, are shown in Table 2.2. These data were provided by the Sicilian *Assessorato Regionale Bilancio e Finanze*, that is, the regional finance office. As a matter of fact, it was impossible to obtain these figures from the *Soprintendenze* themselves, or from the *Assessorato Regionale dei Beni Culturali e Ambientali*.[9] The aggregate amounts shown in Table 2.2 have been calculated by processing and summing the raw data obtained from the *Assessorato Regionale Bilancio e Finanze*.[10]

This trend is somewhat different from those in Table 2.1. In particular, from 1995 onwards, both allocation and expenditure increased despite the reduction in allocation and expenditure of the Sicilian regional government and the *Assessorato*. This happened because the *Soprintendenze* obtained resources through new sources of funds from national or European projects for the funding of cultural heritage. Nevertheless, the last figures recorded

(1998) demonstrate a dramatic fall compared to 1997.

Comparing the funds allocated to the *Soprintendenze* to those of the Sicilian regional government, we see that the former were, on average, 0.6 per cent of the allocation and 0.5 per cent of expenditure of the regional government. This proportion diminished drastically in 1998, when it corresponded to only 0.3 per cent for both figures. Therefore, though only a small proportion of regional resources is used for culture (cf. section 3), an even smaller amount is devoted to heritage maintenance.

Table 2.2 Allocations and expenditures on cultural heritage:
    Soprintendenze, *1990–98 (billion lire)*

Total allocations awarded to the *Soprintendenze*								
1990	1991	1992	1993	1994	1995	1996	1997	1998
94	197	172	164	162	178	153	150	70
Total expenditures of the *Soprintendenze*								
1990	1991	1992	1993	1994	1995	1996	1997	1998
29	93	91	80	80	107	100	90	44

Note: 1 euro = 1,936.27 Italian lire.

Source: Our calculations from data furnished by the Assessorato Regionale Bilancio e Finanze.

5. THE DISTRIBUTION OF FUNDS FOR HERITAGE BETWEEN THE NINE *SOPRINTENDENZE*

The distribution of resources among the nine *Soprintendenze* by the *Assessorato Regionale dei Beni Culturali e Ambientali* is illustrated in Figures 2.2 and 2.3 which respectively refer to allocation and expenditure.[11] They clearly show the remarkable differences in the quantities of funds assigned to (and spent by) the various provincial institutions.

Looking at the distribution of funds to the *Soprintendenze*, it is evident that in the period under investigation, the *Soprintendenza* of Palermo obtained and spent the highest share of resources. It received twice the amount of funds assigned to the other *Soprintendenze* that obtained the highest share (Syracuse, Agrigento and Messina). However, the differences were not so notable, at least during the first few years.

Figure 2.2 Allocations awarded to the nine Soprintendenze, *1990–98*

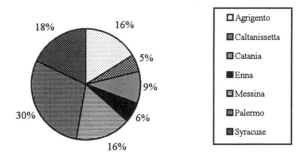

Source: See Table 2.2.

Figure 2.3 Expenditures of the nine Soprintendenze, *1990–98*

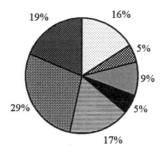

Source: Table 2.2.

Figure 2.4 indicates the amount of resources distributed to each *Soprintendenza* every year. It is evident that, from 1994 onwards, the sums assigned to Palermo rose sharply compared to those given to other offices.

This can be explained by the fact that, since 1993, this *Soprintendenza* has been given an extra 5 billion lire for the restoration of a specific item (Monreale Cathedral) foreseen under a national policy. In the same period, funds linked to national or international (EU) policies for culture and heritage were also given to the other eight Sicilian *Soprintendenze*, though the amounts were smaller. Even so, in the following years, these resources were not sufficient to counterbalance the general reduction in funds which the regional government assigned to heritage.

Figure 2.4 Allocations awarded to each Soprintendenza *per year (million lire)*

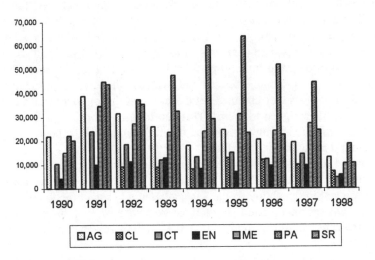

Note: 1 euro = 1,936.27 Italian lire.

Source: Table 2.2.

6. THE SPENDING CAPACITY OF THE REGIONAL GOVERNMENT, THE *ASSESSORATO REGIONALE DEI BENI CULTURALI E AMBIENTALI* AND THE *SOPRINTENDENZE*

As already mentioned, not all the financial resources of the Sicilian regional government, the *Assessorato Regionale dei Beni Culturali e Ambientali* and the *Soprintendenze* are spent. The particular procedures necessary for using the funds delay, and often prevent their actual use. The ratio of expenditure to allocation constitutes an indicator of the central or local institutions' capacity to spend the resources obtained. It can also be considered an indicator of administrative efficiency. This ratio varies according to the kind of expenditure it relates to. On average, however, the Sicilian regional government spent 75 per cent of its allocation, while the *Assessorato Regionale dei Beni Culturali e Ambientali* spent only 63 per cent of the amount it received. For the nine *Soprintendenze*, the ratio, on average, was 53 per cent for the 1990–98 period.

This finding partially contradicts the complaints of the officials interviewed. In fact, they mostly blamed the scarcity of resources obtained for not allowing them to undertake all the activities necessary to implement heritage policy. Yet, according to our findings, around half the funds allocated to every *Soprintendenza* were left unused.[12] There are, however, differences among the various provinces and within each of them. For example, over the period studied, this ratio swings from 72 per cent to 23 per cent in Agrigento and from 30 per cent to 69 per cent in Messina. The *Soprintendenze* of Agrigento, Messina and Syracuse showed a high capacity to spend the resources they obtained but it seems that this did not result in an increase in funds assigned to them. This confirms the impression that the distribution of funds among the various institutions is done without taking into account their actual performance.

In general, during the period considered, the expenditure to allocation ratio increased. On the one hand, this may lead us to believe that there was an improvement in the ability by the *Soprintendenze* to spend the funds they received. On the other hand, it must be remembered that there was a general reduction in the resources that the Sicilian regional government assigned to the *Soprintendenze* through the *Assessorato Regionale dei Beni Culturali e Ambientali*. Therefore, the resources could be mainly being used for administrative expenses. However, these ratios have limits in indicating the ability and speed of the *Soprintendenze* to use the resources which have been assigned to them. As a matter of fact, it also depends on the kind of expenditure to be made: the execution of restoration work or an excavation requires more funds and more time than the ordinary maintenance of a cultural good.[13] This is why it would be more useful to look at the particular objective to be accomplished with the assigned funds but unfortunately the information to do this is not available.

7. CONCLUSION

What can be inferred from the investigation of the data regarding the funding of heritage in Sicily? The amount of funds devoted to heritage administration constitutes a very small percentage of the total regional expenditure and also of the portion awarded to culture. The lack of financial resources is considered by those involved to be the main obstacle to a successful heritage administration, as the limited amount of money allows for 'ordinary maintenance' only and impedes any special kind of activity to prevent further heritage damage.

However, our analysis has shown that the funds available are not used in their entirety. On average, only half of the available funds are actually spent. The difficulty and slowness of the bureaucratic procedures to be followed in order to obtain resources from the *Assessorato Regionale dei Beni Culturali e Ambientali* and to use them is considered to be the principal cause of this. Thus, a simplification of the bureaucratic procedures appears to be essential to achieving a better use of funds for heritage and for the arts in general.

The determinants of financing, that is, the system adopted in allocating the funds to the different *Soprintendenze*, is also still unclear. The actual pattern does not give an incentive to officials working within the local and central institutions to improve their performance. There seems to be no control over their activity and correspondingly there is no system to reward those offices or officials who are more active or efficient. The lack of control and incentives is a typical problem of bureaucracies; nevertheless, it appears particularly serious for the Sicilian institutions responsible for heritage. The central office even seems to ignore how much of the resources have been used and how much are still available before the end of one year.

The present system seems to be bound by too many rules and dominated by the role of the *Assessorato Regionale dei Beni Culturali e Ambientali*: it takes all the decisions while the *Soprintendenze* can only make proposals. The activity of the latter is, therefore, limited by the power of the central office. These arrangements are far from the decentralised model which Sicilian regional laws intended to introduce following the devolution of power to the Sicilian regional government.

NOTES

* I am grateful to Monica Castro with whom I started the research project which was the basis for this work. The first part of this chapter is a summary of Castro and Mignosa (1999). Errors remain my responsibility.

1. Recently constitutional reform of a federalist kind has been approved and the role of regions is likely to change in the near future.

2. This study is based on the results of research conducted by the Department of Economics and Quantitative Methods at the Faculty of Economics, University of Catania.

3. That is, the regional central office responsible for culture and education, although, the department concerned with education is not considered here.

4. The heads of the *Soprintendenze* are the *Soprintendenti*.

5. Recently the post of Regional S*oprintendente* has been created but his role is still limited.

6. Things are due to change in the very near future because of recent managerial reforms of the regional bureaucracy.

7. They were undertaken during the research which was the basis for this study (see note 1 above).

8. However, other *Assessorati*, that is, those responsible for tourism or for public works, can also assign part of their funds to cultural purposes.

9. At present, regional law establishes that the *Soprintendenze* have to present an annual budget on the activity undertaken during the year and a plan for the following year. These reports, however, are not published so we still do not know if they contain these figures.

10. We are aware that these are only partial figures and do not include the total amount of expenses run up by the *Soprintendenze*, as part of them does not get recorded by the regional finance office.

11. The data gathered do not refer to all nine *Soprintendenze*. The *Soprintendenze* of Ragusa, Enna and Caltanissetta were introduced only in 1985 (regional law no. 26/85), and until recently their organisation was still incomplete. This is the reason why there are no data for the *Soprintendenza* of Ragusa and the figures for Caltanissetta refer to the 1992–98 period. Similarly, though the *Soprintendenza* of Trapani was introduced within the first group (regional law no. 80/77), its organisation has been closely connected to that of the *Soprintendenza* of Palermo so, for example, funds destined for Trapani passed through the *Soprintendenza* of Palermo. This explains why we obtained only partial data for Trapani.

12. These characteristics are in line with the findings of similar studies conducted in the rest of Italy: the ratio between the amount of money assigned to cultural objectives and that actually spent is very similar. See Bodo (1990).

13. Interesting proof of this assumption has been provided by Causi and Mazzanti (2001).

REFERENCES

Bodo, C. (1990), 'La Spesa Regionale per i Beni Culturali', in *Camera dei Deputati – Indagine Conoscitiva sui Beni Culturali*, Roma: Camera dei Deputati.

Castro, M. and Mignosa, A. (1999), 'The Administration of Cultural Heritage in Sicily', Research Report, Catania: Department of Economics and Quantitative Methods (DEMQ), University of Catania.

Causi, M. and Mazzanti, M. (2001), 'Investimenti Pubblici nelle Infrastrutture Culturali: Metodi e Processi per la Valutazione e il Monitoraggio', paper presented at the Conference on 'Cultural Supply: Promotion, Management and Funding', Rome, 9–10 February 2001.

Sicilian Regional Government, Assessorato Regionale Bilancio e Finanze, *Annual Budget*, 1990–98.

3. Heritage Conservation: The Role of Heritage Authorities[*]

Ilde Rizzo

1. INTRODUCTION

This chapter explores some aspects of conservation, using Sicily as a case study; the size and importance of heritage is such that conservation policy is a significant area of activity for the regional government.

As has been explained in Chapter 2, conservation policy is carried out by nine heritage authorities, the *Soprintendenze*, which can be considered the 'right hand' of regional government in this field. Given the crucial role they play, it seems important to investigate their activity in order to better understand the features of regional policy, looking particularly closely at their regulatory role. This chapter, therefore, looks at the activity of the *Soprintendenze* in Sicily and, using a political economy approach, offers some thoughts on the more general issue of heritage regulation, that is, the set of specific constraints or directives aimed at heritage preservation or conservation, which affect the behaviour of individuals, firms and institutions.

The analysis is as follows: section 2 briefly reviews the main arguments put forward in related literature to provide a rationale for public intervention in heritage. The main tools of public policy are outlined and special attention is paid to regulation, pointing out the particular features with regard to heritage and those policy implications which can be drawn from it. In section 3, theoretical arguments are used to comment upon the issue of conservation of heritage in Sicily and the role of the *Soprintendenze*, the heritage authorities. In section 4, some concluding remarks are offered.

2.   PUBLIC POLICY TOOLS FOR HERITAGE

2.1 The Rationale for Government Intervention

From the economist's point of view, the most widely accepted rationale for government intervention in the cultural sector recognises that culture is socially important and that markets are imperfect and need to be corrected according to individuals' preferences.[1]   This approach provides a well-established framework for studying public policies in the cultural sector.

Following this conventional normative approach based on 'market failure', and according to the prescriptions of welfare economics, a long-sighted government, adopting a 'public interest' stance, is assumed to provide efficient remedies to 'market failure' through the use of different policy tools. As far as efficiency is concerned, the well-known arguments developed in cultural economics literature on option demand, bequest demand, national prestige, public goods and externalities are usually put forward to justify public intervention in order to avoid underprovision of heritage services.

Moreover, as Throsby (1994) stresses, the normative case for public intervention might also rest on arguments which are outside the conventional assumption of well-informed individuals that underlies welfare economics. Among the issues raised regarding this matter,[2] is the argument that in the arts field, individuals are ignorant and not fully informed: as a consequence, they might make decisions which are not in line with their own interest and public intervention might be required. The concept of *cultural capital*,[3] recently put forward in related literature, stresses the non-economic dimension of heritage.

These normative arguments are too well known to merit further attention here:[4] what is important to stress is that on these grounds government policies are called for.   The question discussed here is whether administrative organisation has an impact on the way policy objectives are achieved.

2.2 Policy Tools: Public Expenditure, Taxation and Regulation

Different mixes of government policy instruments – public expenditure, taxation and regulation – can be adopted, depending on prevailing economic and institutional settings.

Public expenditure can take various forms, each of which has different economic implications: publicly produced goods and services (that is, restoration activities, purchasing of buildings of artistic importance) as well as subsidies and/or loans to private and/or public institutions for conservation purposes.

Taxation can be used as a tool to support private expenditure in heritage in many ways: tax allowances for donations aimed at conserving public historical buildings, tax allowances for owners of historical buildings both on direct taxes (wealth or income tax) and on their private expenditure on conservation of the building.

Regulation is aimed at controlling the stock of heritage; the fulfilment of this objective is usually pursued by listing historical and archaeological sites, as well as individual buildings: owners of designated buildings are obliged to comply with the prescribed requirements,[5] which are enforced by directives and involve penalties for non-compliance.

In this field, as Throsby has pointed out, 'regulation, in the sense of specific constraints or directives affecting behaviour, is possibly the most widely used tool in heritage conservation, despite the fact that in most circumstances it is the instrument least favoured by economists' (Throsby, 1997, p. 19).

Regulation on heritage can be imposed in different ways: preventing the demolition of a building or a group of buildings; imposing restrictions on the uses to which the building can be put, on its appearance and the way restoration and re-use is carried out; and imposing limitations on the use of land affecting heritage buildings.[6]

2.3 Links between Different Policy Tools

Different links may exist between regulations and other forms of government intervention. As Giardina and Rizzo (1994) suggested, regulation may be used as an independent tool as well as a complement to, or a substitute for, other policies. A 'classical' area is placing restrictions on private property by defining the limits of private property rights on heritage items. Regulations may be used as a complement to other policies whenever cultural private activities are publicly funded:[7] for instance, if a private owner receives public financial support for restoration work, he/she will be compelled to carry it out following precise rules and to allow the public to visit the restored building. Finally, regulations may be considered a substitute for public funding whenever a public activity relating to heritage is privatised. For instance, if a publicly owned building is sold to the private sector to be re-used, regulation can be used to ensure that government objectives are fulfilled.

In the analysis which follows, we concentrate on regulation and public expenditure, given that taxation is not a feasible tool available to the regional government in Sicily because it cannot levy autonomous taxation. However, it enjoys considerable autonomy in allocating resources. Before looking at the Sicilian case, some general issues can be pointed out.

2.4 Decision-making Process in the Regulation of Heritage

Leaving aside the 'public interest' rationale, closer consideration of the collective decision-making process[8] suggests some specific features of regulation which need to be stressed:

1. The regulator, that is, the heritage authority, enjoys much more freedom than regulators operating in other sectors of the economy. In fact, not only the choice of instruments and their intensity but also the scope of regulation depends on the regulator, because the size of the regulated sector is not well defined *ex ante*.[9] The identification of what cultural heritage is and, moreover, what deserves to be protected, varies through time[10] and a growth in the extent of conservation has actually been observed in some countries.[11]

2. The identity of the regulator depends on the institutional features of the regulatory decision-making process which may vary among countries.[12] Broadly speaking, it might be assumed that the decisions regarding *what* should be regulated and its ranking are taken at a political level based on the judgement of experts, while the decisions on *how* to regulate usually lie with administrators who are charged with implementing policies (for instance, imposing limitations, issuing constraints, levying penalties for non-compliance and so on). Because of the information problems related to the artistic and historical features of heritage, specialists often play a central role in the process of identification of cultural heritage. In most cases, as happens for instance, in Sicily, bureaucrats in the *Soprintendenze* are experts themselves and intervene in the identification process.

3. A high degree of uncertainty seems to result from the discretionary features of regulatory decisions. In fact, as Pignataro and Rizzo (1997) stressed from a more general perspective, since there is no objective way of identifying what deserves conservation and what priorities are to be established in setting the agenda for public intervention, the stock of cultural heritage, as well as its composition and relative importance of its elements,[13] strongly depends on the decision of experts (art historians, archaeologists and so on) and they are influenced by their specialisations.

2.5 The Impact of Regulation on Private Investment in Heritage

The strength of the restriction imposed by regulations affects the mix of public/private ownership and this creates consequences both for the possibility of conserving heritage and for satisfying society's demand for conservation. If regulatory decisions are taken adopting a 'conservationist' stance,[14] investment costs associated with conservation, maintenance costs as well as costs arising from the restrictions on use will be severely affected and, as a consequence, private investment could be discouraged.

It should be pointed out that under existing laws the *Soprintendenze* usually act according to a rule of thumb that calls for the stopping of any activity which is perceived as inimical to conservation, regardless of the economic implications of the decision taken. The concept of heritage conservation that is usually adopted is strict, the *Soprintendenze* themselves being liable for any damage that may be sustained from the activities carried out on the site.[15] However, they bear no responsibility for the economic loss caused by the restrictions they impose. For instance, a much-debated issue is the use of historical or archaeological sites or buildings for cultural events such as concerts or theatrical performances or even fashion shows: these events, in fact, regardless of their important economic benefits, are, in some cases, banned by the *Soprintendenze* because they are perceived as not being compatible with heritage (state of conservation, prestige and so on).

The above points bear consequences for the feasibility of conservation itself and, therefore, on the ability of local governments to use cultural goods as 'economic resources'. For instance, whenever a heritage item is the result of the combination of different styles and historical periods, as often happens in Sicily, any discovery made while the work is in progress may reduce the scope for planned use because the *Soprintendenze* may give priority to the preservation of the new discovery and, as a consequence, will interrupt the work and/or will impose changes compatible with the new discovery. The likely result is that private investors who intend to restore and rehabilitate a building might be discouraged by such a high degree of uncertainty.[16] It is the unintentioned consequence of a highly 'conservationist' stance which discourages private investment, crowds out private resources and, as a consequence, may result in a very low degree of conservation, that is, yielding the opposite effect to that desired.[17] This can be the starting point of a vicious circle which, because of a lack of funds and pressure on them, produces further decay, further pressure on public funds, and so on.

Severe constraints, in fact, are likely to arise as far as the availability of resources is concerned, especially in an era of budget stringency such as the present one. The problem becomes particularly severe in regions such as Sicily with a huge and widely dispersed artistic endowment, where conservation, if carried out on a large scale, can impose such high costs that they are simply too great for the public budget.

Moreover, we cannot ignore the fact that the costs imposed by heritage regulation on society include not only the costs borne directly by those who are regulated and who have to comply with prescriptions but also the costs imposed on society in terms of public resources used to implement regulations and the indirect costs imposed on any activity which may interfere with heritage at large.[18] To ignore all three of these elements would be to underestimate the full cost of heritage preservation.

2.6 Regulation of Heritage and Urban Renovation

The regulation of heritage is likely to have an impact on urban planning: this impact will depend on the 'stance' conservation policy takes and on the prevailing distribution of functions among different levels of government. This issue is particularly important whenever heritage is dispersed all over the country, as is the case in Sicily and, as a consequence, almost all local authorities are extremely interested in the role heritage can play in local development.

Restrictions on the use of buildings, their appearance and the way in which restoration and re-use is carried out might impinge upon the possibility of restoring and revitalising historical centres, which is usually one of the main objectives on local authorities' political agenda. Any historical centre, in fact, is considered a cultural good *per se*,[19] apart from the importance of each building within it, and therefore every activity within it is constrained by the need to ensure the conservation of such a public good. Indeed, this is in keeping with the objective of revitalising historical centres and transforming them into a 'resource' for the local community. It is important to stress that in many cases, a 'conservationist' approach impinges not only on private interests but also on the ability to pursue public interests. This is the case when major urban renovation is carried out by public institutions and the planned re-use is considered by the *Soprintendenze* to be incompatible with the building's features, for instance, because it would imply major changes to the interiors, even if they are considered compatible with local zoning prescriptions.

The existing distribution of functions in Sicily is such that a potential conflict is likely to arise;[20] no institutional links have been established between the *Soprintendenze* and local authorities even though their powers of regulating heritage conservation have important implications on urban policy carried out at local level.

2.7 The Role of Society in the Regulatory Process

From the above arguments, it follows that the process by which heritage decisions are taken is crucial: if it is driven only by specialists' interests, it is likely to bring about consequences in contrast with the claimed objectives of regulation itself, leaving society's demand unsatisfied. The extent of such an argument depends upon the degree of autonomy experts are granted and on the incentive schemes faced by the bureaucrats, that is, on the institutional features of the decision-making process.[21]

The issue of the role that society is expected to play in this process is crucial[22] and controversial: while it is widely agreed that taxpayers also have a legitimate claim in influencing public decisions on this matter, it is at the same time true that specific knowledge and expertise is involved so that these decisions cannot be left entirely to taxpayers.

Given the importance of the process, forms of greater public participation in decision-making[23] as well as compulsory assessment consultation or review procedures should be included in the regulatory process, though the benefits should be weighed up taking into account the likely increase in administrative costs and decrease in the process which would derive from it. The use of direct democracy tools, such as referenda, has been advocated to assess public evaluation of heritage policies[24] but again, the costs cannot be underestimated.

Another argument is that devolution[25] increases the accountability of government: in fact, in the heritage field, the positive effects of devolution seem to be even stronger than is usually claimed because the links between regional/local communities and heritage are very close[26] and there is a vested interest at decentralised level in the preservation and upkeep of heritage for the beneficial external effects that such an intervention can exert on a local economy (via its positive effects on tourism). Moreover, with it being easier to identify those who gain and those who lose from regulations and their interaction, members of the latter group may have more room to organise themselves, acting as watchdogs rather than being only passive adjusters to heritage authority decisions. From this point of view, Sicily offers an interesting case study to see whether devolution results in the regulatory process being more attuned to the wishes of the general public.

3. CONSERVATION IN SICILY: THE ROLE OF HERITAGE AUTHORITIES

3.1 The Role of the *Soprintendenze*: 'Active' and 'Passive' Conservation

As explained in Chapter 2, heritage conservation in Sicily comes under the competence of the regional government and is carried out by nine *Soprintendenze*.[27] They are fundamental to the decision-making processes underlying conservation[28] because any decision regarding heritage in Sicily is subject to their evaluation. Their activity therefore offers an interesting case study for understanding the features of conservation policy in Sicily and generally, to stress the role of the regulator in the heritage field.

Soprintendenze are a rather peculiar type of regulator, if compared with the abstract model described in the literature.[29] For expository reasons, only two different types of activity on the part of the *Soprintendenze* are distinguished: for simplicity, in what follows, we refer to them as 'passive conservation' and 'active conservation'. The former pertains to the activity of providing rules and monitoring their implementation, that is the regulation activity for both public and private heritage situated in the territory of competence; the latter refers to direct intervention to provide conservation, that is spending activity.

It might be argued that such a distinction is questionable given that active and passive conservation activities are closely interconnected. A clear case for making the connection is given by the research and study activities which underlie both. Moreover, in some cases these activities can be considered interdependent. For example, the discoveries resulting from archaeological excavations might call for imposing constraints; at the same time, expropriation is preliminary for direct intervention on the site. Notwithstanding the importance of these links, it is, however, useful to introduce the above distinction between active and passive conservation activities because it somehow recalls the conventional distinction between public policy tools – that is spending and regulation – and therefore it is useful for understanding the complexity of conservation activities from an economic point of view.

3.2 Passive Conservation

Many different administrative acts, which are enforceable on both private and public owners, are implied by passive conservation activity. Such a complex output can be summarised with the following list,[30] in which each item has a different degree of strength:

1. restrictions: limitations on the use of heritage, their strength depending on the type of heritage;[31]
2. taking the case to the judicial authority;
3. demolition orders; and
4. authorisations: consent to carry out activities (such as restoration, rehabilitation and so on) of heritage.[32]

In some cases the type of regulation adopted depends on the demand of the owners (this is the case, for instance, of permission to make alterations) while in other cases it can also be a spontaneous measure to restrict owners' activities (for instance, restrictions due to the listing of buildings) or to punish violations which have been committed (for instance, demolition orders).

Soprintendenze are responsible for the above-mentioned measures and enjoy a considerable degree of autonomy;[33] their decisions are taken on technical as well as administrative grounds, given that their staff is made up of experts, and are subjected only to judicial review, if those affected by these decisions go to court.

3.3 Active Conservation

A wide array of activities, including making a census or inventory, scientific research, giving staff specialised training, and updating, excavations and restoration, that is heritage conservation put in practice requiring a direct expenditure, are included in the category of active conservation. To carry out this last type of activity, *Soprintendenze* hire external contractors to do the work and sometimes also to draw up the related project.

A few issues deserve attention. First of all, the degree of autonomy enjoyed by the *Soprintendenze* is very high at the planning level while it is low at the operational level. Once the yearly programme of action that is submitted by each *Soprintendenza* is approved at regional level, it becomes obligatory and no discretionary variation is allowed. Nor does autonomy exist as far as the operation of funds is concerned, given that any expenditure decision, even within the programme, has to be approved at regional level. The *Soprintendenze* are 'free' to spend only in the so-called situations of 'high emergency'.

Expenditure by the *Soprintendenze* is constrained by the availability of funds. The amount of funds received from the regional government does not usually correspond to the amounts asked for in advance. Moreover, the regional budget law is rarely approved on time so that resources are usually only available by the middle of the year in question.

The lack of funds is perceived by the *Soprintendenze*[34] as the main cause of difficulties in carrying out direct provision for heritage conservation. Another problem, which has been indicated as relating to the lack of funds, is the impossibility of carrying out 'diagnostic' activity. If carried out on a permanent basis, it can be a useful and direct way of understanding the 'health status' of heritage; it would allow for conservation activity to be targetted where it is most needed with the likely consequence of improving the overall effectiveness of the allocation of resources in this sector.

3.4 Policy Implications

Having briefly described the aims and tools of regional government policy in the heritage field, it is interesting to turn to the implications of this mixture of functions. In what follows, some issues for further discussion and development are raised and a few tentative conclusions are put forward.

The first question to address is how each *Soprintendenza* establishes a trade-off between the main outputs it is expected to produce, that is the above-mentioned active and passive conservation. In defining such a trade-off, it is likely to take into account exogenous constraints as well as its own preferences as determined, among other things, by existing incentives.

Constraints seem to be different in the two cases. As was pointed out above, the possibility of carrying out active conservation measures is somehow constrained by the availability and timing of financial resources assigned by the regional government to each *Soprintendenza*.[35] Nor are there specific incentives to stimulate such an activity, given that the budget is not assigned on the grounds of past performance.[36] *Ceteris paribus*, financial constraints are less severe for passive conservation, where direct spending is less crucial, since it is only a marginal aspect of regulatory activity.[37]

At the same time, there is room for exploring whether active conservation is more important for gaining prestige and reputation among specialists, than passive conservation. In both cases, in fact, research is involved but, in the active conservation case, the restored building or the archaeological excavation are testimonies to the expertise of the *Soprintendenza* specialists involved in such an activity. Moreover, being experts themselves, these specialists are directly interested in any active conservation activity which offers scope for new discoveries, historical interpretation and, therefore, allows them to gain professional prestige. Such an attitude also tends to prevail when discoveries take place by accident, for instance during a public work such as the construction of a road; the interest of the *Soprintendenza* experts may lead to the work being suspended in order to allow specialists to investigate the discovery, use their findings for scientific work and improve their own reputation. It might be argued that it is in society's interest to promote knowledge and, therefore, that such an attitude is in line with society's welfare. This is not necessarily the case or, at least, the way the decision-making process works in practice does not allow it to be assessed. In fact, the decisions made by each *Soprintendenza* are usually not evaluated using the criterion of opportunity cost nor are there institutional arrangements for representing local preferences and therefore, as a consequence, the informational advantage enjoyed by the experts drives decisions.

As far as the demand for public intervention is concerned, there is no strong evidence to assess whether it is more or less effective in the active conservation case than in the passive conservation case. In the case of passive conservation, there is a strong individual component which has to be taken into account: listing, permissions as well as demolition orders or restrictions on the use of listed buildings are divisible, in the sense that they provide divisible benefits/costs[38] and they affect measures relating to both private and public-owned heritage, thus causing an accountability problem. *Soprintendenza* performance is likely to be monitored by interested parties (individuals as well as public and private institutions) and delays or poor performance are likely to give rise to some form of protest: however, the effectiveness of such a form of monitoring is limited by the fact that performance is not used by the regional government as a tool to provide incentives to the *Soprintendenze*. There is, in fact, no evidence of the existence of specific incentives (financial rewards, career benefits and so on) to stimulate *Soprintendenza* performance[39] (as measured by the length of bureaucratic procedures, the degree of complaints from the public and so on). Such external monitoring, however, is likely to be effective whenever individual bureaucratic responsibility is involved. It is useful to recall that the *Soprintendenza* is liable for any damage heritage suffers because of its action (or lack of action) with regard to any work or activity that third parties carry out on heritage.[40] Public concern may then provide an incentive to concentrate attention on passive conservation activities, allocating available resources, such as personnel, to those activities subject to stronger external control.

On the other hand, the role of public opinion seems to be less relevant whenever benefits/costs of a public good nature rather than private benefits/costs are involved. Public opinion, in fact, is interested in monitoring *Soprintendenza* activity because of its impact on the local economy and on the conservation of local artistic patrimony. Though the role of the public is important, since heritage is closely related to the identity of each community, the effectiveness of public opinion on the outcome of the decision-making process does not seem evident. Indeed, the fact that conservation is devolved to regional government does not in itself guarantee that local preferences are adequately represented.[41] The lack of institutional forms for representing local opinion in the regulation decision-making process is likely to limit the beneficial impact of devolution. Nor is *Soprintendenza* performance adequately monitored at regional level: in fact, as was pointed out above, no evidence emerges that an incentive system exists[42] on a generalised basis to induce *Soprintendenze* to fulfil government objectives, however defined.[43]

As a consequence, conservation would seem to be mainly driven by the specialists and experts within the *Soprintendenze* according to their own objectives and preferences.

4. CONCLUDING REMARKS

The main features of the heritage conservation decision-making process have been described, with particular attention paid to regulation, using the evidence from the Sicilian experience as a case study.

The peculiar feature of public policy in heritage – namely, that the area of policy cannot be clearly defined – suggests that the process by which heritage decisions are taken is crucial; the range and intensity of regulation appear more and more to be the endogenous product of the public decision-making process rather than the appropriate tool for fulfilling the stated objectives of government policy in the heritage field. The outcome of this is the tendency towards a 'conservationist' approach in the sense of enlarging the extent of regulation. The issue is of great importance in Sicily where, because of the huge dimension of heritage and the existence of severe resource constraints, a highly 'conservationist' stance may result in a very low degree of actual conservation because of its discouraging effect on private investment.

The evidence found in the Sicilian case also suggests that devolution as such is not enough to provide a framework of rules enhancing the accountability and responsiveness of heritage administrators to public opinion. Political instability has so far reduced the ability to control the administration; no evidence emerges that in Sicily any incentive system exists on a generalised basis (in terms of the size of budget or private benefits for bureaucrats such as career, salary and so on) to induce *Soprintendenze* to fulfil government objectives whatever they are. As a consequence, the choice of the output mix (active and passive conservation) is mainly driven by the specialisms and preferences within the *Soprintendenze*, in accordance with their own objectives. In keeping with such a framework, more attention is likely to be paid to the demand for public intervention when private benefits/costs are involved rather than when benefits/costs of a public good nature are implied.

Moreover, the distribution of functions is such that there is a potential conflict between different levels of government, with the power of regulation being assigned at regional level and implemented by the *Soprintendenze*, with implications on local urban policy.

NOTES

*. I am grateful to Anna Mignosa for helpful discussions, suggestions and critical comments.

1. Another approach is to provide support to the arts, considered as a 'merit good'. This argument is controversial. On one hand, it is argued that it shows a 'paternalistic' philosophy which is difficult to justify on rational grounds; on the other hand, it might be argued that in adopting a concept of multiple individual preferences, the contrast between merit goods and the consumer's sovereignty becomes an open question. According to Musgrave (1987), the conservation of art and culture may be considered a merit good in the sense that consumers' sovereignty is substituted by another rule; individuals support and finance culture and arts because they accept the 'community preference', even though their personal preferences may diverge.

2. Other aspects raised by Throsby (1994) refer to the fact that individual behaviour might be inconsistent because of misperception, weakness of will or fluctuation of preferences and that cultural goods can be defined as 'irreducibly social goods' because they provide benefits which cannot be attributed to a single individual.

3. Cultural capital is defined as 'an asset that embodies, stores or provides cultural value in addition to whatever economic value it might possess' (Throsby, 2000, p. 46). Elements such as aesthetic value, spiritual value, social value, historical value, symbolic value and authenticity value contribute to the aggregate cultural value of heritage.

4. See Towse (1994) and Peacock (2000).

5. Indeed, this is a very simplified way of summarising the complex array of legislation existing in different countries; a comparison between British, French, Italian and Spanish cases is provided by Bobbio (1992).

6. Throsby (1997) defines these forms of regulation as hard regulations, in order to distinguish them from what he calls soft regulations, that is non-enforceable directives (Charters, Codes of Practice, Guidelines and so on) implemented by agreement and not involving penalties.

7. Rules and prescriptions are aimed at inducing the beneficiaries of public subsidies to behave in accordance with the policy objectives underlying the subsidy.

8. It is assumed that regulators do not necessarily aim at pursuing public interest and that regulated producers are not 'passive adjusters' to regulations. The way in which policy may depart from an efficient outcome is complex and depends on various circumstances. This issue is investigated in Rizzo (1998).

9. This is not the case in most sectors where regulation is applied, for example in the electric industry, water supply, telecommunications and so on, where the

scope of regulation is well defined.

10. On this issue, see Guerzoni (1997).

11. Benhamou (1996) points out two reasons for the extension of the objects included in the set of cultural heritage: first, 'historical additions', since 'ever more recent buildings are included as they represent the national heritage of the future'; and second, 'typological extension', since 'new listings included gardens, original decor in restaurants, cafés, shops and swimming pools, parts of the nation's industrial heritage'.

12. Independent agencies can operate or, alternatively, decisions are taken at political level and implemented by bureaucracies. The policy implications of different institutional frameworks have been investigated by Mazza and Rizzo (2000).

13. On this issue, see Chapter 6 in this book.

14. This is the case when the list of buildings, sites and so on claiming historical importance is enlarged and the preservation orders imply strict requirements.

15. Such a liability refers to the fact that the bureaucrats, being public officials, can be taken to court.

16. This issue has been explored by Pignataro and Rizzo (1997) by looking at a specific case study, the rehabilitation of the Benedictine Monastery in Catania (Sicily).

17. The same negative result is reached if private owners, because of the stringency of prescriptions, undertake their activities without complying with existing rules; the likelihood of this is greater, the lower the risk of punishment. When the extent and intensity of regulations are relevant, monitoring, in fact, cannot be exerted effectively because of the amount of resources required for it.

18. Peacock (1994) refers to the considerable hidden costs involved in planning regulations imposing the diversion of roads to protect archaeological sites.

19. A 'polar' case is given by the so-called 'heritage cities', that is, those cities where the historical centre coincides with the city itself, raising specific issues as far as conservation and value of heritage are concerned (see Mossetto, 1992).

20. Such a potential conflict is more severe at national level where *Soprintendenze* are local branches of the Ministry and at local level, five different *Soprintendenze* operate. Some features of the Italian case are addressed in Chapter 14 in this book.

21. This issue is explored by Mazza and Rizzo (2000).

22. The problem that there is a need for a governance structure to define a mechanism available to society to restrain the discretionary scope of regulators is common to regulation in general (see Levy and Spiller, 1996).

23. Peacock (1994) proposes that public participation could be enhanced if greater openness were to characterise the appointments of 'lay' persons to decision-

making bodies and if citizens who are active in heritage matters were allowed to vote for their own representatives within these bodies. See also Chapter 13.

24. Swiss referenda offer interesting evidence on public attitudes towards the arts. Frey (1997) examines the arguments for extending the use of such a method in cultural decisions.

25. The term devolution implies a stronger content of autonomy than the term decentralisation and, in fact, with respect to cultural policy in general, is used to refer to the movement of responsibility to a lower level of government so that such a level has a complete autonomy as far as policy-making, finance, management and performance are concerned, decentralisation being limited to the last two responsibilities (Schuster, 1997).

26. A hierarchy of buildings might be established in terms of the geographical distribution of benefits deriving from conservation, whether it be national, regional or local, in order to decide upon the appropriate level of decision-making.

27. The fundamental conservation principles, however, derive from Italian national law (law 1039/1939) and they constitute a compulsory framework for further regional legislation in the field.

28. For simplicity, adopting the Lichfield (1988, p. 26) classification, policies on cultural built heritage, which can be regarded in general terms as conservation, include: (1) prevention of deterioration; (2) conservation; (3) consolidation; (4) restoration; (5) rehabilitation; (6) reproduction; (7) reconstruction. In practice, these different types of intervention are variously combined.

29. For a general overview, see Sugden (1993).

30. The list does not include import and export licences because they refer to works of art (paintings, objects, sculptures, manuscripts and so on) which are outside the scope of this chapter.

31. These restrictions include different items: those on monuments, prohibitions on making alterations and constraints on landscape.

32. The strength of this act depends on the type of heritage and on the restrictions to which it is subjected: for instance, the more severe ones include interiors, if the building is listed, while the less severe ones are if the building, being located in the historical centre, is only subject to restrictions on its outward appearance.

33. In some cases, for instance, when a monumental constraint is imposed, the procedure ends up with a formal act, a decree, issued by the *Assessore*, based on a proposal put forward by the *Soprintendenza*.

34. See Chapter 2. In the first stage of the research into the operation of heritage authorities in Sicily, interviews were conducted with senior bureaucrats in each of the nine *Soprintendenze* and a questionnaire was submitted. The questionnaire contained questions on output (both active and passive

conservation), input (personnel), financial resources and also on 'qualitative'
aspects such as relationship with local governments, role of procurement and so
on.

35. As was pointed out in Chapter 2, however, evidence shows that on average
     Soprintendenze only manage to spend half the resources they obtain.

36. Indeed, the figures describing the budget of each *Soprintendenza* (see Chapter
     2) were not even easily available and this gives an idea of the lack of
     consciousness at regional level for the adoption of any incentive system. A
     study of the determinants of *Soprintendenza* finance will be one of the further
     developments of the present research.

37. For instance, this is the case for expenditure on demolition and expropriation.

38. Of course the strength of the regulation put into practice is another question
     and relies on the discretion the *Soprintendenza* enjoys in carrying out its
     regulation activity.

39. See Chapter 4.

40. The concept of bureaucratic risk aversion can offer a useful explanatory
     framework (see Mazza and Rizzo, 2000).

41. One possible explanation lies in the fact that the accountability of regional
     government in Sicily has been very low: lack of real fiscal autonomy coupled
     with a proportional political system has so far implied a very low degree of
     political accountability. The voting system changed very recently: in 2001 for
     the first time, the regional governor was elected directly by voters.

42. The recent reform of regional bureaucracy (regional law no. 20/2000) has
     introduced a new contractual scheme which is about to be enacted and is likely
     to create new incentives for *Soprintendenti*.

43. In Sicily, political instability has reduced the instruments of control over
     bureaucracy (Chapter 4).

REFERENCES

Benhamou, F. (1996), 'Is Increased Public Spending for the Conservation of Historic
     Monuments Inevitable?', *Journal of Cultural Economics*, (20), 115–31.

Bobbio, L. (ed.) (1992), *Politiche dei Beni Culturali in Europa*, Bologna: Il Mulino.

Frey, B. (1997), 'The Evaluation of Cultural Heritage: Some Critical Issues', in M.
     Hutter and I. Rizzo (eds), *Economic Perspectives on Cultural Heritage*,
     Basingstoke: Macmillan, pp. 31–49.

Giardina, E. and Rizzo, I. (1994), 'Regulation in the Cultural Sector', in A. Peacock
     and I. Rizzo (eds), *Cultural Economics and Cultural Policies*, Dordrecht:
     Kluwer, pp. 125–42.

Guerzoni, G. (1997), 'Cultural Heritage and Preservation Policies: A Few Notes on the History of the Italian Case', in M. Hutter and I. Rizzo (eds), *Economic Perspectives on Cultural Heritage*, Basingstoke: Macmillan, pp. 107–32.

Levy, B. and Spiller, P.T. (eds) (1996), *Regulations, Institutions and Commitment*, Cambridge, New York and Melbourne: Cambridge University Press.

Lichfield, N. (1988), *Economics in Urban Conservation*, Cambridge: Cambridge University Press.

Mazza, I. and Rizzo, I. (2000), 'Public Decision-making in Heritage Conservation', paper presented at the 11th International Conference on Cultural Economics, Minneapolis, 28–31 May.

Mossetto, G. (1992), *L'Economia delle Città d'Arte. Modelli di Sviluppo a Confronto, Politiche e Strumenti di Intervento*, Milan, Etas Libri.

Musgrave, R.A. (1987), 'Merit Goods', in J. Eatwell, M. Milgate and P. Newman (eds), *The New Palgrave: A Dictionary of Economics*, London: Macmillan, pp. 452–3.

Peacock, A. (1994), *A Future for the Past: The Political Economy of Heritage*, Edinburgh: The David Hume Institute.

Peacock, A. (2000), 'Public Financing of the Arts in England', *Fiscal Studies*, vol. 21, 171–205.

Pignataro, G. and Rizzo, I. (1997), 'The Political Economy of Rehabilitation: The Case of the Benedettini Monastery', in M. Hutter and I. Rizzo (eds), *Economic Perspectives of Cultural Heritage*, Basingstoke: Macmillan, pp. 91–106.

Rizzo, I. (1998), 'Heritage Regulation. A Political Economy Approach', in A. Peacock (ed.), *Does the Past Have a Future? The Political Economy of Heritage*, London: Institute of Economic Affairs, pp. 55–73.

Schuster, J.M. (1997), 'Deconstructing a Tower of Babel: Privatization, Decentralization and Devolution as Ideas in Good Currency in Cultural Policy', *Voluntas*, vol. 8, (3), 261–82.

Sugden, R. (ed.) (1993), *Industrial Economic Regulation*, London: Routledge.

Throsby, D. (1994), 'The Production and Consumption of the Arts: A View of Cultural Economics', *Journal of Economic Literature*, (32), 1–29.

Throsby, D. (1997), 'Seven Questions in the Economics of Cultural Heritage', in M. Hutter and I. Rizzo (eds), *Economic Perspectives of Cultural Heritage*, Basingstoke: Macmillan, pp. 13–30.

Throsby, D. (2000), *Economics and Culture*, Cambridge: Cambridge University Press.

Towse, R. (1994), 'Achieving Public Policy Objectives in Arts and Heritage', in A.T. Peacock and I. Rizzo (eds), *Cultural Economics and Cultural Policies*, Dordrecht: Kluwer, pp. 143–65.

4. Organisation and Decision-making in the Heritage Sector in Sicily

Isidoro Mazza

1. INTRODUCTION

In the growing field of the economics of the arts, a considerable amount of attention has been devoted to the analysis and evaluation of public policy (for a review, see Throsby, 1994; Towse, 1997; Blaug, 2000).

This literature has investigated both the normative aspects, such as the justification for public support, and positive aspects, such as the activity of specific institutions in different countries (see, for example, Bobbio, 1992; Brosio and Santagata, 1992; Giardina and Rizzo, 1994; Peacock 1994b, 1994c; Towse, 1994). A general tenet underlying this analysis has been the objective of social welfare maximisation by those who formulate and implement cultural policies, although their perception of what should be financed and how much, can differ from that shared by the public (Peacock, 1994b, 1994c). On the contrary, there are relatively few political economic studies on the subject allowing for self-interested, non-benevolent decision-makers.[1] From this point of view, the political economic analysis of the arts seems little developed in contrast to a recent trend of public economic studies in other areas. In my opinion, this is rather surprising because the analysis of the policy-making process is particularly meaningful and important for evaluating public policy for the arts, due to the fact that justifications, objectives, means and the extent of intervention are often difficult to define, if not outright controversial. Furthermore, in some countries like Italy, the dimension of historical heritage is such that it involves a considerable amount of national resources and, therefore, may well attract the attention of interest groups who can benefit substantially from influencing political decision-making.[2]

In this chapter, a 'public choice approach' is adopted in order to analyse the hierarchical organisation of the regional administration of cultural heritage in Sicily. Unlike all other Italian regions, Sicily enjoys a unique comprehensive autonomy in this matter; in fact, the state authority concerning libraries, heritage, art, museums and the safeguarding of the landscape is fully delegated to the regional legislator.[3] In particular, we focus on the unusual organisation of the decentralised bureaux with specific responsibility for the cultural heritage, the *Soprintendenze*.

In Sicily, each *Soprintendenza* is responsible for all the policies concerning the whole cultural heritage of a specific province, whereas, in the rest of Italy, *Soprintendenze* are generally responsible for certain categories of cultural heritage or work carried out in a specific region. The investigation of these institutions provided here considers them as endogenous, in view of the objective of the legislator: they are supposed to be designed and to evolve in order to best serve the interests of the government. Therefore, in the presence of potentially different objectives between the political sector and those who implement public programmes, bureaucratic institutions may be designed by the political sector in order to guarantee supervision of the activity of the former.

This study suggests a political economic interpretation of the observed centralisation of policy-making in Sicily, particularly as far as financial aspects are concerned (see Chapter 2). It is shown that centralisation may be supported by institutional design that allows the central government to control the decisions made by local offices. In particular, we show that the specific design of the Sicilian *Soprintendenze*, unlike their Italian equivalents, favours this control in an uncertain environment where the life span of government is very short.[4] It is also argued that such a specific organisation strengthens the power of local, politically influential groups to exert their influence on regional policies.

The investigation presented here sheds light on the decision-making process underlying the regional policy on cultural heritage, arguing the importance of political determinants of public expenditure on cultural goods. From this point of view, the propositions presented here could be the basis for empirical studies testing for political bias in the geographical distribution of regional resources. In addition, this study provides more general insights into the effect of political instability on the decision to decentralise.

The chapter is organised as follows: section 2 offers a brief presentation of the basics of the public choice approach and recalls some literature on political institutional design which will be used as a basis for the theoretical issues presented in this chapter. Section 3 identifies some characteristics of the administration of cultural heritage in Sicily, while section 4 interprets these characteristics in the light of the main theoretical models. Section 5 presents the main thesis of this work, concerning political instability and its effect on the design of the regional administrative framework. Finally, section 6 concludes with a few comments on the broader implications.

2.   A PUBLIC CHOICE APPROACH

Public choice has been defined as 'the economic study of non-market decision-making' (Mueller, 1989, p. 1). The spread of the field has been extraordinary in the last forty years and has generated a huge amount of literature on a large variety of subjects. A very brief overview of the main topics would probably require more pages than those in this book and is beyond the scope of this study; however, in order to help the reader who is unfamiliar with public choice, I present some basic topics in public choice theory on which the analysis presented in this chapter rests.

2.1 Some Basic Issues

The study of the policy-making process is obviously a very complicated matter. The variety of institutions, the substantial number of actors involved and the complexity of relationships among them are already sufficient to give insight into the difficulty of such an analysis.   In the economic literature, we can distinguish two main theoretical approaches to the study of public policy-making.   One approach presents a fundamental assumption that the activity of the public sector is especially directed at the achievement of public interests. A different approach, which is followed in this chapter, considers that individuals fulfil personal objectives in collective decision-making just as they do in the market.   Policy-makers therefore react to economic incentives and strive for their position because of the economic advantages they can derive from it although they could also concentrate on public welfare.   This hypothesis applies to each participant in the public sector, political representatives as well as bureaucrats: the former are responsible for the policy selection and the latter for policy implementation. Of course, it is reasonable that these actors have different interests because politicians are elected and generally bureaucrats are not.

Delegation of authority from a political principal to a bureaucratic agent may cause a loss of political control of the former over government output. With complete information, agenda-setting and gate-keeping powers provide the bureaucrat with a substantial influence over policy outcomes.   When there is asymmetric information, agencies have an additional instrument, namely their superior knowledge, to control the public decision-making process and deceive the legislator, if the latter has different goals.[5]   The extent of bureaucratic compliance with the objectives of their political principals is related to several factors, such as the magnitude of information asymmetries, the diversity of interests and the availability of incentive contracts and/or monitoring instruments (Noll, 1989). The public outcome, therefore, will depend on the characteristics of relationships between the political principals and bureaucratic agents.

Moving our attention from the supply to the policy demand side, we see that not all individuals have the same influence on public outcome. Politicians need the support of their constituency if they want to be elected but not all individuals are informed about the policy formation process. Voters are 'rationally ignorant' about politics as they have a negligible impact on the electoral result. In addition, organisational costs and free-riding problems, due to collective benefits deriving from policies, hinder lobbying activities by large heterogeneous groups. By contrast, relatively smaller groups with specific interests face low transaction costs and high per capita stakes from favourable policies. They could therefore have a selective incentive applicable only to them, for overcoming free-riding, for being informed about politics and for investing resources to influence policy-making (Olson, 1965).[6] Redistribution to these groups has a political cost to the elected policy-makers, due to the dissatisfaction of those who pay for that redistribution. These kinds of costs, however, are presumably low for the politicians because of the lack of information that common voters have and because the per capita cost of redistribution to the narrow group will be marginal, since it is distributed among a large number of individuals. Clearly, not only politicians but also bureaucratic officials can be targets for lobbying by interest groups.

The more autonomy those officials have from political superiors and the greater their importance in the policy-making process, the more likely this is to happen; moreover, the autonomy of an office is positively related to its informational advantage. The possibility of bureaucratic capture by interest groups has to be taken into account by the political principal when deciding the degree of autonomy to delegate and/or when designing the incentive-compatible contracts capable of inducing the bureaucrat to act according to the preferences of the principal.

2.2 Endogenous Institution Formation

After having indicated the main actors in a general process of political decision-making, we have to consider the institutional environment within which they interact. This section draws specifically on recent literature regarding the endogenous formation of political institutions. According to this theory, institutions are designed and evolve in a way that guarantees benefits for their members, according to their relative power. This approach is in line with the indications of the new economics of organisation, presenting the institutions within the firm as designed to reduce transaction costs, as well as the problems of moral hazard, adverse selection and shirking due to asymmetric information and contract incompleteness.[7]

Recent studies have investigated the justification for the separation of powers that we observe in the organisation of the public sector and in politics. For example, Laffont and Martimort (1998, 1999) show that the fragmentation of regulative powers in many agencies increases welfare benefits and therefore the payoff of the legislator because it reduces the information monopoly rents that a single regulator would enjoy. Persson et al. (1997) address the issue of institutions allowing the voters to oversee their representatives. They show that the separation of agenda-setting power between parliament (or congress) and government (or president) introduces a system of checks and balances that may induce the representatives to fulfil the preferences of the voters.

The study most closely related to this is probably Banks and Weingast (1992). In that paper, the legislator is unable to observe the performance of bureaucratic agencies and the outcome of bureaucratic agencies is relevant for the re-election chances of the legislator, because his/her constituents are consumers of the agencies' services. Banks and Weingast suggest that this information problem can be solved by the activities of interest groups who may benefit from transferring valuable information about the activity of the agencies to the legislator. The main consequence in institutional terms is that the value of the information transmitted by the groups may induce the legislator to create those agencies that can be more easily monitored.

A similar idea is advanced in this chapter. I argue that the design of the regional administration and of the provincial agencies is advantageous for the legislators in order to solve the problems of overseeing bureaucracy and to serve the interest of their constituents, when governments are short-lived. Before explaining this thesis in more detail, it would be helpful to look closely at some characteristics of the regional administration of cultural heritage.

3. THE ADMINISTRATION OF CULTURAL HERITAGE IN SICILY

Sicily enjoys special autonomous powers compared to other Italian regions, and a complete autonomy as regards the preservation, conservation and valorisation of Sicilian cultural heritage.[8] It is therefore paradoxical that Sicily, which represents the main laboratory for experimenting with fiscal federalism in Italy, is characterised by a heavily centralised system as far as the administration of cultural heritage is concerned. At the top of the hierarchical organisation of the regional administration, we find the *Assessorato Regionale dei Beni Culturali e Ambientali e della Pubblica Istruzione* and, at a lower level, there are nine provincial heritage authorities, the *Soprintendenze* with specific competences compared to their national equivalents.   In particular, each Sicilian *Soprintendenza* has jurisdiction over a sub-regional territory, the province, and is divided into seven technical sections (archaeological heritage, architectural heritage, libraries, archives, historic and artistic goods, etc.), whereas in the rest of Italy the *Soprintendenze* have jurisdiction over a whole region and they are differentiated according to working area.[9] The specific competences of the Sicilian *Soprintendenze* are usually justified on the grounds that they provide a comprehensive and co-ordinated administration of the local heritage existing under one (provincial) jurisdiction.[10] Theoretically, the inclusion of more technical offices in one sector may be explained with the goals of easing the co-ordination of activities and/or allocating resources efficiently by minimising the variance of their output (Cremer, 1980).

Concentration of functions may, however, reduce welfare as it increases the power of an agency to assign rents through regulation and therefore induces those interest groups favoured by regulation to lobby (that is 'to capture') that agency (Laffont and Martimort, 1998, 1999). Moreover, the existence of several dimensions of output may make it more difficult to evaluate the performance of an office. An additional problem caused by multifunctionality concerns Sicily in a specific way. This is related to the rule that the head of the *Soprintendenza* (the *Soprintendente*) is selected from among the directors of the different sections. This rule has been criticised because it gives an evident advantage to the section from which the *Soprintendente* comes.[11]

In addition to having more functions, the regional *Soprintendenze* are characterised by a superior constraint and control over their decisions or power of decision-making. A first constraint is represented by the limited budget that makes them depend fully on regional transfers for their functioning and the completion of local projects. Regional transfers are contingent on specific projects and activities proposed by the *Soprintendenza*. A similar centralisation applies to regional museums: the earnings from ticket sales are remitted to the regional administration and then the *Assessorato* finances their expenditure.[12] The determinants of the regional transfers are, however, unclear. It appears from our investigation that there is no officially defined scheme regulating the allocation of funds. This allegedly large discretion over the budget provides the regional *Assessorato* with an effective authority over local agencies. That authority is strengthened by the fact that the *Assessorato* appoints the heads of each provincial *Soprintendenza* (that is the *Soprintendente*) and the directors of regional museums for five years.

In order to explain the reasons endogenously for this centralised administration and the functions of *Soprintendenze*, we need to investigate the advantages for the political system from which it originates.

4.   JUSTIFICATIONS FOR CENTRALISED DECISION-MAKING

As mentioned above, the organisation of the decision-making process is a rather complicated matter for the information asymmetries affecting the relationships between elected representatives and bureaucrats within a governance structure. The problem of obtaining some kind of performance from bureaucrats is based on the difficulty in observing and measuring their performance. For example, when the legislator generally observes some 'product' in the office, he/she is uncertain about the underlying behaviour of the bureaucrat. Moreover, the impossibility of designing complete contracts that spell out the conduct of the bureaucrat in every circumstance exacerbates opportunistic behaviour from the latter.

When the preferences of the executive are frequently in conflict with those of the bureaucrat, the former may have an incentive to reduce the autonomy of the latter. For example, in the context of cultural goods, it may be expected that *Soprintendenti* have a more conservationist approach than the *Assessore*, because of different cultural backgrounds, institutional roles, personal goals as well as responsibility they have regarding the conservation of monuments. Moreover, the *Assessore*, as a member of the government, may be biased towards the exploitation of heritage for social events with the aim of attracting electoral support. On the contrary, *Soprintendenti* are non-elected bureaucrats and likely to be less willing than the former to exploit cultural sites for collective uses and, instead, more inclined to preserve cultural heritage.

The centralisation of decision-making may also produce some benefits in terms of policy co-ordination in addition to ensuring policies that closely reflect the preferences of the principal. In spite of the above problems, legislators may nonetheless be induced to delegate the implementation of policies to bureaucracy for several reasons. In a nutshell, the de-centralisation of policy-making in line with the principle of subsidiarity, has the advantage of empowering agents who are more informed about local preferences and more competent than central government. Moreover, there are several instruments available for reducing the risk of bureaucratic drift or abdication caused by delegation. Monitoring is a rare option because of its costs in terms of time and resources. Similarly, it may be rather difficult to design an appropriate system of *ex ante* incentives/constraints and *ex post* penalties, for the information requirements of the legislator.

Other, probably more feasible systems exist for improving political control (Weingast and Moran, 1983). Firstly, the political sponsor could stimulate competition between agencies for the allocation of resources (for example see Breton and Wintrobe, 1982). Secondly, bureaucrats can be appointed by the principals and fulfil their preferences because of career concerns (Peacock, 1994a; Tirole, 1994). Thirdly, as already mentioned, organised groups may have incentives to monitor the activity of the bureaucrats and alert the legislator to protecting their rights against abuses by the administrative system (Banks and Weingast, 1992; see also McCubbins and Schwartz, 1984).

The effectiveness of the above instruments in controlling the bureaucrats and inducing them to act according to the principals' preferences should, however, not be overstated. For example, competition between bureaucrats may transform into collusion. Furthermore, bureaucrats may go against those who appointed them with little risk to their careers when they have become indispensable to the organisation. Finally, interest groups may have the incentive to behave strategically in their surveillance and sound alarms even when they are not needed. It may then be difficult to separate true problems from false alarms, if there are insufficient penalties for lying or if the preferences of lobbies and legislators are too different to make the former credible (see Lupia and McCubbins, 1994).

Political principals can also induce bureaucracy to act according to their goals by introducing criteria and procedures that substantially restrict the range of bureaucratic activity and improve the effectiveness of controls (Epstein and O'Halloran, 1994). This rather extreme solution, however, nullifies a great deal of the previously discussed advantages of decentralisation. In conclusion, the delegation of decision-making implies a fundamental trade-off for the legislators between the benefits deriving from information held by the bureaucrats and the cost of bureaucratic drift; where the latter has to be compared to the cost of defining laws and incentive schemes to limit that drift.

In the light of the above observations, we can finally interpret the cultural heritage administration in Sicily.

5. POLITICAL REPRESENTATION AND INSTITUTIONAL DESIGN

In this section, I would like to present an explanation of the unusual centralised decision-making process we observe in the Sicilian administration of cultural heritage which is endogenous to the specific political setting.

Sicilian governments are generally characterised by a rather short life span. The electoral system, based on proportional representation, causes a frequent political turnover: fifty-two regional governments, from 1947 to 1998. This political instability has some important consequences for the choice of decentralised administration and the design of bureaucratic institutions. In particular, the frequent turnover of governments reduces the instruments of control over bureaucracy. For example, the power of appointment does not represent a powerful device for discipline. As mentioned above, the *Soprintendenti* and the director of regional museums are appointed by the regional government (*Assessorato*) and stay in power for five years. A government will, therefore, often find a pre-existing bureaucracy. In this case, the use of informal agreements between a political principal and bureaucratic agents (see Breton, 1995) is hindered by government turnover, which makes politicians' promises less credible.

Thus, if we look at the instruments indicated in the previous section, the remaining control instruments are basically the budget allocation, which can stimulate competition between the provincial agencies (*Soprintendenze*) and scrutiny by interest groups. The use of the first instrument seems corroborated by empirical observation since *Soprintendenze*, as well as regional museums, only have a very limited autonomous budget. They totally rely upon regional transfers. As for monitoring by interest groups, this is facilitated by the particular structure of the *Soprintendenze*. In particular, the characteristic that all the main sectors are grouped into one office with jurisdiction over a limited territory (the province) makes monitoring by local interest groups easier than with institutions such as the state *Soprintendenze* in the rest of Italy. In that case, each local group has to provide information about several offices, instead of one; and for the policy-maker, it can be difficult to co-ordinate information coming from different sources.

More importantly, I would argue that the regional *Soprintendenze* are designed in such a way as to reduce costs for the legislator serving the interests of his/her constituency. Suppose, for example, that a regional secretary wants to favour the group of his/her electors that one may reasonably assume to be located mainly within the boundaries of a jurisdiction and they require more expenditure for all the cultural goods in their province.[13] If *Soprintendenze* were structured as in other Italian regions, with a single institute having authority over the whole regional territory, the legislator would not be able to use the budget instrument to support his/her constituents. In fact, an increase in the budget of one *Soprintendenza* may, in principle, benefit any jurisdiction in the region and there is no guarantee that the office will allocate the resources to favour that specific constituency of the legislator giving the grant. Furthermore, it would be costly for the regional legislator to lobby each *Soprintendente* to favour a specific jurisdiction. On the contrary, by designing institutions with authority over the whole heritage of a province, the legislator could be confident that the interests of the constituents will be served by biasing the allocation of resources towards that office. Furthermore, the legislator would need to exert pressure only on one *Soprintendente*, if required to support the constituency's welfare.

The existence of a politically uncertain environment suggests that the legislator would try to shape institutions to guarantee a centralised decision-making structure. On the contrary, when there is certainty concerning the incumbency, a government may be willing to give autonomous power to lower bureaucracy. Since every government, however, expects to last for a rather limited period of time, it may have strategic reasons to 'hard-wire' the bureaucracy chosen by itself: the imposition of strict procedures would reduce the advantages that bureaucracy can provide to future (potentially rival) governments. In addition, because with each potential new government there is a high probability of finding a bureaucracy selected by a different and potentially hostile government, the political system would endogenously be inclined to support the choice of a bureaucracy with restricted authority.

One could argue that national Italian governments have also been short-lived in the recent past and therefore the fact that we do not observe a similar organisation as in other regions seems inconsistent with the above thesis.

This discrepancy might be justified by the observation that members of the national government find it difficult to serve narrowly located interests because of institutional and political constraints. In particular, a redistribution of national resources to local subregional jurisdictions might find more opposition within the government and the party of affiliation than a redistribution to a region because of the different effects that they have in terms of political support. From this point of view, the region would represent the lowest jurisdictional level to which redistribution policies can be pushed forward by the national Ministry and the organisation of the *Soprintendenze* would be of little relevance in fulfilling redistribution objectives. In other words, the regional interests would represent a target for the national Ministry equivalent to the provincial interests for the regional *Assessore*.

From the above discussion, the administrative organisation which we have seen at national level seems to offer little control to central government over regional policy-making. In line with the concept of endogenous institution formation and with other issues concerning political supervision of bureaucracy, it is interesting to note the recent introduction of the *Soprintendente Regionale* for every region except Valle d'Aosta, Trentino Alto Adige and Sicily, which have the power to co-ordinate the activity of the *Soprintendenze* in their region, intervening in regional planning, verifying the outcome and expenses of *Soprintendenze* as well as their functional needs in order to optimise the allocation of human resources.[14] In my opinion, this institutional reform favours a greater control of central government on the activity of the regional office. In fact, the *Soprintendente Regionale* is more likely to be informed about the activity of regional offices than the *Ministro per i Beni e le Attività Culturali*, because of its institutional role and its auditing role which will therefore improve the oversight of the latter over regional administration.

6.   CONCLUDING COMMENTS

In this chapter I have tried to present some explanations for the centralised decision-making process characterising the administration of cultural heritage in Sicily. According to the analysis provided, the institutional framework seems consistent with the hypothesis that the regional legislator aims to serve the interests of his/her constituency. Moreover, it has been argued that the choice of centralisation may be directly connected to the uncertainty concerning the term of government.

The topics presented here also offer interesting insights into the political economic analysis of fiscal federalism. It is suggested that the decentralisation of functions is dependent on the control that a higher-level policy-maker can exert on the performance of the lower-level decision-maker. This control is weakened by the uncertainty concerning the duration of the central government which hinders the use of several instruments (such as informal contracts, the power of nomination and competition) which can be used to direct the decisions of lower-level government. Incidentally, this outcome seems strikingly consistent with what we observe in Italy, where the recent reform process towards decentralisation coincided with the replacement of proportional representation by a majority system which produced more stable governments, while Sicily maintained proportional representation.

NOTES

1. Exceptions are, for example, Grampp (1989) and Mossetto (1994) examining

rent-seeking in the performing arts and visual arts and Mazza and Rizzo (2000a, b) investigating rent-seeking in the regulation of urban heritage conservation.

2. As for the entity of expenditure of the Sicilian region on cultural goods, see Chapter 2 in this book.

3. *Decreti del Presidente della Repubblica* n.635/1975 and n.637/1975.

4. For a complete description and analysis of the functions of the *Soprintendenze*, see Chapter 3 in this book.

5. The political representatives may be induced to delegate the implementation of policies to bureaucracy because of time and competence constraints and in order to guarantee expeditious intervention. The existence of many specific problems needing specific information that is costly to acquire and process leads to the creation of information-managing hierarchies (Radner, 1992, 1993). De-centralisation and specialisation can reduce the time needed to process information but may imply a cost for the delay in internal communication. An efficient communication network should therefore have, for a given degree of specialisation, a number of communication links that cannot be reduced without worsening the performance of the organisation (see Bolton and Dewatripont, 1994).

6. Therefore, a policy bias in favour of narrow interest groups would originate from their superior ability, with respect to the general public, in overcoming the free-riding problem of information acquisition and monitoring the legislator (Lohmann, 1994).

7. In their seminal paper, Weingast and Marshall (1988) apply these concepts to the US committee system, suggesting that it is designed to institutionalise vote trading and solve the problem of *ex post* enforceability of bargains. They assume that each congressman has the goal of re-election and therefore he/she serves the interests of politically important groups in his/her district without being constrained by the political party. To do so, each legislator needs to trade votes with others, with obvious problems caused by the non-simultaneity of the exchanges and benefit flows, for example.

8. See Chapter 2 in this book.

9. For example, in Liguria there is one *Soprintendenza* for archaeological sites, another for archives and so on. The same reasoning applies in other regions. In some special cases with particularly substantial and important heritage, we can have *Soprintendenze* with a more limited jurisdiction, which include more provinces or only one, as in the cases of Rome or Naples; occasionally, *Soprintendenze* may include an even smaller territory, as in the cases of Pompei and Venice. However, in these instances, *Soprintendenze* also refer to a single institute (that is archaeological heritage, architectural heritage, or archives and so on).

10. A standard explanation for the choice of a limited jurisdiction is efficiency. By fragmenting the regional administration into provincial jurisdictions we can fulfil local preferences, assuming that external effects are irrelevant. There are at least two kinds of problems with this interpretation. Firstly, the completion of a decentralised system would mean more autonomy for the local agencies and a separate budget. Secondly, there is no evident connection between the decisions of the *Soprintendenze* and the preferences of the residents in the provinces. For example, the project of having local councils putting forward the needs of local communities has not been implemented yet.

11. The recent reform of regional bureaucracy (regional law no. 20/2000) has introduced a different system for appointing the *Soprintendenti* and new incentives for them.

12. For a detailed overview of the administration of Sicilian cultural heritage, see Chapter 2.

13. Of course, it is assumed here that each province does not internalise the costs imposed on other jurisdictions.

14. See the D.Lgs. no. 368/1998 and D.P. no. 441/2000, which provide the legislative framework.

REFERENCES

Banks, J.S. and Weingast, B.R. (1992), 'The Political Control of Bureaucracies Under Asymmetric Information', *American Journal of Political Science*, **36**, 509–24.

Blaug, M. (2000), 'Where Are We Now On Cultural Economics', *Journal of Economics Surveys*, **15** (2), 123–43.

Bobbio, L. (1992), *Le Politiche dei Beni Culturali in Europa*, Bologna: Il Mulino.

Bolton, P. and Dewatripont, M. (1994), 'The Firm as a Communication Network', *Quarterly Journal of Economics*, **109** (4), 809–39.

Breton, A. (1995), 'Organizational Hierarchies and Bureaucracies: An Integrative Essay', *European Journal of Political Economy*, **11**, 411–40.

Breton, A. and Wintrobe, R. (1982), *The Logic of Bureaucratic Conduct*, Cambridge, UK: Cambridge University Press.

Brosio, G. and Santagata, W. (1992), *Rapporto sull'Economia delle Arti e dello Spettacolo in Italia*, Turin: Fondazione Agnelli.

Cremer, J. (1980), 'A Partial Theory of the Optimal Organization of a Bureaucracy', *The Bell Journal of Economics*, **11**, 683–93.

Epstein, D. and O'Halloran, S. (1994), 'Administrative procedures, information, and agency discetion', *American Journal of Political Science*, **38**, 687–722.

Giardina, E. and Rizzo, I. (1994), 'Regulation in the Cultural Sector', in A. Peacock and I. Rizzo (eds), *Cultural Economics and Cultural Policies*, Dordrecht: Kluwer, pp. 125–42.

Grampp, W.D. (1989), 'Rent-seeking in Arts Policy', *Public Choice*, **60**, 113–21.

Laffont, J.J. and Martimort, D. (1998), 'Transaction Costs, Institutional Design and the Separation of Powers', *European Economic Review*, **42**, 673–84.

Laffont, J.J. and Martimort, D. (1999), 'Separation of Regulators Against Collusive Behaviour', *Rand Journal of Economics*, **30**, 232–62.

Lohmann, S. (1994), 'Electoral Incentives, Political Intransparency and the Policy Bias Toward Special Interests', mimeo.

Lupia, A. and McCubbins, M. (1994), 'Learning from Oversight', *Journal of Law, Economics and Organization*, **10** (1), 96–125.

Mazza, I. and Rizzo, I. (2000a), 'Public Decision-making in Heritage Conservation', paper presented at 11th International Conference on Cultural Economics; Minneapolis, 28–31 May.

Mazza, I. and Rizzo, I. (2000b), 'Scelte Collettive e Beni Culturali', mimeo.

McCubbins, M. and Schwartz, T. (1984), 'Congressional Oversight Overlooked: Police Patrols vs. Fire Alarms', *American Journal of Political Science*, **28**, 165–79.

Mossetto, G. (1994), 'Cultural Institutions and Value Formation on the Art Market: A Rent-seeking Approach', *Public Choice*, **81**, 125–35.

Mueller, D.C. (1989), *Public Choice II*, Cambridge, UK: Cambridge University Press.

Noll, R.G. (1989), 'Economic Perspectives on the Politics of Regulation', in R. Schmalensee and R. Willig (eds), *Handbook of Industrial Organization*, vol. II, Amsterdam: North-Holland, pp. 1253–87.

Olson, M. (1965), *The Logic of Collective Action*, Cambridge, MA: Harvard University Press.

Peacock, A. (1994a), 'The Utility Maximizing Government Economic Adviser: A Comment', *Public Choice*, **80**, 191–7.

Peacock, A. (1994b), 'The Design and Operation of Public Funding of the Arts: An Economist's View', in A. Peacock and I. Rizzo (eds), *Cultural Economics and Cultural Policies*, Dordrecht: Kluwer, pp. 167–84.

Peacock, A. (1994c), 'A Future for The Past: The Political Economy of Heritage', Edinburgh, UK: The David Hume Institute.

Persson, T., Roland, G. and Tabellini, G. (1997), 'Separation of Powers and Political Accountability', *Quarterly Journal of Economics*, **112**, 1163–202.

Radner, R. (1992), 'Hierarchy: The Economics of Managing', *Journal of Economic Literature*, **30**, 1382–416.

Radner, R. (1993), 'The Organization of Decentralized Information Processing', *Econometrica*, **61**, 1109–46.

Throsby, D. (1994), 'The Production and Consumption of the Arts: A View of

Cultural Economics', *Journal of Economic Literature*, **32**, 1–29.

Tirole, J. (1994), 'The Internal Organization of Government', *Oxford Economic Papers*, **46**, 1–29.

Towse, R. (1994), 'Achieving Public Policy Objectives in the Arts and Heritage', in A. Peacock and I. Rizzo (eds), *Cultural Economics and Cultural Policies*, Dordrecht: Kluwer, pp. 143–65.

Towse, R. (1997), *Cultural Economics: The Arts, the Heritage and the Media Industries*, Cheltenham, UK and Lyme, USA: Edward Elgar.

Weingast, B.R. and Marshall, W.J. (1988), 'The Industrial Organization of Congress; or, Why Legislatures, Like Firms, Are Not Organized as Markets', *Journal of Political Economy*, **96**, 132–63.

Weingast, B.R. and Moran, M.J. (1983), 'Bureaucratic Discretion or Congressional Control? Regulatory Policymaking by the Federal Trade Commission', *Journal of Political Economy*, **91**, 765–800.

PART II

Supply of Heritage

5. Measuring the Efficiency of Museums: A Case Study in Sicily

Giacomo Pignataro

1. INTRODUCTION

Museums represent an important part of the supply of cultural goods in Sicily.

They mostly belong to the public sector and, therefore, the analysis of their efficiency is crucial for the evaluation of cultural policies. 'Museums may be viewed as productive units "firms" which, in order to achieve certain objectives, engage in the transformation, via a production technology, of inputs into a mix of outputs' (Johnson and Thomas, 1998, p. 75). Despite the particular nature of the 'output' produced by museums, this view stresses the fact that museums use valuable resources to carry out their activity and, therefore, they should be made accountable for the way they organise the transformation of inputs into outputs. The nature of the output produced, however, is relevant to the techniques that can be applied to measure the efficiency of the production process of museums.

The issue of measuring the performance of museums has been addressed in many studies. One of the notions that has been used to analyse the efficiency of museums, especially US museums, is cost minimisation. Heilbrun and Gray (1993) develop their analysis of art museums in the USA by focusing on the financial aspects of their management. Deaccessioning, one of the hottest issues in the economics of museums, is usually discussed as a problem of efficient financial management of museums' collections (see Frey, 1994). Cost minimisation is an important dimension to be considered when evaluating the efficiency of museums but there must be serious doubts as to whether it properly measures their performance. Cost minimisation is related to the optimal choice of inputs and therefore it implies that museums' managers should be able to control the main inputs used in the different activities in which a museum is involved. This is not always true for every museum, particularly in those countries where most museums belong to the public sector and operate within a set of more or less tight constraints. Sicily surely represents a case in which museums' managers are exogenously constrained in the choice of inputs they employ. They do not have a budget and cannot select the people who work in the museum because they are employees of the regional administration. It would, therefore, be completely inappropriate to judge the efficiency of these museums by looking at their financial performance. This is the main reason why we have decided to look at the technical efficiency of museums as a possible measure of their performance.

Technical efficiency occurs when an organisation produces the maximum output, given the available inputs. Perelman and Pestieau (1988) think of technical efficiency as a 'natural' objective of any organisation, public or private. 'The only objective for which no extenuating circumstances can be invoked is that of technical efficiency (for a given input pattern, more of any outputs cannot be produced). This objective is thus compatible with all the other objectives. In other words, there are no good justifications of any sort for not producing more with the available inputs' (Perelman and Pestieau, 1988, p. 433).

The common method of measuring technical efficiency in most empirical studies on museums is represented by productivity indicators.[1] Among the most widely used indicators are those measuring the number of visits per unit of the different categories of personnel, the number of visits per square metre of display space, the attendance trend, which is defined by Ames (1997) as the ratio of each year's total attendance to the average of the preceding 3 years' attendance.[2] The productivity indicators are able to provide some information on specific aspects of the museums' management. The production process in museums, however, is multidimensional, both from the input and output sides. Indicators then fail to provide a general representation of the production process. The wide range of indicators[3] does not allow for a clear-cut evaluation of the efficiency of each museum. Moreover, when comparing the values of the same indicator for different museums, the relevance of the comparison is limited by the fact that quantities of output, multiples or submultiples of that achieved by any given museum, are not necessarily technically attainable by employing multiples or submultiples of the inputs used by that museum. There is a need, therefore, to use more advanced techniques that take into account the multidimensional nature of museums' production process. This is why we measure technical efficiency of museums through the method of efficiency frontiers, using a non-parametric technique, Data Envelopment Analysis (DEA), and showing its advantages with respect to more traditional methods, such as productivity indicators. Efficiency frontiers or, as they are sometimes called, *best practice* frontiers are sets of the best production units. The particular advantage of the methodology of non-parametric efficiency frontiers, including DEA, with respect to simple productivity indicators, is to establish a sort of 'best' reference, those museums which are on the efficiency frontier (that is they are 100 per cent efficient), without the need to impose any assumption about the shape of the frontier.

The empirical analysis is restricted to a sample of Sicilian museums, those which fall under the responsibility of the Sicilian regional administration. The regional museums belonging to our sample are the Archaeological Museum of Agrigento, the Archaeological Museum of Messina, the Aeolian Museum of Lipari, the Archaeological Museum of Camarina, the Salinas Archaeological Museum, the Palazzo Abatellis Gallery in Palermo, the Paolo Orsi Archaeological Museum, the Palazzo Bellomo Museum in Syracuse, the Conte Agostino Pepoli Museum in Trapani and the Ceramics Museum in Caltagirone. Their choice is justified by their particular importance in the Sicilian context, both for the number of visits and for the broad scope of their collections. Data were collected through questionnaires filled out by museum managers, in co-operation with their administrative and technical staff. The data requested in the questionnaire cover the 1986–96 period. Later, we obtained more detailed data on personnel for the 1993–98 period from the central offices of the regional administration and further data on visits for the years 1997 and 1998. Given the purpose of our analysis, we have considered only data on personnel and visits. For financial data on museums, see Chapter 2 in this book.

The measurement of technical efficiency implies the identification of the physical inputs used by museums and the outputs produced, in other words the production process, discussed in section 2. Once inputs and outputs are clearly identified, it is necessary to apply a technique to measure efficiency. After a brief presentation of DEA and some summary statistics of data in section 3, in section 4 we will show the results of the measurement of technical efficiency of Sicilian museums in our sample. Concluding remarks are drawn in section 5.

2. THE PRODUCTION PROCESS

Whatever techniques are used, the measurement of technical efficiency emerges from a relation between the inputs used in the production process and the output(s) eventually attained. The definition of the characteristics of the production process administered by museums is therefore preliminary to any attempt to measure their technical efficiency. The main problem encountered here is connected with a clear identification of what constitutes the output(s) of museums. In their seminal work, Peacock and Godfrey (1974, p. 17) assert that 'a gallery/museum presents a range of products in the form of exhibits which satisfy a desire for visual enjoyment or for instruction ... Consumer participation is essential to the process of production'. Heilbrun and Gray (1993, p. 172) refer to museums as 'essentially a collection of objects that have been systematically gathered to provide information and stimulation to the attending public'. Finally, Hutter (1998, p. 100) says that the 'output [of museums] can be divided into three disparate segments: 1) expansion, maintenance and documentation of a collection, 2) display services and 3) add-on product and service offers'. From all the above definitions, we get the idea that production in museums is a complex process that makes use of several inputs and generates multiple outputs. Moreover, some of these outputs can be considered as intermediate products, which serve as inputs for the production of other outputs. It is obvious for instance that the extent of exhibitions is strictly related to the activity of collection of objects.

Figure 5.1 is simply an attempt to provide a rough illustration of a typical museum's activities. There are inputs which are specialised in the production of specific outputs (display spaces for the display of objects), and others which serve the preparation of different activities in museums. At the same time, the arrows in the chain of production stress the fact that there are intermediate outputs that are used as inputs for the production of other outputs. The fact that visits have been considered among the outputs of museums reflects the view that those managing museums must regard the promotion of attendance as part of their duties, of what they must produce, since 'Consumer participation is essential to the process of production'.

The museums' activities probably deserve a more refined representation than that contained in the diagram in Figure 5.1. However, when we want to evaluate museums' efficiency, we must refer to the overall process of production, no matter how complex it is.

3.   MEASUREMENT OF MUSEUMS' EFFICIENCY

3.1 The Technique

We measure the technical efficiency of museums through the use of DEA. DEA is a mathematical non-linear programming technique elaborated by Charnes et al. (1978). It can be considered as a generalisation of the traditional approach to productivity indicators in a multiple-output multiple-

Figure 5.1 Inputs and outputs in the production process of museums

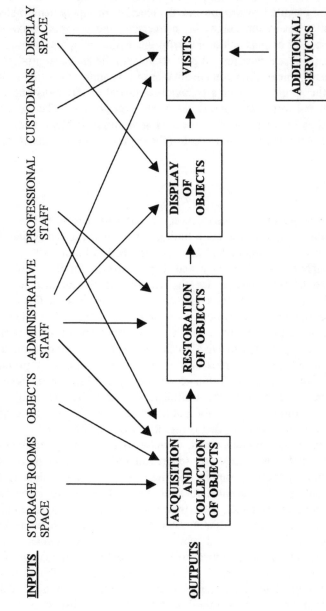

INPUTS STORAGE ROOMS   OBJECTS   ADMINISTRATIVE   PROFESSIONAL   CUSTODIANS   DISPLAY
SPACE   STAFF   STAFF   SPACE

OUTPUTS

ACQUISITION AND COLLECTION OF OBJECTS

RESTORATION OF OBJECTS

DISPLAY OF OBJECTS

VISITS

ADDITIONAL SERVICES

69

input context like the production of museum services. It allows for measuring the potential maximum radial reduction in inputs achievable to keep production levels unchanged or, conversely, the potential maximum radial expansion of outputs achievable with the available inputs. Moreover, DEA provides different measures of pure technical efficiency and production scale efficiency. One of the main advantages of this approach is that it does not require the specification of a behavioural model of museums and of a precise functional form representing the production process. The measures are computed as the solution of a linear programming problem, under the hypotheses of constant returns to scale (CRS) or variable returns to scale (VRS).

3.2 The Data

As already mentioned in the introduction, the database used in this analysis is severely limited. One of the main limitations is related to the availability of data for some of the inputs and outputs described in Figure 5.1. We do not have complete data for storage and display spaces, for the number of objects owned by museums or for the number of objects displayed by museums. We are not able, therefore, either to measure the efficiency of some of the activities of museums depicted in Figure 5.1, such as conservation or restoration, or to attempt an evaluation of their overall efficiency. The application of DEA in this chapter is therefore limited to estimating the efficiency of museums in using their inputs to promote attendance. This has the unfortunate consequence of not being able to exploit all the potentiality of the technique employed but we think this application is a useful exercise for pointing out benefits and costs of a method of measuring efficiency that is essentially new to this field.[4]

As far as the inputs are concerned, we have used data on administrative and technical staff, custodians and square metres of display space. As already mentioned, the only output on which we had reliable data is the number of visitors. We decided to split personnel into two categories, custodians and other personnel, since their contribution to the production of the selected output is of a different nature. While the employment of custodians is directly connected with exhibitions and therefore with attendance, the technical, administrative and scientific staff may also be regarded as a sort of 'indirect' input because they contribute to the production of general services, conservation and research activities, which are valuable inputs in the 'production' of attendance. The display space is a sort of proxy measure of the capital employed in museums' activities, not only *per se* but also because it may reflect the size and number of the objects exhibited.

Some summary statistics of the data employed in the analysis of efficiency are presented in Table 5.1.

Table 5.1 Summary statistics

Year	Statistics	Visitors	Tech.+Admin. Personnel	Custodians	Display space
1993	Mean	36,616	23	32	2,340
	Stand. Dev.	27,514	13	16	1,452
	Min	7,490	1	3	350
	Max	99,543	39	52	5,000
1994	Mean	44,138	25	34	2,340
	Stand. Dev.	36,168	13	10	1,452
	Min	10,000	6	18	350
	Max	119,329	43	48	5,000
1995	Mean	53,533	25	33	2,340
	Stand. Dev.	45,293	12	9	1,452
	Min	10,330	7	18	350
	Max	113,416	41	48	5,000
1996	Mean	53,881	24	31	2,340
	Stand. Dev.	40,430	12	11	1,452
	Min	10,747	7	18	350
	Max	141,745	42	44	5,000
1997	Mean	26,142	23	32	2,340
	Stand. Dev.	22,652	11	10	1,452
	Min	0	6	16	350
	Max	73,308	41	45	5,000
1998	Mean	40,435	23	29	2,340
	Stand. Dev.	30,385	12	11	1,452
	Min	10,710	9	12	350
	Max	108,520	43	43	5,000

Source: Author's questionnaire.

4. THE RESULTS

First of all, we have computed, for the inputs and the outputs considered in this analysis, an overall measure of technical efficiency for each museum in each year, whose results are shown in Table 5.2 below.[5] The efficiency values may range from 0 (for totally inefficient observations) to 1 (for a fully efficient observation on the efficiency frontier).

The mean value in each year under observation is quite low, ranging from

0.475 in 1995 to 0.59 in 1996. These measures have a quite straightforward interpretation. In 1995, on average, museums in our sample had to reduce their inputs to 47.5 per cent of their actual level in order to be fully efficient.

Table 5.2   Computations of overall technical efficiency for museums in Sicily

Museums	1993	1994	1995	1996	1997	1998
Palazzo Abatellis	0.375	0.332	0.294	0.447	0.541	0.602
Palazzo Bellomo	0.260	0.382	0.382	0.565	0.543	0.547
Agrigento	0.953	0.841	0.863	1	0.882	0.761
Caltagirone	1	0.492	0.518	0.705	0.571	0.579
Lipari	1	1	1	0.972	1	1
Messina	0.324	0.267	0.234	0.246	0.259	0.485
Palermo	0.232	0.257	0.299	0.360	0.219	0.225
Camarina	0.931	0.765	0.732	0.994	0.854	0.874
Syracuse	0.387	0-339	0.344	0.446	0.388	0.482
Trapani	0.177	0.098	0.085	0.170	0.093	0.109
Mean	0.564	0.477	0.475	0.590	0.535	0.566

The values show an alternate pattern over time with a decrease in the first three years, an increase in the following two years, and again a decrease in the last year under observation. The variability of results among the museums is quite high but that is probably due to the restricted number of observations. Only the museum in Lipari is always on the efficiency frontier, except in 1996 (its efficiency score in that year was, however, 97.2 per cent of full efficiency).

Five museums are on the frontier for just one year, while the remaining four are never considered as efficient. Overall technical efficiency measures provide us with information on the 'best' performances in the sample and on the relative inefficiency of all other museums with respect to the former. Inefficiency may, however, have different explanations. It may well be that a museum is behaving efficiently thanks to the combination of inputs it is using for 'producing' its attendance. It is not, however, as efficient as a museum on the frontier because the production technique used by the latter (in other words, the 'optimal ratio' of outputs to inputs) is optimally exploited only when the 'scale' of production is exactly at the level of the fully efficient museum.[6] If the current production process of museums is such that, at a different scale, the return of inputs in terms of outputs is variable, then the inefficiency signalled by overall measures of efficiency may be simply due to an inefficient scale of production, and it is not attributable to managers' behaviour. This is why it is useful to decompose the overall measure of efficiency into two separate measures: pure technical efficiency and scale efficiency.[7]

The values of pure technical efficiency are computed on the basis of the VRS assumption. The estimates are shown in Tables 5.3 and 5.4 below.

Table 5.3 Pure technical efficiency

Museums	1993	1994	1995	1996	1997	1998
Palazzo Abatellis	0.386	0.511	0.506	0.534	0.556	0.614
Palazzo Bellomo	0.389	0.554	0.596	0.963	0.710	1
Agrigento	1	1	1	1	1	1
Caltagirone	1	1	1	1	1	1
Lipari	1	1	1	1	1	1
Messina	0.349	0.5	0.5	0.471	0.481	0.522
Palermo	0.234	0.482	0.502	0.424	0.361	0.337
Camarina	1	1	1	1	1	1
Syracuse	0.388	0.407	0.416	0.463	0.432	0.507
Trapani	0.217	0.542	0.566	0.442	0.483	0.529
Mean	0.596	0.700	0.709	0.730	0.702	0.751

Table 5.4 Efficiency of scale

Museums	1993	1994	1995	1996	1997	1998
Palazzo Abatellis	0.972	0.650	0.580	0.836	0.972	0.980
Palazzo Bellomo	0.669	0.690	0.641	0.586	0.764	0.547
Agrigento	0.956	0.841	0.863	1	0.882	0.761
Caltagirone	1	0.492	0.518	0.705	0.571	0.579
Lipari	1	1	1	0.972	1	1
Messina	0.927	0.535	0.467	0.522	0.540	0.928
Palermo	0.989	0.534	0.596	0.849	0.607	0.665
Camarina	0.931	0.765	0.732	0.994	0.854	0.874
Syracuse	0.996	0.831	0.828	0.965	0.897	0.949
Trapani	0.818	0.181	0.150	0.385	0.192	0.206
Mean	0.926	0.652	0.637	0.781	0.728	0.749

The main advantage of using the VRS assumption is the gain in precision of the measurement of the inefficient behaviour of museum managers in the short run, given the size of each museum. The efficiency scores in Table 5.3 reveal that more museums can be regarded as efficient if we take account of their current size. Some of the inefficiency measured under the CRS assumption is then due to an inefficient scale of production, as can be seen from the results in Table 5.4. It is also possible to be more precise on the nature of scale inefficiency. All museums, with the exception of the ones in Agrigento and Lipari,[8] present increasing returns to scale. In other words, their size (measured either in terms of inputs or outputs) is smaller than what would be optimal.

Furthermore, for each museum it is possible to compute the exact reduction in the quantity of each input for attaining target levels that would locate the museum on the efficiency frontier. The analysis of the values of targets, as far as personnel is concerned, does not reveal special inefficiencies connected to one of the two categories.

Finally, it is possible to consider the variation in the efficiency scores over time which are usually referred to as productivity changes. These changes may be due to movements towards or away from the efficiency frontier (efficiency changes) or to movements of the efficiency frontier itself (technological changes). It is possible to compute the so-called Malmquist index[9] of productivity changes and to decompose it in a measure of technological change and one of efficiency change. The latter in turn can, as usual, be decomposed in pure efficiency and scale efficiency changes. The results are shown in Tables 5.5 and 5.6. In Table 5.5 the changes are measured for all museums in each year with respect to the previous year, starting with 1994. In Table 5.6 the measures refer to each museum as an average of the annual changes.

Table 5.5 Malmquist index summary of annual means

Year	Total factor productivity change	Technological change	Efficiency change	Pure technical efficiency change	Scale efficiency change
1994	1.024	1.199	0.853	1.307	0.653
1995	1.183	1.207	0.980	1.017	0.963
1996	1.083	0.824	1.315	1.017	1.293
1997	0.858	0.997	0.861	0.962	0.895
1998	1.109	1	1.109	1.074	1.033
Mean	1.045	1.035	1.010	1.069	0.944

Table 5.6 Malmquist index summary of museums' means

Museums	Total factors productivity change	Technological change	Efficiency change	Pure technical efficiency change	Scale eff. change
Palazzo Abatellis	1.161	1.056	1.099	1.098	1.002
Palazzo Bellomo	1.225	1.056	1.160	1.208	0.960
Agrigento	1.020	1.068	0.955	1	0.955
Caltagirone	0.768	0.857	0.896	1	0.896
Lipari	1.063	1.063	1	1	1
Messina	1.145	1.056	1.084	1.084	1
Palermo	1.045	1.052	0.994	1.076	0.924
Camarina	1.036	1.049	0.987	1	0.987
Syracuse	1.108	1.060	1.045	1.055	0.990
Trapani	0.958	1.056	0.907	1.195	0.759
Mean	1.045	1.035	1.010	1.069	0.944

The values in Tables 5.5. and 5.6 show that over the six years considered in the data set productivity has increased on average about 4.5 per cent per year. The dynamics of efficiency substantially varies across museums and over time. Most of the change in total productivity is explained by a movement of the efficiency frontier, while a minor contribution has been given by improvements in the technical efficiency of single museums. The measures of change in scale efficiency confirm the view that some museums are excessively small.

5.   CONCLUDING REMARKS

Even if the limitations in the sample do not allow us to draw definitive conclusions, some points deserve to be stressed.

As for the nature of the problems of regional museums' performance in Sicily, it seems that the biggest issue is attendance. This emerges from the identity of the so-called *peer* museums. The peers are represented by those museums which are regarded as purely efficient (that is those observations on the efficiency frontier under VRS) and whose input–output combinations provide a reference for the inefficient museums.[10] Only three museums – Caltagirone, Camarina and Lipari – can be regarded as peers in this sense. These are relatively small museums, with the lowest number of personnel and, in the case of Camarina, with the smallest display space. The most important characteristic, however, is that they enjoy a sort of natural flow of visitors, because they are located either in holiday resorts (Camarina and Lipari) with a considerable flow of tourists or in towns which attract people for the production of objects connected to the museum's exhibitions (Caltagirone).[11] The achievement of efficiency in the attraction of visitors to museums therefore seems to be related to factors exogenous to the managers' choices.

The other problem is the relatively high value of inefficiency of scale, which reveals that the museums in the sample generally operate at too low a production scale. Again, since the number of visits to museums is not completely under the control of their managers, this analysis needs to be enriched with an investigation of the main determinants of the differences in efficiency among museums, looking at the properties of the demand for museum attendance and at the qualitative characteristics of the museums' supply. However, a few managerial policy suggestions may arise even from this limited analysis. Any improvement in the efficient use of resources in museums surely involves a co-ordination of efforts by the regional administration and the museum managers. Given the relevance of the inducement of visits due to tourism, the regional administration could develop policies for a better exploitation of the flow of tourists to the island (on this issue, see Chapter 6). They should aim to encourage a better distribution of tourists among the different sites, so that regional museums and other heritage sites could enjoy a number of visits commensurate with the resources employed. At the same time, museum managers should make a bigger effort to develop those services which stimulate people to visit their collections. The development of additional services, moreover, is a way of improving the efficient use of inputs, above all personnel, without any dismissals.

The limitations in the availability of data have not allowed us to show the potentialities of DEA in measuring efficiency in a multiple-input multiple-output context. However, even with this quite constrained data set, it has been possible to point out the additional information coming from the application of this technique. First of all, it provides more information about the nature of the inefficiency of museums, either pure technical inefficiency or scale inefficiency. Secondly, it may provide those who have responsibility for the management of museums with clear indications about the pattern of changes needed to improve performance since, for each input and each output, it suggests the quantitative change needed to be efficient.

The benefits that the application of this methodology can bring about should provide an incentive to further think about the production process of museums and the best way to model it. Any progress in this field can indeed be accompanied by an appropriate empirical methodology capable of incorporating the complexity of the museums' production process.

NOTES

1. For a survey of a wider set of performance indicators for museums, see Jackson (1997).
2. It allows for the representation of the dynamics of visits to museums.
3. The potential number of indicators measuring factor productivity is equal to the number of inputs multiplied by the number of outputs.
4. For other applications of non-parametric techniques in the analysis of efficiency of museums, see Mairesse and Vanden Eeckaut (1999).
5. The overall technical efficiency measures are computed under the assumption that the transformation of inputs into outputs is done through a constant returns to scale technology. Moreover, our efficiency measures are input oriented, that is, they show the maximum radial reduction in inputs needed for each museum to become efficient, given their output.
6. With a one-input–one-output production process, for instance, a production unit

on the frontier uses 50 units of input to produce 100 units of output. However, the production techniques may be such that the maximum output attainable using 25 units of input is less than 50.

7. It has been shown (Banker et al., 1984) that the efficiency of scale of a productive unit can be defined as the ratio of the distance function with respect to the VRS technology to the distance function with respect to the CRS technology. The latter identifies the measure of overall technical efficiency, while the former defines the pure component of technical efficiency, once the effect of variable returns to scale is taken into account.

8. The former presents decreasing returns to scale, while the latter is fully efficient.

9. On the Malmquist index, see Caves et al. (1982).

10. In other words, the inefficient museums would become efficient using an amount of inputs which is a linear combination of the inputs used by *peers*.

11. Caltagirone is famous for its production of ceramics and the museum specialises in ceramics.

REFERENCES

Ames, P.J. (1997), 'Measuring Museums' Merits', in K. Moore (eds), *Museum Management*, London, UK: Routledge, pp. 22–30.

Banker, R.D., Chang, H. and Cooper, W.W. (1984), 'Some Models for Estimating Technical and Scale Inefficiency in Data Envelopment Analysis', *Management Science*, **30**, 1078–92.

Caves, D.W., Christensen, L.R. and Diewert, W.E. (1982), 'The Economic Theory of Index Numbers and the Measurement of Input, Output and Productivity', *Econometrica*, **50**, 1393–414.

Charnes, A., Cooper, W.W. and Rhodes, E. (1978), 'Measuring the Efficiency of Decision Making Units', *European Journal of Operational Research*, **2**, 18–39.

Frey, B. (1994), 'Cultural Economics and Museum Behaviour', *Scottish Journal of Political Economy*, **41**, 325–35.

Heilbrun, J. and Gray, C.M. (1993), *The Economics of Art and Culture: An American Perspective*, Cambridge: Cambridge University Press.

Hutter, M. (1998), 'Communication Productivity: A Major Cause for the Changing Output of Art Museums', *Journal of Cultural Economics*, **22**, 99–112.

Jackson, P.M. (1997), 'Performance Indicators: Promises and Pitfalls', in K. Moore (ed.), *Museum Management*: London, UK, Routledge, pp. 156–72.

Johnson, P. and Thomas, B. (1998), 'The Economics of Museums: A Research Perspective', *Journal of Cultural Economics*, **22**, 75–85.

Mairesse, F. and Vanden Eeckaut, P. (1999), 'Museum Assessment and FDH

Technology: A Global Approach', Université Catholique du Louvain CORE Discussion Paper 9938.

Peacock, A. and Godfrey, C. (1974), 'The Economics of Museums and Galleries', *Lloyds Bank Review*, **111**, 17–28.

Perelman, S. and Pestieau, P. (1988), 'Technical Performance in Public Enterprises', *European Economic Review*, **32**, 432–41.

6. Heritage and Tourism[*]

Giovanni Montemagno

---

1. INTRODUCTION

The last fifty years of international tourism have seen an increase in the demand for cultural destinations; thus, an analysis of their conservation, management and use both for tourists and for the region's inhabitants is called for (Council of Europe, 1999).

One of the two basic characteristics which makes an area the object of tourist demand and supply,[1] is the specific localisation and permanence of its resources. Users must therefore travel in order to express their demand (Montemagno, 1985, pp.80–81). In this chapter attention is concentrated on demand for heritage and tourism. The second characteristic is the potential or effective knowledge of the tourist resources by potential users.

The cultural heritage in a region constitutes an object of demand by tourists who go to a specific region for a specific reason. It is, however, also the object of domestic demand. The two are connected. If resources are expended on heritage to justify tourist flows and the benefits brought by these flows are enjoyed (such as revenue, employment and so on), the quality of life of residents in physical and cultural terms has to be protected (Patin, 1997, p. 127).   The cost of excessive and unchecked tourist flows, from wearing out and changing the environment and its resources, has to be considered. There are also social and cultural costs, with the degradation of the urban and natural environment, culture and folklore.

The hypothesis of overexploitation linked to excessive tourist flows and the possible conflict between foreign and domestic demand calls for some form of public policy aimed at promoting the use of cultural resources, while at the same time, establishing limits and rules. This chapter considers how public intervention can affect the supply of heritage and, as a consequence, tourist demand. To do so, Syracuse will be used as a case study.

2.   THE TOURIST USE OF CULTURAL HERITAGE

Heritage can be also considered an important resource to be used to promote endogenous and sustainable development, an objective which over the last few years has gained attention in regional policy. The term endogenous is used to include all the region's resources: natural, human and scientific, financial and cultural; sustainable means that it must have a positive intergenerational balance from the point of view of environment and resources. Regional heritage is, indeed, linked to cultural tourism and its elements can become tourist resources if properly managed (Pechlaner and Osti, 2000, p. 212).

The use of cultural goods as a tourist resource requires careful planning to keep mass tourism under control, through the definition of an adequate level of access both for the more fragile resources and for those capable of receiving non-stop flows. This is in line with the interest of combining two different objectives: the preservation of heritage for future generations and the development of a significant tourist demand. Well-organised tourism has positive effects on a regional economy, while if badly managed it would no longer be a positive development factor.

To fulfil the above-mentioned objective, useful steps are the creation of an index to check the various elements of heritage and the use of the concept of environment's carrying capacity.[2]

Legal and economic tools can be used to control tourist flows. Legal tools can be restrictions, positive precepts or policy rules aimed at controlling the private activity of those employed in tourism and the organisation of resources. Economic tools are the introduction of charges. Among the various tools which can be used to plan a sustainable growth, we focus attention only upon the policies directed towards heritage, linked to the 'attraction capacity' of cultural resources, that is, the possibility of distinguishing the tourist supply of a region from that of other competitive regions (Wahab, 1996, pp. 60–74).

3.   THE MANAGEMENT OF CULTURAL HERITAGE AS A TOURIST RESOURCE

A rational policy in the management of cultural heritage as a tourist resource must be a careful classification of all the elements that are part of this large, open category, that is the creation of a 'register' of resources. The list should include not only descriptive data and content but also references to the opportunities for and limits of tourist use. The list should go together with a calendar of linked activities which constitute a further attraction for tourists.

The second step should be the creation of the 'tourist product', which is simply the content of the tourist supply; the tourism organisms (tourism offices or departments, town councils and so on) have to create a complex process to integrate the resources with other elements which constitute the integrated tourist product (ITP), that is land use, transport and access infrastructures, hotels, camping sites and other structures, complementary goods and public or private facilities.

A necessary stage between the creation of the register of cultural tourist resources and of 'tourist product' creation is heritage conservation, that is restoration and adaptation needed to transform the cultural heritage from 'visible' or 'open' to 'available'. Integration must therefore be strictly defined and established, drawing up a functional relationship between all the variables, so as to avoid any quantitative or qualitative incompatibility.

However, when we talk about conservation, restoration and adaptation of cultural tourist resources, there are implementation problems. The features of the decision-making process underlying conservation in Sicily as well as the financial problems deriving from the scarcity of resources and the role of *Soprintendenze* have been dealt with in Chapters 2, 3 and 4. As has been already pointed out, the decisions of the *Assessorato* lack planning and rational criteria for the efficient distribution of financial resources.

That is also true of the decisions taken by the *Soprintendenze*, for the distribution in their administrative area. In the latter case, the allocation of resources is likely to be biased by the scholastic and academic training of the majority of managers and civil servants; in most cases, they have a cultural education from archaeological schools, which has always assigned a value to the different elements of heritage according to the era and architectural typology; for example, it is common knowledge that over the centuries, relics of the Middle Ages have never really been taken into consideration compared to relics of classical antiquity. This in turn affects the conservation decisions and, therefore, the supply of heritage, including that for tourist purposes. The consistency of visitor flows, in fact, is influenced by the presentation of monuments and sites, which depends, in turn, on the investment made in them.

Our aim is to offer an example of this bias in the creation of tourist resources and the city of Syracuse will be used as a case study.

4. A CASE STUDY: SYRACUSE

Syracuse is well suited to the role of model or paradigm for analysing the policies aimed at transforming heritage as a tourist resource: in fact, its accumulation and stratification of heritage can be considered the most important in Sicily and possibly in Europe.

Established by the Corinthians in 784 BC, Syracuse was the most important city in the Mediterranean area in the fifth century BC and remained so up until the Roman conquest. Over 25 centuries, all the occupations that followed one another left a large quantity of remains and monuments on the small island of Ortigia and in the 'Neapolis' (New City) now the Archaeological Park, with its magnificent Greek Theatre, two great museums (Archaeology and Fine Arts), the Cathedral and many other buildings.

For the investigation of the policies adopted in the case study, a heritage register[3] was compiled. We then attempted to estimate the range of values which could be attributed to the different elements of heritage, according to age. The following indicators were adopted:[4]

1. quotations in tourist guide-books or brochures;
2. tourist itineraries drawn up by travel agencies;
3. questionnaires supplied to schools and qualified 'witnesses';
4. number of visits to cultural sites; and
5. applications for funding and recovery plans.

The analysis of indicators supports the hypothesis that, leaving aside motivational factors which are difficult to investigate and which lead us to favour certain goods over others (the myth of classicism), tourists' or residents' perceptions of the value of cultural goods are in some way determined by factors that contribute to the image that the city conveys. In the case of Syracuse, the implication was to use heritage goods belonging to classical antiquity.

The value that these remains contribute to the history of humanity cannot be denied but undoubtedly the potential inherent in goods belonging to other historical ages has been undervalued, a potential which would keep the tourist *in situ*, extending his/her travel programme and making use of all the linked activities in the economic sectors which rely on tourism. It is, therefore, worth looking more closely at the indicators mentioned above.

As we know, tourist books and brochures aim to inform the tourist about the attractions of a site and provide essential information which permits him/her to have a worthwhile experience; anything not mentioned in these books, or mentioned only briefly, risks remaining undiscovered or being undervalued by the potential visitor. Therefore, the number of times cultural goods are mentioned in tourist books constitutes an important indicator of their appreciation.[5]

Tourist books present Syracuse mainly as a classical town; 60 per cent of what is mentioned deals with monuments from the Greek, Roman and late Roman periods. This percentage increases considerably with lower category tourist books available in souvenir shops which are very popular among tourists. Only 15 per cent of descriptions concern Byzantine, Swabian, Norman and Gothic monuments and only 23 per cent of the total is reserved for Renaissance and Baroque palaces. Finally, only 2 per cent mention buildings built in modern or contemporary times (nineteenth and twentieth centuries).

A similar argument has been put forward for tourist itineraries proposed by tourist agencies that set stopping-off points, reducing the tourists' choice margin by only showing them what the agencies regard as important. Tourist itineraries are provided almost exclusively for excursions to places of classical antiquity within the city and places conserving their relics or ruins: the Neapolis Archaeological Park – with the famous Greek Theatre, the 'Ear of Dionysius' and so on, the famous Paolo Orsi Archaeological Museum, the Roman catacomb of S. Giovanni, Apollo's Temple and the Cathedral (with the Athenaion). These itineraries are mostly prepared and conducted by official guides provided by tourist offices or by group guides and occasionally by local tourist agencies. Incoming activity is almost completely absent in Syracuse: in fact, there are only two private agencies which do this and even then, not exclusively.

We also used questionnaires for the research. In our case the questionnaire was not designed for tourists but for samples of residents. In fact, it has been a valid analytical instrument because it permitted us to acquire information directly from qualified sources, that is from people expressing their preferences concerning cultural goods. The questionnaires, distributed in schools and to some 'informed observers', showed that insiders and experts mainly determine the values and range of opinions on heritage goods that are considered more valuable within the city context and that they all prefer classical antiquity goods.

The questionnaires distributed in schools and to 'informed observers' were structured differently. The first one (for schools), showed that there is a perfect correlation between the most visited and studied sites and those considered by school heads and teachers as best representing the city. Once again, it was Greek culture which dominated all the others, particularly the Neapolis Archaeological Park and the Paolo Orsi Museum.

As far as the second type of questionnaire is concerned, a list of thirty monuments was given to each interviewer, with an equal number of monuments belonging to classical antiquity and the Middle and Modern Ages. In the questionnaire, they were required to give a score between 1 and 5 to each monument, following a historical–cultural criterion rather than an aesthetical one. In all the questionnaires, the Greek Theatre, the Cathedral, and the Archaeological Museum received the highest scores.[6]

This result is more significant than the others, because some of the informed observers were officers and managers from agencies which manage cultural heritage.

As expected, from the above indicators, the strong appeal of Greek and Roman sites to tourists and residents was underlined by the number of visitors. This provides the answer to how the cultural and tourist image of Syracuse is presented.

We used the Neapolis Archaeological Park, the Paolo Orsi Museum, the Catacombs of S. Giovanni and the Regional Gallery of Bellomo Palace (Museum of Fine Arts) as sample sites to analyse visitor numbers. This choice was made as they are the only sites where a ticket is required to enter.

Visitor data show a considerable discrepancy between the use of the first site and the others. The number of visitors to the Archaeological Park in 1998 exceeded the other sites by 3.7 times, and the places of classical antiquity attracted more than 80 per cent of the visitors, while the regional Gallery of Bellomo Palace, which mainly houses masterpieces from the Middle Ages and modern times, remained the least visited site.

Finally, as expected, we discovered that the financial resources for heritage conservation were allocated mainly to archaeological sites. At present, the most important plan for the recovery and exploitation of cultural heritage is the *Programma Operativo Urban Siracusa 1994/1999* (EU grants given to the region and town councils). It should be pointed out that this programme, together with the detailed plan for the restoration of the historical centre of Ortigia, is primarily aimed at the economic and social renewal of this run-down area of the city, using the restoration of buildings as a tool. Tourist motivation has been secondary and incidental, even though the last few years have seen an increased interest in its tourist value.

Besides Ortigia, the only other important recovery and restoration works with a high tourist value appear to be archaeological sites, and grants from the region and the EU aim to improve their use.

Other interesting facts have emerged from the analysis of funding distribution by the *Assessorato Regionale dei Beni Culturali e Ambientali* to the peripheral organs in the province of Syracuse between 1993 and 1997. We found that 77 per cent is assigned to the *Soprintendenza*, 15 per cent to the town councils, 6 per cent to the Paolo Orsi Archaeological Museum and 2 per cent to the Regional Gallery of Bellomo Palace. Although these data refer to the province, most of the funds go to the city of Syracuse, and as the *Soprintendenza* directly manages all the most important archaeological sites, while the town councils own architectural and landscape goods, the data clearly show a bias towards favouring the archaeological sector. Finally, the difference between financial support to the two museums, the first one being archaeology while the second one is mainly dedicated to works from the Middle Ages, is further confirmation of our hypothesis.

5. FINAL REMARKS

So far we have reached two conclusions: the first one is that cultural authorities have focused their attention and resources on a particular heritage typology, that of Greek–Roman archaeology. The second conclusion is the concentration of visitors exclusively to archaeological sites indicated by tourist organisations who are following set cultural guidelines.

We cannot investigate the criteria that have determined the attribution of a first- or second-class label to the different categories of heritage any further but the mechanism behind this vicious circle is quite evident. Increased care of classical antiquity has increased visitor flows thus producing an ever-increasing care, and so on. It would be useless to question how this process began or where the more or less conscious responsibilities lie; what is really needed is a completely different policy, both for heritage and tourism.

Of course, the first step towards change must be in the policies of cultural authorities who need to understand that good practice cannot focus solely on a single typology of heritage, even if it is famous or very important. Attention, planning, funding and restoration work are to be distributed by taking the situations of physical risk into consideration (decay, collapse and so on), or by giving due weight to the impact of the availability and valorisation a new site or monument will have on tourism.

An efficient supply needs, therefore, to be organised and so the creation of appropriate tourist itineraries is required, based on new typologies that have previously been overlooked and, where possible, linked with other sites in the province that present similar elements of heritage (such as Augusta, Noto and Palazzolo Acreide) (Montemagno, 1986, p. 99). Secondly, a new policy of urban and regional marketing for Syracuse is required, which no longer simply classifies it as 'the city of classical civilisation' but as 'a city through 25 centuries of history and art', or 'the city of a hundred facets', and so on. These are only a few ideas for a new marketing policy, but serious action must be taken to create a more efficient management of both heritage and tourism.

As for tourism, two very important goals which could be achieved by following our proposals have to be underlined. The first one is the distribution of tourists over a wider range of destinations, avoiding or reducing the risks deriving from the concentration of mass tourism in the few areas where they go to at present. In addition to the physical benefits, this reduced concentration of visitors would also improve the 'quality' of visits, in terms of time, space, animation and so on. The second goal would be to prolong tourists' stay in the city or region. The increased number of monuments, buildings and sites worth visiting would undoubtedly reduce the one-day trips and short visits, producing a growth in visits lasting three, five or more days. If we add a certain number of visitors attracted by the resources of the new products, we can easily forecast an increase in overnight stays which could have quite a significant and positive economic impact in terms of employment and direct, indirect and induced income.

These new policies could effectively contribute to improving the quality of the tourist phenomenon in the region, as well as to the general growth of the region and *Mezzogiorno* in Italy, a growth which remains the most important goal of economic and social policies (Montemagno, 2001, pp. 53–61).

NOTES

*   The author wishes to thank Alessandro Arangio, for his valuable contribution to this study.

1.   Demand refers to the demand for goods and facilities on the part of tourists, who move and stay in a place that is not their usual residence; supply refers to the production and selling of goods and facilities, in both the areas of origin and destination, by private or public agents.

2.   The carrying capacity concept refers to the maximum number of tourists which a territory can cope with and the physical capacity of tourist facilities in a wider sense. This concept was first applied in the 1960s to determine recreation management strategies aimed at highlighting environmental and social impact.

3.   This register, obviously incomplete but fairly significant all the same, has been drawn up classifying heritage according to the categories quoted in the law and, within each, according to the specific typology. General information on the heritage site (location, ownership and so on) as well as on tourist use was included, too.

4.   A lot of other possible indicators were excluded from our list, such as: eating areas near the cultural sites; means of transport, their timetables and costs; entry times and their flexibility; willingness of visitors to pay to enter the sites, related to their importance, one of the most common scientific criteria; the quality of services and amenities offered; and visitors' evaluation through regular questionnaires.

5.   No significant data could be obtained from brochures produced and distributed by public bodies (local authorities, tourist offices and cultural boards); in Syracuse, in fact, only a few exist and even they are poorly distributed. Public

bodies do not seem to rely upon this kind of tool to reach certain user targets.

6. The monuments belonging to classical antiquity received an average score of 4.15, while the monuments from the Middle Ages and those from modern times received an average score of 3.81 and 3.72, respectively.

REFERENCES

Council of Europe (1999), *Tourism and Environment: The Natural, Cultural and Socio-economic Challenges of Sustainable Tourism*, Proceedings of the Riga Conference, Latvia.

Montemagno, G. (1985), Turismo e Beni Culturali: dalla Relazione Teorica all'Integrazione Sistemica, in *Quaderni dell'ANIEST*, n. 5, Atti del Convegno Nazionale 'Lo Sviluppo del Turismo e la Protezione dell'Ambiente', Rome 6 December, pp. 77–88.

Montemagno, G. (1986), Funzione e Valutazione dei Beni Culturali negli Itinerari Turistico-culturali del Mezzogiorno, in *Quaderni dell'ANIEST*, n. 6, Atti del Convegno Nazionale 'Turismo e Beni Culturali', Rome 12 December, pp. 99–128.

Montemagno, G. (2001), 'Italian Dualism and New Tourism Trends: The Challenge of Mezzogiorno', in Apostolopoulos, Y., Loukissas, P. and Leontidou, L. (eds), *Mediterranean Tourism – Facets of Socioeconomic Development and Cultural Change*, London and New York: Routledge, pp. 53–62.

Patin, V. (1997), *Tourisme et Patrimoine en France et en Europe*, Paris : La documentation française.

Pechlaner, H. and Osti, L. (2000), 'Cultural Heritage and Destination Management - Contributions to Sustainable Tourism', in *Lights, Camera, Action: Spotlights on Tourism in the New Millennium*, Travel and Tourism Research Association (TTRA) 31st Annual Conference Proceedings, San Fernando Valley, California, 11–14 June.

Wahab, S. (1996), Balancing Culture Heritage Conservation and Sustainable Development through Tourism, in *Toward a Sustainable Future: Balancing Conservation and Development*, Proceedings of the International Conference on Tourism and Heritage Management (ICCT), Yogyakarta, Indonesia, pp. 60–74.

7. The Role of Non-profit Organisations in the Finance of Heritage

Salvo Creaco

---

1. THE MAIN ECONOMIC DIMENSIONS OF THE ITALIAN NON-PROFIT SECTOR

1.1 An International Perspective

From a historical point of view, the Italian non-profit sector has a tradition which goes back to the Middle Ages and to church-related institutions. Over the centuries, the number of non-profit organisations has grown and has been consolidated, particularly in the period from the nineteenth century to the first half of the twentieth, because of the lack of provision of public institutions in the supply of goods and services in the different fields of social welfare (Zaninelli, 1997; Cova, 1997).

A comprehensive evaluation of the economic dimensions of the Italian non-profit sector is unfortunately hindered by inadequacies of statistical data: an up-dated register of organisations acting within the sector is lacking and alternative systems of information, such as those based on data banks of public origin is unsatisfactory. Such information is, nevertheless, essential to understanding what the scope and features of this non-profit sector really are and what its potential is for satisfying the new demands being placed upon it in the Italian economy and society. In this respect, lacking a more recent in-depth analysis (Barbetta, 2000), we will make reference to the results contained in a major inquiry into the scope, structure, history, legal position and role of the non-profit sector in a broad cross-section of nations (Salamon and Anheier, 1994; Salamon et al.,1996; Barbetta, 1996, 1997). Figure 7.1 and Tables 7.1, 7.2, 7.3 and 7.4 summarise the main aspects of this inquiry for 1990.

In every modern economy, the non-profit sector has experienced rapid growth. As Figure 7.1 demonstrates, there is, however, a wide variation in

Figure 7.1 Composition of the non-profit sector in selected countries (per cent of expenditure)

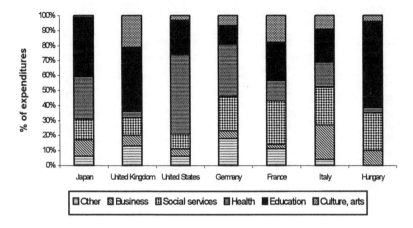

Source: Salamon and Anheier (1994).

the distribution of non-profit activities from one country to another.

Fundamentally, the relative importance of non-profit organisations differs from one country to another mainly because of differences in government attitudes towards the creation of organisations that could be a source of competition to traditional public policies and because of the interactive features between institutional structure and other aspects of the overall socio-economic context (Rose-Ackerman, 1996). This perspective, that of the relationship between non-profit organisations and government, implies that the expansion of the non-profit sector reflects an increase in the divergence between perceived social needs and government supply of public-type services (Weisbrod, 1975).

In 1990, according to the data in Table 7.1, in terms of the number of paid workers, the Italian non-profit sector employed approximately 418 thousand standard employment units, constituting 1.8 per cent of total employment. This percentage is not high when compared with that of France, Germany, the United Kingdom, the United States and Japan, and indeed is only higher than that of Hungary. Although representing a comparatively low position in terms of numbers employed, the Italian percentage of the labour force employed is nevertheless important from a national perspective; in fact, it produces the same amount of employment as the insurance and banking sectors put together. With reference to the ratio of the operating expenditure (excluding capital expenditures) of the sector to the Italian gross national product, the indicator for Italy is lower than those

Supply of Heritage

in other countries, with the exception of Hungary, as would be expected from
the employment considerations.

Table 7.1 The economic dimensions of the non-profit sector

Countries	Standard employment units (thousands)	% of employment of the total economy	Operating expenditures as % of GDP
France	803	4.2	3.3
Germany	1,018	3.7	3.6
Japan	1,440	2.5	3.2
Italy	**418**	**1.8**	**1.9**
UK	946	4.0	4.8
Hungary	33	0.8	1.2
USA	7,120	6.8	6.3

Source: Salamon and Anheier (1994).

Table 7.2 Sources of non-profit revenue (percentages)

Countries	Total public revenues	Private revenues		
		Donations	Others	Total private revenues
France	59.5	7.1	33.4	40.5
Germany	68.2	3.9	27.9	31.8
Japan	38.3	1.3	60.4	61.7
Italy	**40.2**	**4.9**	**54.9**	**59.8**
UK	39.8	12.1	48.1	60.2
Hungary	23.3	19.7	57.0	76.7
USA	29.2	18.5	52.3	70.8

Source: Salamon and Anheier (1994).

Besides its modest economic dimensions, the Italian non-profit sector is
characterised by the particular structure of its financing system (Table 7.2).

Obviously a variety of methods is used to finance non-profit organisations
and each has different implications in terms of equity and efficiency.
Incentives also matter, taking into account that the mechanisms used to fund
non-profit activities affect, and are affected by, the nature of those activities.[1]
On the whole, it is useful to group these sources of finance into two major
categories: public and private revenues. The relationship between revenue
from government and that from the private sector can take many forms and
the lines that divide them are difficult to define in different institutional

contexts. Nevertheless, viewing the data in Table 7.2, at first glance it appears that non-profit organisations are more dependent on private revenues in one form or another and less so on public resources. Only in France and Germany do public revenues account for more than 50 per cent of total revenue, while private donations account for less than 5 per cent in three of the seven countries studied.

Within this financing process at international level, the Italian scenario stands out for the distinctive role played by the commercialisation of non-profit activities. In fact, fees, sales of products and other sources represent the main component of finance. This broad tendency of organisations to sell their goods and services on the market, however, is accompanied by a dependence on public finance that is lower only than that of France and Germany.

Due to the predominance of these sources of finance, private donations account for a negligible amount of the total revenues of non-profit organisations: the percentage of donations is in fact higher only than that of Germany and Japan. Since donation behavioural patterns of giving have established the existence of strong links between levels of donating and changes in the tax-defined price of giving, it is reasonable to assume that in Italy the small amount of private donations can be, to some extent, attributed to the fragmentation of the fiscal discipline that discourages such private action.

1.2 The Activities of the Italian Non-profit Sector

Table 7.3 shows the main economic dimensions of the Italian non-profit sector broken down into its various groups. Obviously, the different groups of activities carried out by non-profit organisations assume a specific importance according to the particular variable under consideration. Nevertheless, five of the groups of activities (culture and recreation, education and research, health, social services, and business and professional associations and trade unions) always represent more than 90 per cent of the sector whichever distinctive parameter is considered. The five remaining groups therefore play an extremely modest role within the Italian non-profit sector.

With reference to the size of the culture and recreation sector, including the organisations aimed at promoting the safeguard of cultural and artistic goods, it accounts for just over half the 52 per cent of the total of the non-profit sector according to the number of organisations. Its capacity to mobilise volunteers puts the culture and recreation group at the top of the ranking, ahead even of social services.

Table 7.3 Groups of activities of the Italian non-profit sector (per cent of the whole non-profit sector)

Groups of activities	Organis.	Expend.	Empl.	Volunteers	Value added by volunteers	Total value added
Culture and recreation	**51.62**	**11.4**	**6.3**	**30.3**	**31.3**	**16.2**
Education and research	23.17	20.7	28.5	9.2	9.5	20.1
Health	3.28	17.8	14.1	12.8	16.4	16.7
Social services	17.88	21.4	33.4	35.3	25.3	23.5
Environment	0.51	0.2	0.2	1.6	0.6	0.3
Development and housing	1.24	1.6	4.5	2.9	1.3	1.6
Law, advocacy and politics	1.39	2.3	2.1	1.7	2.2	2.4
Philanthropic intermediaries	0.29	0.9	0.5	0.1	0.1	0.3
International	0.62	1.7	1.4	1.5	1.7	1.6
Business and professional associations, unions	n.a.	22.0	8.8	4.5	11.7	17.3

Source: Barbetta (1997).

Moreover, the value added by volunteers is very high when compared with that of other groups of activities. Generally speaking, therefore, it seems that the culture and recreation group possesses important opportunities for further development to the extent that it is effectively co-ordinated by paid personnel. In fact, 'volunteer work as a resource for increasing the quantity and quality of the services supplied by organisations and for containing costs' (Barbetta, 1997, p. 125) is not highly fruitful in the absence of any permanent supervision that only paid staff are able to guarantee.

The culture and recreation sector consists of three subgroups:

1. culture and arts (for museums, theatres, concert organisations, publishers, radio and television stations);
2. recreation (with tourist organisations and local tourist boards, sports organisations and local branches of large national cultural and recreational organisations); and
3. service clubs (with organisations such as the Lions or Rotary clubs, or company pensioner clubs).

Each subgroup is characterised by specific aspects. Financial characteristics are shown in Table 7.4.

*Table 7.4 Culture and recreation: percentage breakdown of revenue
          sources in Italy*

References	Culture and recreation subgroup			Subgroup	Non-profit sector
	Culture & arts	Recreation	Service clubs		
Grants and contracts	5.8	2.0	1.4	4.3	27.9
Statutory transfers	17.4	5.0	0.0	12.6	7.8
Third-party payments	0.2	1.3	0.0	0.6	4.5
Total public revenues	**23.3**	**8.3**	**1.4**	**17.5**	**40.2**
Donations	10.8	1.5	13.8	7.4	4.9
Fees and sales of prod.	48.2	72.7	0.0	56.5	26.1
Dues	3.6	10.0	84.1	7.1	20.5
Investment income	7.7	1.6	0.6	5.3	2.8
Other income	6.6	5.8	0.0	6.2	5.5
Total private revenues	**76.7**	**91.7**	**98.6**	**82.5**	**59.8**

Source: Barbetta (1997).

For each subgroup, private funds exceed public resources. This trend is perfectly in line with that registered by the non-profit sector as a whole. It is worth noting, however, that in the culture and recreation sector in Italy, the incidence of private funds is still much more important than in the sector as a whole, as shown in the last column of Table 7.4, demonstrating that a broad share of the organisations' services is first assigned to the general collectivity rather than to a particular class of customer.

Within this sector, the private source of finance of the culture and arts sub-sector is smaller, not only than the average value of the sector itself but also of that registered by the other two subsectors: recreation and service clubs.

With regard to the culture and arts subsector, the weight of public sources is mostly represented by statutory transfers made up of grants and contracts and indirect third-party payments, which are either of lesser importance, as in the former, or absolutely insignificant, as in the latter case.

1.3 The Modest Size of the Italian Non-profit Sector

An exhaustive interpretation of the modest weight of the Italian non-profit sector compared with that of other countries goes beyond the purpose of this chapter. In any case, a vast amount of literature already exists on this issue (Borzaga, 1999), pointing out that the small economic dimension of the

Italian non-profit sector is connected with a set of structural factors rather than a single element. These structural factors are usually linked to:

1. the presence of a legal framework which is absolutely unsatisfactory and in any case hardly designed to stimulate the growth of the sector as a whole, mainly because it appears as the result of successive laws, rather than the outcome of any clear logical design of the sector;
2. the existence of long and complex procedures for the institutional acknowledgement of the organisations acting within the sector;
3. the inadequacy of the fiscal system to favour and facilitate the typical activities of the sector;
4. the extent of direct provision by the state and other public agencies in the supply of goods and services in the different fields of welfare; and
5. the existence of a 'family' structure that frequently supports its own members on the basis of a mutual principle.

1.4 The Organisational Structure of the Italian Non-profit Sector

In describing the main aspects of the Italian non-profit sector, reference was made to an analysis having twin aims: to supply solid, objective information about individual countries and to permit cross-national comparisons in a systematic manner. For this purpose, the analysis identified organisations as falling within the non-profit sector according to a structural–operational definition of the subjects to be taken into consideration. To be more specific, an organisation was deemed to belong to the non-profit sector whenever it met the following criteria:

1. formal constitution: the organisation must be formally constituted, that is, having a charter or some other founding constitution;
2. private legal status: the organisation must not be a part of the public sector of the economy;
3. self-government: the organisation's decision-making process must not be controlled by other organisations, of a public or private nature;
4. non-distribution constraint: the organisation must not distribute profits gained through the implementation of its activities; and
5. voluntary to some meaningful extent: volunteers carrying out some activity receive salaries or wages that are less than the market price for the work.

By adopting this broad set of criteria, the non-profit sector appears to be made up of a vast amalgam of organisations (Rossi and Boccacin, 1997). This intricate network can be analysed according to different factors in order to identify homogeneous groups. If we refer to the terms most commonly used to analyse the non-profit sector as a whole, the structure of the non-profit sector itself seems to be constituted by organisations falling within one of the following categories:

1. voluntary service;
2. social co-operativism;
3. associationism ; and
4. foundation.

In the course of the years, each type of organisation has become responsible for specific fields of the non-profit sector in the different institutional contexts. From a general point of view:

1. Voluntary service, carried out individually but more often by members of specific organisations, tends to concentrate on the most typical areas of the welfare system, such as health and social services, displaying altruism and a social conscience towards the weaker members of society.
2. Social co-operativism is mainly concerned with its members' needs, rather than with those of society in general. Because of this aspect, social co-operatives have assumed an important role, essentially in situations in which a complex organisation structure is needed in order to supply services with a wide base of paid personnel necessary to guarantee the continuity of the activity.[2]
3. Associationism is when groups of people who join together to share funding establish a formal structure and act to achieve one or more common goals in almost all fields of social life, from sport to culture, from religion to social services. Within the association, reciprocal exchange or gift exchange remains a widespread means of obtaining goods and services as a solution for the difficulties in having access to a variety of commodities through anonymous market alternatives (Kranton, 1996).
4. Foundations are organisations structured primarily as a permanent collection of endowed funds, the earnings of which are used for achieving particular welfare purposes. These organisations have a governing body, nominated in accordance with established principles and procedures, which operates either directly through the implementation of specific projects (operating foundation) or indirectly through the provision of funds or other assistance to particular charitable entities (grant-making foundations).

1.5 The 'Foundation' Case

The 'foundation' case deserves further investigation. Because of the criteria adopted in the cross-national study by Salamon and Anheier, a definition of the non-profit sector capable of attaining two joint aims, that is, the comparison between countries with very different socio-economic features and the measurement of the quantitative dimensions of the sector, it was not possible to adequately describe the quantitative dimensions of the sector. The inevitable outcome of this has led to inaccuracies in the estimation of the actual position in specific institutional contexts. In particular, with reference to the Italian case, the recourse to a structural–operational definition has resulted in, among other things, the inclusion within the non-profit sector of the foundations ruled by the Civil Code[3] but not of the banking foundations, which were created by the transformation of publicly owned banks as a result of the Amato-Carli law (Law 281/1990).

Recently in Italy, banking foundations have ended up playing a growing role within the third type of market, particularly in the provision of collective consumption goods (Filippini, 2000; Ferrari, 2000). Such a view has been accompanied by increasing attention by economists, especially by those who believe that banking foundations may well represent an appropriate answer to the important problems of organisation, legitimacy and finance of the modern welfare systems (Scandizzo, 1999; Segre, 2000). As a consequence, not having included such organisations within the Italian non-profit sector actually means that an important element was excluded from the picture. In order to discover the current and potential future capacities of banking foundations within a little-understood segment of the economy, the next section analyses in detail one of the two banking foundations functioning in Sicily, in particular, looking at the role that this organisation may play in the conservation and safeguard of cultural and artistic heritage.

2. THE FOUNDATION OF THE BANK OF SICILY

2.1 Origin of the Foundation

The Foundation of the bank of Sicily was set up in 1991 under the Amato-Carli law which aimed to privatise state-owned banks. On the same day, the joint-stock company, Bank of Sicily, was set up with a registered stock, which was at first entirely held by the Foundation itself. At present, the Foundation owns little more than 18 per cent of the shares of the Bank of Sicily. Besides these shares, the Foundation owns all the works of art exhibited in the Bank's offices both in Sicily and in the rest of Italy.

From a historical viewpoint, the Foundation has a long tradition, going back to the Foundation for the Cultural and Economic Development of Sicily, which was started in 1923, thanks to the initiative of the Bank of Sicily, with the aim of promoting specific sectors in Sicily, especially in the field of agriculture, mining and tourism.

The Foundation is presently completing the transformation process from state-owned bank to a non-profit organisation under a recent national law. This transformation has also given rise to the identification of new aims and goals: conservation and promotion of artistic and cultural goods, development of entrepreneurial skills, economic growth and support for those on low incomes.[4]

The Foundation has its offices in Palermo, capital of the Sicilian Region, in Villa Zito, a magnificent neoclassical architectural building, built at the start of the eighteenth century. Villa Zito, which bears witness to the old cultural role of the Bank of Sicily, contains the historical and artistic works of the Ignazio Mormino Museum, which was named after the director of the Bank of Sicily during the 1950s, under whose auspices the Foundation for the Cultural and Economic Development of Sicily acquired both importance and splendour.

Various collections are exhibited in the Museum. Apart from an important collection of Greek pottery, the Museum has an interesting collection of Sicilian coins from the Aragonese and Bourbon reigns, a beautiful collection of both Sicilian and continental majolica pieces and a valuable collection of rare stamps with specimens from Angevin times to the nineteenth century.

There is also a very valuable library in the Museum with more than seven thousand books, with specialised sections on Sicilian archaeology, stamp collections and history. This library plays a very important cultural role since it contains certain publications, which are either not available in other Sicilian libraries, public and private, or which cannot be consulted very easily.

The above-mentioned collections are not the only elements of the artistic and cultural possessions owned by the Foundation. In fact, the space available in the Museum does not seem to be big enough and many important articles are still stored in warehouses waiting to be found a suitable home.

The artistic, historical and cultural assets of the Museum can be enjoyed by visitors without paying an entrance fee. The Foundation, whose aim is the promotion of culture and art, also organises or hosts conferences, meetings and debates on these themes with the purpose of spreading information on the history and culture of Sicily.

2.2 Expenditure by the Foundation of the Bank of Sicily on Culture and Art

Between 1997–98 and 1998–99, funds available for expenditure by the Foundation of the Bank of Sicily fell from 1,154 to 789 billion lire or from 41 to 33 per cent of asset earnings. All Italian banking foundations tended to earn low rates of return during this period, especially when compared to low risk investments such as Treasury Bills (Messori, 1999). In 1997–98, the highest rate of return was 3.4 per cent. However, the Foundation of the Bank of Sicily earned only 0.5 per cent.

Expenditure of the Foundation was divided between culture and art, research and education and social assistance.   Table 7.5 shows the breakdown of the percentage of total expenditure on culture and art rose from 5 per cent to 63 per cent over the period on both its own projects and on grants to projects of third parties. However, the amount of expenditure fell very considerably both in total and on culture and the arts, where it was reduced from 673 million lire to 30 million lire. This notable decline was due in part to the lower return on the Foundation's assets but much more to the significant rise in management costs and taxes, which together reduced the net margin of resources available for expenditures from 41 to 33 per cent.

Table 7.5 Foundation of the Bank of Sicily: expenditure by sector (in million lire), 1995–96 and 1998–99

Institutional sector	1995–96						1998–99					
	Own projects		Third-part projects		Total		Own projects		Third-part projects		Total	
	Value	%	Value	%	Value	%	Value	%	Value	%	Value	%
Culture and art	**279**	**21**	**394**	**30**	**673**	**51**	**13**	**27**	**17**	**35**	**30**	**62**
Research and education	140	11	472	36	612	46	6	12	10	21	16	33
Social assistance	38	3	0	0	38	3	2	4	0	0	2	4
Total (rounded)	457	35	866	66	1,323	100	21	43	27	56	48	100

Source: Foundation of the Bank of Sicily.

From this analysis it must be concluded that the Foundation of the Bank of Sicily has substantially abandoned its role of grant-making, in terms of both the number of its projects and their value. Its expenditure to culture and art has more or less been reduced to the management of the Mormino Museum and the offices of the Foundation and restoration of works of art and books and the updating of its library collections.

3. CONCLUDING REMARKS

Banking foundations in Italy have very considerable resources that they can use to support welfare projects, particularly if compared with other non-profit organisations. In this chapter, the resources of the Foundation of the Bank of Sicily have been analysed and data on its expenditure on culture and the arts have been presented. It is clear that not only have both declined but also that the Foundation is far from fulfilling its own institutional duties. It does not operate effectively or efficiently either with respect to investment of its assets or with respect to planning suitable projects for grant-making.

In relation to culture and art, it is acknowledged that there are problems, as revealed in recent discussions on the third sector. Organisations that seek grants must have clear objectives and goals, even though these are not easily stated in the cultural field compared to those of other sectors: all objectives cannot be gauged under the same value systems (Greffe, 1999). Even though progress has been made on rationalising the economic and social rationale of cultural heritage, it remains a controversial topic that presents difficult decisions (Forte and Mantovani, 1999; Allison et al., 1996).

With specific reference to the banking foundations, improvements to their governance structure could assist in the decision-making process. They must be able to better serve their original aims and also have board membership that allows them to maintain their traditions and roots at local level.

NOTES

1. As Weisbrod (1998, p. 2) points out, the rationale for the special tax treatment and subsidies of the non-profit sector 'rests on the belief that it provides services that are materially different from, and preferred to, the services that private enterprises provide'.
2. In general terms, co-operatives provide work, goods, or services for their members under better conditions than are available on the market-place. Paramount examples of these are self-help groups and housing co-operatives.
3. Articles 12–34 of Book I of the Civil Code deal with these foundations. The role of such organisations within the Italian non-profit sector is analysed by Demarie (1997).
4. All the values expressed from here onwards, as far as the Foundation Bank of Sicily is concerned, refer to the situation of the Foundation as on 31 December 2000.

REFERENCES

Allison, G., Ball, S., Cheshire, P., Evans, A. and Stabler, M. (1996), *The Value of Conservation? A Literature Review of the Economic and Social Value of the Cultural Built Heritage*, London: The Royal Institution of Chartered Surveyors.

Barbetta, G.P. (ed.) (1996), *Senza Scopo di Lucro*, Bologna: Il Mulino.

Barbetta, G.P. (1997), 'The Economic Dimensions of the Non-profit Sector', in Barbetta, G.P. (ed.), *The Non-profit Sector in Italy*, Manchester: Manchester University Press, pp. 104–70.

Barbetta, G.P. (2000), *Il Settore Non-profit Italiano*, Bologna: Il Mulino.

Borzaga, C. (1999), 'L'Evoluzione del Welfare Mix in Italia', in L. Fazzi and E. Messora (eds.), *Modelli di Welfare Mix*, Milan: Angeli, pp. 29–44.

Cova, A. (1997), 'La Situazione Italiana: Una Storia di Non profit', in G. Vittadini (ed.), *Il Non Profit Dimezzato*, Milan: Etas Libri, pp. 29–45.

Demarie M. (1997), 'Le Fondazioni in Italia: un Profilo Empirico', in AA.VV. (eds), *Per Conoscere le Fondazioni*, Turin: Fondazione G. Agnelli.

Ferrari, P. (2000), 'La Gestione del Patrimonio delle Fondazioni Bancarie Italiane: Un Confronto con la Realtà Europea e Statunitense', *Studi e Note di Economia, Quaderni*, special issue, (4).

Filippini, L. (ed.) (2000), *Economia delle Fondazioni*, Bologna: Il Mulino.

Forte, F. and Mantovani, M. (1999), 'La Valutazione dei Beni Artistici nella Strategia delle Fondazioni Bancarie', *Fondazioni*, (1), 63–93.

Greffe, X. (1999), 'Managing Foundations: The Case of Cultural Activities', paper delivered at the Conference on 'The Banking Foundations and the Italian Economy', Ravello.

Kranton, R.E. (1996), 'Reciprocal Exchange: A Self-sustaining System', *American Economic Review*, vol. 86, (4), 830–51.

Messori, M. (1999), 'Banche e Fondazioni Bancarie', *Bancaria*, (9), 32–52.

Rose-Ackerman, S. (1996), 'Altruism, Nonprofits, and Economic Theory', *Journal of Economic Literature*, vol. 34, June, 701–28.

Rossi, G. and Boccacin, L. (1997), 'Il Volontariato: un Soggetto Fondamentale del Terzo Settore Italiano', in G. Vittadini (ed.), *Il Non Profit Dimezzato*, Milan: Etas Libri, pp.125–52.

Salamon, L.S. and Anheier, H. (1994), *The Emerging Sector: An Overview*, Baltimore, MD: Johns Hopkins Institute for Policy Studies.

Salamon, L.S., Anheier, H.K., Sokolowski, W. and associates (1996), *The Emerging Sector: A Statistical Supplement*, Baltimore, MD: Johns Hopkins Institute for Policy Studies.

Scandizzo, L. (1999), 'Le Fondazioni Bancarie: Origine, Razionalità ed Evoluzione', *Fondazioni*, (1), 25–61.

Segre, G. (2000), 'Fondazioni senza Fondatore. Storia, Natura e Modello di

Funzionamento delle Fondazioni Bancarie Italiane', in L. Filippini (ed.), *Economia delle Fondazioni*, Bologna: Il Mulino, pp. 199–231.

Weisbrod, B.A. (1975), 'Toward a Theory of the Voluntary Non-profit Sector in a Three-sector Economy', in E.S. Phelps (ed.), *Altruism, Morality, and Economic Theory*, New York: Russell Sage Foundation, pp. 171–95.

Weisbrod, B.A. (ed.) (1998), *To Profit or not to Profit: The Commercial Transformation of the Non-profit Sector*, Cambridge: Cambridge University Press.

Zaninelli, S. (1997), 'Historical Developments', in G.P. Barbetta (ed.), *The Non-profit Sector in Italy*, Manchester: Manchester University Press, pp. 80–103.

8. New Technologies and Heritage

Maria Musumeci

1. INTRODUCTION

Sicily has the richest cultural, historical and environmental heritage in Europe. The successive series of invasions and integration of different cultures, starting from the earliest times, have left a diversified legacy that in some way sums up the history of Sicily and the role it has always played in Italian and European culture.

Of the 31 villages designated as being of high cultural interest, 19 have a historical centre that stands on an archaeological site. In fact, 62 *Polis*, three of them in the town of Agrigento, have been found in Sicily, not to mention numerous smaller centres, settlements, areas of archaeological interest and the so called 'isolated assets' such as towers, castles, convents, farms and so on, which today represent a patrimony of more than two thousand archaeological items. Among existing Sicilian villages, 43 developed around old archaeological sites, 128 are of medieval origin, while 132 towns were founded in the period between the 'Baronies' (approx. 1400) and the beginning of the nineteenth century.

According to the Southern Development Plan for Sicily 2000–2006, there are more than twelve thousand architectural items in the town centres and 800 historical centres and settlements in Sicilian towns. Moreover, Sicily boasts 256 museums, 334 historical town archives and about 1,700 libraries. Sicily, therefore, has a heritage of monumental, archaeological, historical and artistic significance and value. It represents one of the most remarkable concentrations of cultural and environmental assets in the south of Italy, providing an attraction for tourists and a resource in the field of archaeological preservation and restoration with a considerable spin-off, both at local and national levels.

However, the standard of the Sicilian artistic heritage is considered low, both in how cultural heritage is exploited and in the adequacy of services offered. For example, the availability of informative material is poor, as is interactive relations with visitors in general: from advertising and telebooking aspects to telematic support before and during the visit, things are generally badly organised. As we shall see later, the use of new technologies in cultural assets is extremely limited and provides only a partial and disjointed service that does not meet the changing needs of potential visitors.

This chapter aims to study the possible implications in using new technologies in the field of artistic heritage, both for restoration and preservation. In particular, we will try to test the kind of quantitative and qualitative reaction that the introduction of innovative processes produces on the supply of culture, as well as on the demand for enjoyment of cultural heritage itself. The aim is to indirectly offer a few ideas on Sicilian cultural heritage, starting from some innovative plans already carried out in other cultural institutions, in order to encourage the use of web and multimedia technologies, enlarge the range of available services and thus offer a cultural product on a par with those of other national and international cultural institutes. These improvements could increase demand and stimulate cultural tourism.

2.   CULTURAL TOURISM AND HERITAGE

Before examining the main innovative factors applicable to the supply of artistic heritage services, some information on the stream of tourists recorded over the last few years in Sicily provides a context.

The exploitation of Sicilian cultural patrimony produces a positive impact on the regional economy, particularly on those areas that are better equipped from a cultural and tourist point of view. Until a few years ago, many Sicilian archaeological sites and monuments were considered 'secondary' ones because they were not situated near the traditional cultural cities such as Rome, Venice, Naples and Florence, but thanks to a new strategy employed in recent years by the Heritage Ministry to promote visits to museums and archaeological sites through the introduction of new services, cultural tourism in Sicily has become more important. The number of visitors to Sicilian cultural heritage has increased considerably in recent years due to the introduction of plans for improvement, which were included in European Community programmes.

Table 8.1 shows the growth of visitors in the period from 1998 to 1999.[1] In particular, there was an increase of about 3 per cent. However, this was due to growth of free admissions (students, soldiers and so on), compared to paying visitors who decreased by 1.7 per cent. The consequences for revenues can be seen in Table 8.2; overall, revenues fell by 1.4 per cent, with considerable variation by province.

Table 8.1 Visitors per province in Sicily, 1998–99

	Paying			Free			Total		
	1998	1999	%	1998	1999	%	1998	1999	%
Agrigento	305,226	282,493	-7.5	236,072	222,382	-3.3	535,298	504,845	-5.0
Caltanissetta	7,834	5,898	-24.7	13,890	14,477	4.2	21,724	20,375	-6.2
Catania	13,889	8,991	-35.2	36,559	28,206	-23.1	50,528	37,197	-26.4
Enna	249,281	246,548	-0.9	183,625	204,304	11.3	432,908	451,152	4.2
Messina	590,873	596,468	0.9	228,679	276,301	20.8	819,552	872,769	6.5
Palermo	447,073	449,530	0.5	312,145	331,331	6.1	759,218	780,861	2.8
Ragusa	11,338	9,781	-13.9	16,015	17,093	8.7	27,353	26,854	-1.8
Syracuse	346,362	341,788	-1.3	259,920	255,907	-1.5	606,282	597,893	-1.4
Trapani	402,993	392,226	-2.7	178,387	265,139	46.8	581,380	657,385	13.1
Total	2,374,869	2,333,733	-1.7	1,465,292	1,615,140	10.8	3,834,243	3,949,331	3.0

Source: Assessorato ai Beni Culturali.

Table 8.2 Tourist revenues per province in Sicily, 1998–99

	Revenue (in thousand lire)		
	1998	1999	%
Agrigento	1,451,996	1,347,444	-7.20
Caltanissetta	31,336	23,592	-24.71
Catania	91,860	67,744	-26.25
Enna	997,124	987,392	-0.98
Messina	2,447,364	2,533,752	3.53
Palermo	1,960,241	1,960,824	-0.02
Ragusa	63,738	54,000	-15.28
Syracuse	1,575,016	1,547,932	-1.72
Trapani	1,629,972	1,582,304	-2.02
Total	10,248,647	10,104,984	-1.41

Source: Assessorato ai Beni Culturali.

After a remarkable drop in the number of visitors registered in 1992, owing to the outrages perpetrated that summer (the murders of Giovanni Falcone and Paolo Borsellino), from 1994 onwards, tourism in Sicily has shown a clear sign of revival. In 1999, about 3.6 million arrivals were registered, which corresponded to a 5.6 per cent increase compared to the previous year. The data show that the highest growth was of foreign tourists (nearly 10 per cent between 1996 and 1997).

However, the tourists' average stay in Sicily seems steady during the period. It corresponds to little more than three days, thus resulting in a lower level than the national average (approximately four days). A possible explanation is firstly that Sicilian tourism is often influenced by certain special events such as performances at the Greek theatre in Syracuse, which take place every two years. Secondly, although some improvements have been made, there are still problems linked to infrastructure, transport, socio-environmental conditions and the professional competence of some tour operators.

The positive trend of visits to Sicilian cultural heritage can be linked to the flow of tourism recorded in Sicily during the same period. That is, the data regarding the presence of Italian and foreign tourists in Sicily, compared to that of regional visitors to cultural heritage, show that the percentage of tourism in Sicily is linked directly and indirectly to the exploitation of cultural assets.

In fact, if we compare the 11.2 million Italian and foreign guests registered in 1998 in accommodation facilities, with the 3.8 million visitors to Sicilian cultural assets in the same year, this suggests that about 34 per cent of tourism in Sicily is in some way linked to its historical and artistic heritage. In the same way, for the year 1999, the percentage of 'cultural tourism' is about 33 per cent.

All things considered, therefore, it appears that in the last three years, despite some difficulties, Sicilian tourism, as well as cultural tourism, has experienced steady growth.

3. PRESERVATION OF CULTURAL HERITAGE AND NEW TECHNOLOGIES

There are two phases in which new technologies may be applied to cultural heritage: the first is preservation and restoration and the second is its enjoyment. Here we will deal with the first phase, concentrating on the economic effects rather than on the technical aspects of cultural supply.

As far as the preservation of cultural heritage is concerned, new technologies may be employed at two different stages: the preservation of cultural heritage and the discovery or 'rediscovery' of cultural assets. As regards the restoration phase, new technologies can delay the process of decay of cultural heritage. Moreover, the use of information technology for certain kinds of restoration enables faster operation, thus protecting and preserving the material at the same time. A recent example is the reconstruction of the frescoes in San Francesco's church in Assisi, damaged by an earthquake. The numerous pieces were first of all passed through the scanner and then put side by side on the computer to create the original drawing like a large 'automatic' jigsaw, which avoided handling the pieces. Other innovative techniques allow us to look 'inside' a work of art without opening it, in other words, make diagnostics possible by using multi-spectral images with a high resolution in order to foresee and prevent possible damage to the work. Among these 'non-destructive' tests, as they are technically defined, are infrared reflectography which highlights pictorial elements lying under the surface layer, fluorescent ultraviolet photography, which detects previous restoration work and some of the materials used, and thermography and radiography.[2]

Sophisticated information technology instruments not only open up new restoration methods but also allow for archaeological discoveries including entire towns which have been buried for thousands of years. All this is possible thanks to the use of magnetic waves, which can locate an underground structure, allowing for precise detection of the excavation site. The Etruscan graves in Tarquinia, the ruins of the old town in Crotone and the Etruscan Mantua are examples of the use of such technology. A rural settlement has also been brought to light in Sicily in the area near Calascibetta in the so-called Vallone Canalotto. It consists of approximately 30 caves and has been defined as one of the most significant examples of Byzantine domination in Sicily.

Technical innovation can also be used in the field of security, which guarantees better protection both for museums and archaeological sites, which are often subjected to vandalism; in fact, in recent years some cultural sites in Sicily have been the victim of vandalism. The Paolo Orsi Archaeological Museum in Syracuse, for example, suffered considerable damage with numerous pieces being stolen. The Roman Villa at Piazza Armerina has been damaged four times by unknown assailants who spilt black paint on the mosaic floors. In fact, one of the most innovative security systems available has recently been installed at the Villa to prevent further attacks. The system surrounds the whole site with a sophisticated alarm and television camera system, allowing guards to control the archaeological area 24 hours a day.

A lot of work on artistic and cultural heritage can, in fact, generate effects that also have a monetary value. Without taking into account the allocation of expenditure to restoration, we can look at the effects caused on the wider macroeconomic variables (income, consumption and employment).

A restored museum or monument can attract a large number of visitors and consequently produce greater revenue from the increased number of tickets sold. The profits of hotel owners and restaurateurs, as well as all those running a commercial business in some way connected to the restored museum or monument, can also increase. That can also be the case even if the restoration is of a monument with free admission, run by public institutions (Di Maio, 1999).

The use of new technologies in relation to cultural heritage also promotes professional courses for skilled workers and involves large high-tech specialised companies.

In conclusion, the improvement of cultural heritage not only represents an attraction for tourist consumption but can also offer an occasion to develop new productive opportunities, technological growth, a specialisation of human capital and, above all, the creation of new jobs.

4. NEW INFORMATION AND COMMUNICATION TECHNOLOGIES AND THE EXPLOITATION OF HERITAGE

New information and communication technologies can influence both the supply of cultural heritage and the demand for it.

The spread of telecommunication nets and the interaction between the telecommunication field with that of audiovisual and multimedia technologies has allowed cultural institutions to improve and increase the variety of cultural supply. The web technologies offer a huge quantity of information to a potentially huge number of consumers via hypertext and hypermedia. Through text, sound, images and simulations it is possible to stimulate interaction between cultural organisation staff and visitors and thus increase the possibilities for strengthening consumer relations.

Digital technologies have significantly changed the way in which cultural heritage itself is exploited. Before the introduction of new technologies, the exploitation of artistic heritage consisted mainly in a visit to the cultural institution (museum, archaeological site), following a planned route. Nowadays, however, consumers can approach the cultural sites in a different way (virtual visit), create their own routes according to their needs, closely study those aspects which they are more interested in, giving up a passive role for a leading active role of enjoyment (Micelli and Di Maria, 2000). Thus, web technologies represent an effective means of providing information and knowledge to art consumers while, at the same time (interactive and multimedia technologies), creating new possibilities and methods of exploitation together with other means of communication (Pilati, 1996).

4.1 Computerisation and Cultural Heritage in Sicily: An Outline

In the field of Sicilian culture, the use of multimedia information systems appears to be very limited compared with other cultural institutions in Italy and abroad. There are various reasons for this, starting with a shortage of funds for buying the necessary technology and programmes to develop multimedia products, and a lack of personnel in museums and archaeological sites with skills in multimedia systems. The only significant amount of information available over the Internet refers to regional museums (less so to archaeological sites). For each of them, the heritage authorities provide information about location, days and opening hours, ticket prices and so on. Moreover, the building of each museum and its collections are described, with some details about the way they are displayed. The site also gives some historical and artistic in-depth studies, together with some digital photos.

As far as the provinces in Sicily are concerned, none of them (on their own web sites) provide information about the museums in their area though town councils, on the other hand, generally provide information, though often poor, about their cultural patrimony. Most of the time it is just basic information (opening hours, ticket prices and so on), together with a short description of the museums mentioned in the site. However, information is often scanty; giving little or no useful information about the visit and collections; some city council web sites, such as Enna, Trapani, Agrigento, Ragusa and Messina do not even mention the museums or archaeological sites in their area.

4.2 Cultural Supply and New Technologies

As we already know, cultural supply includes the preservation and improvement of cultural heritage, organisation and management of activities and services, and relations with consumers and other institutions. The new information and communication technologies can be used to make improvements in each of these areas.

A starting point for these improvements is the creation of an effective information system capable of exploiting the possibilities given by web connections, both external (Internet) and internal (Intranet). In fact, web connections offer favourable advantages not only as regards the diffusion of information and knowledge but also concerning costs: costs of transmission and distribution of data, sounds and images decrease remarkably as they are averaged over all the net subscribers. Moreover, the introduction of a new subscriber to the net produces a low marginal cost and may contribute to a further reduction in fixed costs, since the expense can be shared among a wider number of consumers. We will now look more closely at how technological innovation can influence the cultural supply in its different aspects by looking at examples of museums that have exploited these new technologies as a means of achieving better results.

Admittance to museums
At the Forum in Rome, the traditional entry ticket to museums has been replaced by a magnetic band card that can be bought both at the entrance to the Forum or at ticket counters in any museum, theatre or at any monument around the city, as well as any travel agency or hotel. The use of this card, besides admission to the site, also grants access to a series of information services. A different kind of tariff rules the system of remote access. Using the card in the interactive information stations, you can also book seats for guided tours and shows organised by different Roman structures. The interactive station records all the questions received, creating a chart for each kind of consultation, and asks the visitor to fill out a short questionnaire about his/her motivation for and valuation of the visit to the Forum. So, the card is not only a more rational system for accessing the area but also a way of building up a database on the characteristics and behaviour of the visiting public (Perego, 1997).

Multimedia information
The multimedia information system represents the main innovative factor that characterises the new supply of many museums and archaeological sites.

Looking once again at the Forum in Rome, films, audiovisuals and multimedia programmes transmitted on wide screen and interactive monitors, placed on local platforms and the Web, have been produced. The aim is to create a visitor's route with interactive programmes that assist the cognitive process. From the highest points along the route you can, for example, observe virtual landscapes of the ancient town on the monitor or touch lifelike reproductions of objects and architectural details or listen to lifelike sounds, voices and noises reproduced from ancient Rome and so on. For those (students, researchers or more enquiring visitors) who wish to further their knowledge about the history of the Forum, there is a multimedia laboratory, organised in a hall and connected to the Internet, which allows you to view in real time, the work that architects and archaeologists are carrying out to implement the museums' information system. It provides information about the techniques and methods employed in restoration, preparation, virtual reconstruction and so on (Perego, 1997).

Another example, this time in Sicily, is the multimedia and simulation laboratory in the *Progetto Catania-Lecce*[3] which has created a multimedia informative system capable of storing and processing an extraordinary amount of heterogeneous data (a cultural heritage of remarkable dimensions, images, texts, films, virtual reconstruction and so on).

On line restoration
From the beginning of 2001, a technologically up-to-date site has been

produced, where it is possible to follow the live restoration of Moses and Jules II's grave by Michelangelo with the help of web-cams. The site is available 24 hours a day, with images and news about the event from the restoration and exhibition organised at San Pietro in Vincoli to all the activities which will take place throughout the year (interviews, concerts, meetings and so on) to support the event itself. This project, known as *Progetto Mosè*, enables everyone from researchers and art lovers to ordinary consumers to follow the restoration work without the traditional obstacles of crush barriers and scaffolding. Moreover, it is possible to make a virtual visit to the monument and church where it is situated, thanks to a three-dimensional reconstruction, which is faithful to the original one, while a special chat line gives you the opportunity to communicate, inside the church, with other Internet subscribers. This project, due for completion in September 2001, surely points the way to a new idea on restoring artistic heritage.

Virtual restoration
An experimental field, which is becoming increasingly successful, is the virtual restoration of archaeological sites and above all, of severely damaged paintings and frescoes.

For the restoration of paintings the computer mainly plays a role of project analysis in supporting the restorer. This means that the operator must not only be a computer scientist, but also an art expert in painting; the restorer must be able to reconstruct the missing parts of the work, using a highly technological instrument instead of a brush. Compared with 'manual restoration', virtual restoration of a painting offers some advantages. First of all, using a digital technique, the restoration work can be modified several times before choosing the best solution to employ in the final phase of manual change. In other words, by virtually reconstructing the missing part of a painting, it is possible to project and preview restoration work before actually carrying it out. Previewing the work which will actually be carried out on the works of art not only simplifies the restorer's task but also helps the expert, researcher and heritage authorities to estimate, in advance, the feasibility and convenience of the work to be done.

Virtual restoration not only offers support and help but, in the case of lost architectural assets or completely ruined paintings, can also have a teaching and study aspect, as it provides an idea of what the original work looked like.

The study on the work *Madonna col Bambino e Quattro Santi*, by Rosso Fiorentino and that on the frescoes of *Chiostro Ottagonale di San Michele in Bosco* in Bologna, from the 1600s, which were completely ruined by damp in just a few decades, represents two examples of virtual restoration carried out for teaching purposes. This project, besides allowing for the completion of the final product has created a way of teaching historical, cultural and artistic reconstruction and the collection of materials.

Virtual reality
The purely virtual viewing of museums and exhibitions allows the potential consumer to visit them virtually even if they are closed for restoration. At the moment, about ten halls in the Uffizi Gallery in Florence have already been virtually reconstructed and can be visited through other informative instruments located inside the museum. Moreover, in some cases, the virtual reconstruction of the surroundings can represent an effective historical documentation and it is certainly a great help when planning the layout of works and the organisation of exhibitions.

In conclusion, cultural supply has been considerably changed and with it the way art consumption is conceived, as we shall see later.

4.3 Digital Technologies and New Ways of Exploiting Cultural Heritage

It has been shown that the adoption of new technologies by museums and archaeological sites has resulted in a greater number of tourists and an average increase in length of visits.

Besides providing general information about cultural institutions and programmes, telecommunication and information technology also allows access to museums by providing a virtual visit, thus overcoming spatial and time obstacles. The presence of less well-known museums on the web represents an extraordinary promotional opportunity for them. In fact, the digital transmission of images on national and international nets permits the outside world to gain greater knowledge of the museums' objects, thus arousing an interest in a real visit.

So, the virtual museum represents an instrument of study, information, promotion of distant reality and, if necessary, can compensate for direct experience, although it cannot replace the real museum, only work alongside it (Galluzzi, 1999). The conditions under which the traditional visit to the museum takes place can be complemented and enriched by access routes and remote information. Moreover, virtual routes can include unavailable objects not easily exposed to air and light, or which belong to other institutions. But there are other positive aspects of home consumption.

First of all, it eliminates the sense of constraint that the visitor sometimes feels inside a museum, compelled to stand in long queues, which can prevent him/her from peacefully contemplating the work of art. Modern and sophisticated reproductive visual techniques, on the other hand, allow you to examine a picture in detail, observing particulars which during the visit to a museum can often go unnoticed, or to 'personalise' the visit by choosing some pieces, isolating them on the computer, and focusing your attention on them.

Another advantage is that of 'preserving the memory', as it was called during a recent meeting in Turin; that is, by means of virtualisation, it is possible to preserve cultural assets of historical interest, such as the image of Lingotto from the beginning of the 1900s, before the Fiat car factory (no longer in operation) was modified, and then re-employ them.

Lastly, virtual visits surely reduce the cost of getting into museums or other cultural sites in general as well as the cost of transportation and allow more time to devote to the visit (Santagata, 1999). However, while this is beneficial for 'visitors' it means a lower income both for the museum's hotel owners, restaurateurs and all those who live in the place where the museum is situated, because the tourist stream would be reduced.

Besides the advantages, there are also disadvantages and risks linked to virtual museums which deserve to be underlined. One of the first negative aspects of the reproduction of a work of art, by mechanical and electronic means, is that it provides a qualitative image that is sometimes too 'poor' or too 'strong', but which, in any case, cannot always convey real-life emotions and feelings. The reproducibility of the work also creates some risks during the commercialisation phase of cultural goods. With the selling of cultural products on CD-ROM, it is possible to simulate a work, that is, reconstruct the work of art on the basis of an identikit, by replacing the original one. Moreover, from an artistic point of view, the cultural good loses its value when reproduced on CD-ROM. To this fact we must add another substantial risk that can result from the digital visit: the visit itself becomes uninteresting.

And if the web is used as a game, there is the risk that the 'visitor' could be more impressed by the game than by the object of the game itself.

4.4 New Technologies and Education about Cultural Heritage

The use of electronic files and telecommunication and information connections also contributes to increasing young people's knowledge of cultural heritage. In fact, the information system seems to have a strong attraction for young people who make great use of computers, remaining in contact for a long period of time with interactive electronic guides and crowding the hall with a permanent connection to the web.

Even nowadays, the demand for cultural heritage by schools is still rather low and often limited to annual visits, with inadequate educational preparation. The educational aspect represents one of the most important and difficult aspects of a museum (Binni and Pinna, 1980). Creating an interest on the part of young people who are the future users of the cultural patrimony and making them understand and appreciate the different cultural functions and values of a museums is an important objective.

In 1977 in Turin the *Software Educativo Scuola Arte e Musei on line (SESAMO)* was established with a view to increasing and developing teaching in museums. The project aimed at improving relations between students and cultural patrimony, using new technologies and taking into account the strong attraction that the multimedia systems exert on young people. It is based on multimedia routes planned by the Modern Art Gallery for schools which organise didactic games on the net, providing the stimulus to approach the museum through attentive and interactive participation.

Further museum teaching on the Internet can be found on the site of the Metropolitan Museum of New York which has planned a special section with forms of experimental didactic computer games. In the same way, the Louvre.edu represents the first educational–cultural site created in France and addressed to the educational world. It represents a useful pedagogical instrument as it conveys knowledge about a series of visual, textual and sound resources produced from a database of more than 1000 works at the Louvre museum and 350 building halls, enriched with documentary resources which gather together biographies, information about artists and works, historical notes, illustrations of the halls and more. With particular attention focused on schools, this site exploits all the instruments provided by the World Wide Web, combining promotion on line and forum discussion.

The Egyptian Museum in Turin has also planned an informative area on its site devoted to museum teaching, called 'The Egyptian Museum game'. But the most innovative area is the one known as 'The Egyptian Museum at a touch', devoted to visually impaired users. All the information on the site such as texts and instructions, is given on file, so that the blind can download the whole site in braille at home. A guide for the tactile analysis of findings of the exhibits that they can bring to the museum is also provided, so that they can analyse the different tactile findings detected in the exhibits themselves.

A multimedia and interactive tour route which offers completely new and original ideas is the *Rocca del Borgo Medievale* in Turin. The sound, olfactory and illuminated route, that guides the visitors has been created using highly sophisticated equipment which has been completely disguised and is capable of recreating effects to attract the attention of the public and get them involved. In the soldiers' hall, the fights are evoked through the noise of swords; in the kitchens it is possible to smell the food; in the dome, to listen to religious chants and so on.

5.   CONCLUSION

This chapter has highlighted how the introduction of new technologies influences both the preservation and restoration of cultural heritage as well as ways in which it is offered and exploited. In particular, the spread of telecommunication and information technologies, with the creation of virtual museums, has produced a new way to consume art.

The greatest risk is that the digital transmission of a work of art could be favoured over the pleasure of real-life contemplation. The empirical data seem to exclude this idea. However, to be sure that this does not happen, the use of these new technologies must be strategically aimed at particular works.

As we have already mentioned, art consumption is very different nowadays because it is more personalised and less linked to traditional schemes, so the cultural institution must be able to approach its consumer, even from a distance, by offering its patrimony over the web and being instantly accessible to everybody, wherever they may be, in order to stimulate curiosity and encourage a visit to the place in real life. There is therefore a need not only to increase the adoption of technological knowledge, that is, the use of computers, but also to create new skilled workers, linked to the increase in value of our cultural patrimony. These workers should be able to plan and create a policy of cultural management, promotion and communication, scientific and technological innovation applied to restoration, security and the control of services for informatics. In this, Sicily appears to be slow in fully adopting new technologies for its cultural heritage.

It is believed that one of the objectives of the *Assessore Risorse Culturali*, specified in the POR (Operative Regional Programme) 2000–06, for the recovery of cultural patrimony and the improvement of cultural heritage, could notably contribute to solving this problem. It remains to be seen what the long-run effect on cultural heritage tourism in Sicily will be.

NOTES

1. Bearing in mind the objective difficulty in finding recent surveys about cultural tourism in Sicily, the data we use was processed by the *Assessorato ai Beni Culturali* on a sample of 45 regional sites (the only ones with an entrance fee), 20 of which are museums, 21 archaeological sites and four monument sites. Among the most recent papers is a survey carried out by Cles s.r.l in 1992 on a sample of visitors to 16 different cultural assets opened to the public; the Economic and Social Development Plan 1992–1994 of the Sicilian Regional

Council (Regione Siciliana 1992); and the study by Causi (1995).

2. The insertion of a fibre optic endoscope in the heel on the *Bronzi di Riace*, which allowed for the clearance of salt and soil, is an example of how these techniques can be used. It was possible to use them to restore the original colours and architectural elements in the restoration of the façade of the *Basilica di San Pietro*.

3. It is a co-ordinated plan for the development of information and communication technologies aimed at saving, upgrading and developing the historical, cultural, scientific and natural patrimony of the universities of Catania and Lecce.

REFERENCES

Binni, L. and Pinna, G. (1980), *Museo, Storia e Funzioni di una Macchina Culturale dal Cinquecento ad Oggi*, Milan: Garzanti.

Causi, M. (1995), 'Beni Culturali e Politiche di Sviluppo in Sicilia', *Economia della Cultura*, 1, 63–70.

Di Maio, A. (1999), *Economia dei Beni e delle Attività Culturali*, Naples: Liguori.

Di Maria, E. (2000), 'L'Impiego dell'ICT nella Cultura: Alcune Esperienze Nazionali e Internazionali', in E. Rullani, S. Micelli and E. Di Maria, *Città e Cultura nell'Economia delle Reti*, Bologna: Il Mulino, pp. 95–138.

Galluzzi, P. (1997), 'Nuove Tecnologie e Funzione Culturale dei Musei', in P. Galluzzi and P.A. Valentino (eds), *I Formati della Memoria. Beni Culturali e Nuove Tecnologie alle Soglie del Terzo Millennio*, Florence: Giunti, pp. 111–131.

Galluzzi, P. (1999), 'Musei Virtuali: Istruzioni per l'uso', *Rivista IF*, (2), 41–44.

Micelli, S. and Di Maria, E. (2000), 'Tecnologie di Rete e Rinnovamento delle Istituzioni Culturali nel Contesto delle Città d'Arte', in E. Rullani, S. Micelli and E. Di Maria, *Città e Cultura nell'Economia delle Reti*, Bologna: Il Mulino, pp. 57–89.

Perego, F. (1997), 'Oltre le Pietre le Storie. Il caso dei Fori Imperiali a Roma', in P. Galluzzi and P.A. Valentino (eds), op. cit, pp. 103–121.

Pilati, A. (1996), 'Nuove Tecnologie: Opportunità e Mercati', *Economia della Cultura*, (1), 35–37.

Regione Siciliana (1992), *Piano Regionale di Sviluppo Economico Sociale 1992–94*, Materiale per il progetto di attuazione Beni Culturali, Palermo.

Santagata, W. (1997), 'L'Economia del Museo nell'Epoca delle Reti-mercato Telematiche', in P. Galluzzi and P.A. Valentino (eds), op. cit, pp. 75–89.

Santagata, W. (1999), *Produrre Cultura. Note di Economia sulle Istituzioni e sui Mercati Culturali*, Turin: Celid.

PART III

Demand for Heritage

9. Methods for Measuring the Demand for the Arts and Heritage: Theoretical Issues*

Tiziana Cuccia and Giovanni Signorello

1. INTRODUCTION

Public decision-makers should choose the economic allocation of public funds which maximise social welfare resulting from the aggregation of individual preferences. On the basis of this principle, public intervention in favour of the conservation of cultural heritage (CH) is justified only if social welfare increases. In a context of more and more limited public economic resources, public policies on the conservation of CH have to compete with other social policies that promote public health, social security, education, job opportunities, and so on.

If we consider the different objectives of public policies, it is hard to prove that a public plan for the conservation of CH is more favourable than public policies for public health and social security. The conservation of CH, however, could be among the determinants of the individuals' utility functions. It is surely present in the utility function of heritage experts, such as archaeologists, conservationists and art historians. In wealthy societies with a higher average level of education and per capita income, a larger number of individuals also care about CH and include the conservation of CH in their own preference functions. Markets are the main places where these signals can be perceived. If individuals demand more tradable cultural goods, the market mechanism shows this with a higher market price for the goods. If the cultural asset is traded on the market, we can estimate the demand curve to measure the aggregate consumers' surplus. If the cultural good is not traded, the task becomes more difficult.

Most of CH is not tradable on the market because of its economic characteristics. CH displays the characteristics of public goods in different degrees: if someone enjoys CH, other individuals can enjoy it as well without reducing the enjoyment of the first (non-rivalry in consumption) and there is no technical mechanism that can prevent individuals from enjoying the asset (non-excludability from consumption).   These characteristics make it unprofitable for an enterprise to supply CH because, if no one can technically be excluded, no price can be applied to the enjoyment of CH. The zero-price condition can produce overexploitation of CH and cause irreversible damage to CH. CH becomes 'common goods' and two kinds of rivalry can arise: an intra-temporal rivalry in consumption due to congestion connected to mass tourism and an inter-temporal rivalry because the actual consumption of CH competes with the consumption of future generations.

If the private or public owner can technically make some cultural assets excludable and a price is charged to access these assets, the conservation of CH then essentially depends on what the price signals.

As an example, the price on the real estate market of a privately owned historical building mainly reflects the use value of the building and the historical and artistic qualities of the construction can influence the market price either positively or negatively. On the one hand, consumers could positively appreciate the artistic value because it recreates an old-style atmosphere and the market price could rise. On the other hand, consumers could negatively value the artistic features because they imply higher maintenance costs and the market price could fall. In either case, the market signals are strictly connected with the use value of CH.

Beside the use value, CH has a non-use value, that is the 'existence' value which has to be estimated as a component of the total economic value. Put differently, there are two different demands that may be estimated: the recreational demand expressed by the actual consumers and the conservation demand expressed by non-users.

The market therefore partially signals the economic value of CH, as some components of the economic value of CH are not tradable on the market and this causes underinvestment in the conservation of CH.   Individuals, however, act not only on the market but also in institutions.   When individuals act in the institutions as citizens, they can value the different allocation of public funds proposed by political programmes and can express their preference for the conservation of CH by voting for the political programme which takes care of that.

When decision-makers have to value the net social effect of alternative public investment projects, they adopt cost–benefit analysis (CBA), based on the comparison of social benefits and the cost of each project. The project that generates the highest net social benefits will be favoured. One of the main problems of CBA is how to estimate some social benefits and project costs. This task can be particularly hard if decision-makers are involved in the valuation of projects that directly or indirectly affect CH.

In a project regarding the construction of a road, decision-makers might have to choose between two alternatives: two routes with different financial costs. One is shorter and costs less than the other but passes close to a historical site and disturbs the surrounding view. In such a case, from a strictly financial CBA point of view, the decision-maker should favour the cheaper project but if he/she adds the social costs and benefits of the two alternative projects, the choice could be different. In this example, two different measures of individual preferences could be used: the individual's maximum willingness to pay (WTP) to avoid damage connected to the altered view of the historical site or the individual's minimum willingness to accept (WTA) compensation to tolerate the damage of the altered view or to forgo the benefit of the original view of the historical site. Both are measures of the demand and value of cultural heritage.

To overcome the absence of market information, methods developed and implemented in the fields of public economics and environmental economics are adopted.

In this chapter, after a short review of the main theoretical approaches which require public policies for the conservation of CH, we briefly summarise non-market valuation methods. We focus our attention on the contingent valuation (CV) method which presently seems to be the only method available for the recovery of non-use values. In particular, we describe the application of CV in the arts sector and examine the empirical and theoretical developments in CV studies on the arts sectors and the policy implications of this approach.

2. WHAT DOES VALUING CH MEAN AND WHAT IS IT FOR?

To determine an optimal level of CH conservation, that is, a level of conservation where the social marginal benefit of conservation is equal to the social marginal cost, decision-makers have to take into account all the economic values which make up the total: use value, option value and non-use or intrinsic value. In the economic value of a historical building, for example, we have to include not only the value directly or indirectly connected with the use of the building, but also the value connected with its existence, that is, the non-use value, expressed by the cost of its irreplaceable loss.

The use value includes the actual use of the building, its vicarious use value, that is, the use made by individuals who cannot visit the building but can enjoy seeing it in pictures or on film. These are indirect benefits or costs which, those close to cultural heritage receive from its use for cultural and recreational purposes. The indirect benefits of CH conservation are both pecuniary externalities, revealed by the market mechanism, for example, by higher hotel rates in heritage cities, and benefits which are not registered in the market through the price mechanism (Towse, 1994). If policy-makers do not internalise these positive externalities with economic instruments such as subsidies, we could end up with a suboptimal allocation of resources for CH. Following this economic approach, private owners of historical buildings who personally sustain the burden of CH conservation should receive a public subsidy equal to the positive externalities which individuals receive from the maintenance of the historical building. The problem is, how much subsidy? If CH has, in different degrees, the characteristics of 'public goods', individuals cannot be forced to reveal their preference and can act as free-riders, because it is technically impossible to exclude them from the enjoyment of CH even if they are not willing to pay anything for it.

The willingness to pay in order to secure the possibility of using the goods in the future for their own utility and/or the utility of future generations is called option value and can also be considered as a potential use value to be taken into account.

The existence or non-use value has two main components: an altruistic component and a selfish component. We can look at the case where there are people who are scared of flying but value a monument located at the opposite end of the world just because they enjoy knowing it exists and is conserved, even if they know that they will never visit it (Krutilla, 1967). In the valuation of CH, we can qualify the non-use value with different attributes. On the one hand, a historical building could be appreciated more for its spiritual value than for its aesthetic value (that is a church or a mosque); it could also have a symbolic value (that is St. Peter's Church has a spiritual and symbolic value because it represents the centre of Christianity). The non-use value of other cultural assets could be more a social and historical value than an aesthetic one (that is, monuments to the unknown soldier all over the world, war cemeteries, and so on). On the other hand, aesthetic and authentic value concerns more objective values than anthropocentric opinions of artistic masterpieces. Even if everyone has their say on whether they like an artistic piece or not, the aesthetic and authentic value can be considered a sort of 'intrinsic' value or absolute concept in some philosophical approaches, independent of human behaviour.

The aesthetic value can only be appreciated by a restricted group of experts (paternalistic approach). At an aggregate level, there could be a trade-off among these different motivations which influences individuals' opinions on CH: experts only value the aesthetic worth of CH while other individuals could appreciate more than the other non-use aspects of CH.

The individualistic approach has the great advantage of allowing every individual, expert or not, to express their different motivations of WTP in the same language and monetary terms. The quantification in monetary terms allows decision-makers to rank intervention in CH by taking into account the different motivations and, given a limited conservation budget, establish priorities when a conservation programme has to be planned.

Up until now, policy-makers have generally based cultural policies on experts' judgements. Cultural experts have a very important role in the management of CH because of their informational advantage and only experts, or very well-educated people, can appreciate it and can suggest where and how to intervene. This essential contribution, however, sometimes supports very conservative policies because CH is seen only as an object of research and not as buildings and goods which can be used and opened to visitors. The experts' objective function could oppose the policy-makers' objective function: experts aim to maximise their own scientific prestige in academic circles and policy-makers should aim to maximise access to CH, as CH plays an educational role.

In the restoration plan of a group of historical buildings with a limited financial budget, the priorities and types of intervention expressed by experts should be tested and compared with the preferences of individuals. The individualistic approach mitigates the role of experts even if in policy decisions on CH this role cannot be totally disregarded. In prioritising policy measures, experts can be biased in their interest towards a particular style (that is archaeologists may prefer intervention on archaeological sites rather than on medieval monuments), individuals may prefer a historical building with a high identity value rather than a unique historical building. Policy-makers should balance these different priority ratings and decide what is the level of intervention and on which particular cultural sites (that is, local or central level of public authority).

Public intervention in CH can have a further objective. Individuals' preferences can be considered endogenous and the public authority, through educational plans, can stimulate the demand for CH. The conservation of CH can therefore be considered an essential element in an educational plan: the more individuals are used to living in a stimulating, cultural environment, the more the addictive element of the consumption of cultural goods contributes to increasing the demand for CH.

The asymmetric distribution of information on CH and the ignorance that *ex ante* characterises most individuals when consuming cultural goods justified the normative public finance approach based on the 'merit goods' argument. As a 'merit good', CH is a low demand good because individuals are unfamiliar with CH and therefore cannot appreciate it. This approach, however, assumes that the public authority has a dictatorial approach and

Demand for Heritage

prevails over individuals' preferences. It is in conflict with the fundamental principle of consumer sovereignty on which rational economic behaviour is founded.[1]

Policy-makers should consider individuals' preferences either when they have to establish the priorities of intervention on CH or when they have to choose the instruments and level of intervention: the level of access charges or of tax refunds, the regulation of the tourist flow, and so on.

We therefore focus on the methods of estimating and aggregating individuals' preferences for the conservation and promotion of CH.

3. HOW SHOULD WE VALUE CULTURAL HERITAGE?

The different components in the economic value of CH mentioned above could influence the choice of technique to be adopted for the valuation of CH.

The choice is also influenced by the importance we attribute to the different components. As an example, the relevance of the existence value is particularly difficult to estimate and considering it in cultural project appraisal is quite controversial. A large amount of literature shows that non-use values can be estimated and that the values obtained are usually significant and sometimes exceed current use values by a considerable margin (Morey et al., 1997; Mourato and Pearce, 1999).

In the case of CH, the existence value can be considered a collective concept related to the national prestige that well-preserved heritage produces. If, however, we consider each item that makes up heritage, the existence value can be more or less significant according to how unique or not the item is estimated to be. Monuments of a widely spread art style have a lower existence value than monuments of a unique art style that has to be preserved. According to Randall, this suggests that, in many routine benefit estimation contexts, existence values will be unimportant (Randall, 1991).

Table 9.1 Methods of valuing public goods

	Direct	Indirect
Revealed preference methods	Simulated markets Parallel private markets Replacement costs Referenda	Household production function Travel cost method Averting costs Hedonic price analysis
Stated preference methods	Contingent Valuation method	Conjoint analysis (contingent ranking)

To briefly summarise the most common methods of valuing public goods, it can be useful to adopt a taxonomy based on two dimensions (see Table 9.1) – how preferences are revealed and the type of behavioural linkage (Mitchell and Carson, 1990).

In what follows, we consider the two main classes of methods separately: the revealed preference methods, and the stated preference methods within which we focus on the contingent valuation method (CVM).

4.   REVEALED PREFERENCE METHODS

Revealed preference methods involve the direct or indirect estimation of WTP for a non-marketed item from the individuals' preferences revealed in an associated market or in a different context (referenda).

4.1 Direct Revealed Preference Methods

In direct revealed preference methods, the individuals' preferences for a non-marketed item can be inferred by the market in three different ways:

1. simulating an experimental market set up by researchers where individuals actually trade the item observed. This experiment requires that the essential condition of the excludability needed to institute a market is technically available. Researchers can adopt the simulation market technique only to estimate the WTP for quasi-marketed goods;
2. inferring the value of the publicly provided commodity from the market price of a similar private good; and
3. not valuing the public item less than the opportunity costs to replace it, taking into account not the artistic value but the present use of CH.

In the case of CH, the value of a free admission museum can be estimated either by an experiment market, that is, actually applying an admission charge, because it is technically possible to exclude those who do not pay the admission fee (simulation market) or by the value of a similar museum where an admission fee is applied (appropriate parallel private item market). The value of the museum could be equalled to the opportunity cost to build or rent a different building for a certain number of years and to preserve and exhibit what the museum holds.

Referenda represent a particular case of individual preferences revelation technique.   Preferences are revealed in an institutional context where individuals behave as citizens and with their vote making binding decisions on the provision of public goods.   However, the different context can influence the utility function individuals wish to maximise: a more altruistic behaviour could be more frequent.

4.2 Indirect Revealed Preference Methods

Indirect revealed preference methods include those methods which estimate non-market goods by using consumption behaviour in related markets; in this class we distinguish three methods.

Hedonic pricing (HP) method

This assumes, according to Lancaster's theory of demand, that the price of a marketed good is a function of its different characteristics. The implicit price of a particular characteristic is found by differentiating the market price with respect to the particular characteristic whose economic value we want to estimate (Rosen, 1974). It has often been used in the real estate market to estimate the economic value of each characteristic which makes up the demand for housing. For example, *ceteris paribus* all the other characteristics, two properties can differ only in location: one can be located in a historical area and the other outside. If the individuals appreciate or depreciate the historical zone location of the properties, the positive or negative difference in price shows the implicit value they attribute to the historical centre.

To determine the implicit value of private properties located in a historical zone, the hedonic approach implies two different stages. In the first stage, using econometric techniques, we estimate the hedonic price function that enlightens the relationship between the property's price and the characteristic we want to estimate, also taking into account all the other explanatory variables we think may influence the property's price. In the second stage, an inverse demand curve is estimated, which, for each implicit price deduced from the hedonic price function corresponding to the marginal cost of being located closer and closer to a historical zone, points out the different levels of the characteristic estimated that maximise the individual utility function.

Even if this technique can, in principle, value all the use values (but not the non-use values), several problems can also arise concerning the knowledge of the market examined and some technical aspects which can influence the utilisation of the data. Firstly, this technique works if the market clears, consumers are perfectly informed and can maximise their utility function. Unfortunately, in reality, market clearing does not occur. Secondly, some technical aspects can reduce the reliability of the HP method: the choice of the functional form, the omission of significant variables and the strict correlation between each independent variable included in the hedonic price equation (multi-collinearity) result in imprecise and unstable coefficient estimates. For example, in the housing market, we could overestimate the implicit price of the historical zone location of a property because this variable is strictly related to other variables such as easy access to city services (offices, shops and so on), usually concentrated in the city centre which in turn is very often the historical area of the city.

Averting costs or expenditure approach

This directly infers the value of cultural heritage changes from changes in expenditure on defensive activities (Smith, 1991). If cultural changes and expenditure on defensive activities are perfect substitutes, we can estimate the value of improvement in cultural changes (for example, the opening of a cultural asset) by the expenditure saved in videos or films of the asset's interiors. On the contrary, if cultural changes and the expenditure saved are not a perfect substitute, the estimate of benefit may not be reliable. The averting expenditure could also serve other functions: the tape of a historical site, for example, could be a souvenir of the trip and therefore more a complement to than a substitute for the trip.

Travel cost method (TCM)

This is based on the spatial theory of rent and has been commonly used to estimate the demand for outdoor recreational goods (Clawson and Knetsch, 1966). The proxies for price (origin zone of each user) and quantity (number of trips) are obtained by on-site or off-site surveys. The collected data allow the researcher to estimate the demand curve for the site as a function of the distance covered by the visitors (trips per capita distance decay function). Implementing the TCM is relatively easy. The researcher converts travel and distance into a travel cost, assuming that individuals take trips until the marginal cost of the trip equals its marginal value, and then regresses the number of trips on price (that is the marginal cost) and demographic variables. The estimated function, obtained by using appropriate regression models such as count data models, contains all the necessary information to estimate total and mean consumer surplus (Freeman, 1993). The individual value of a recreational cultural site is equal to the area under the demand curve and above the 'travel cost'; the total value of the cultural site is equal to the sum of the whole area under the individual demand curves.

An alternative to the individual TCM is the zonal TCM where the dependent variable of the estimated demand function of the cultural site is the number of visits per capita from each zone. The single-site TC models, however, (either the individual or the zonal version) in most cases, represent an oversimplification of recreation behaviour.

One of the most commonly discussed weaknesses of the simple TCM is a highly site-specific result. In other words, simple TC models do not adequately account for possible substitution among sites (if they are present in the region) and do not take into account the importance of the quality (characteristics) of the site (Hanley and Spash, 1993).

Attempts to compensate for these drawbacks have included multiple-site models, hedonic TCM, and, more recently, random utility or discrete choice models (RUM). Multiple-site models aim at incorporating possible substitute sites into the simple TC model. Possible substitutes for the cultural site considered are those cultural sites which have the same recreational function because of their location, artistic relevance or functional destination. What can be considered as a substitute for the observed cultural site, though, is questionable.

The hedonic TCM (Brown and Mendelsohn, 1984) attempts to estimate, by individual or zonal travel costs, the economic value of the different characteristics of cultural sites, calculated on samples of visitors at a number of cultural sites. A two-stage approach is usually adopted. Firstly, a travel cost function is estimated for each zone of origin of the visitors as a function of both the distance and different characteristics of the cultural sites (conservation, historic and artistic uniqueness, kind of fruition and so on). Secondly, a demand curve for each characteristic is estimated by regressing site characteristic levels against the marginal cost of the characteristics calculated by the travel cost function. Unfortunately, individuals may appear to place more value on certain characteristics just because they are more evident in a cultural site which is further away (Bockstael et al., 1991).

Unlike traditional single and multi-site travel cost models, RUM can incorporate a large number of substitute sites and can assess the importance of site characteristics at each of these sites to determine their value to users. The RUM assumes that an individual who wants to take a trip faces a set of possible alternative sites with differing characteristics. The RUM, however, estimates the probability that an individual will choose a particular cultural site, depending on the characteristics of that site and the characteristics of the available substitutes. To implement the RUM, the researcher must collect data on site quality from every site in the choice set and on round-trip travel distance from each visitor's origin to every site included in the bundle. The RUM explicitly models the recreation-decision process, recognising that choices can be made at different levels (nested models). In this way, it allows for the non-violation of the assumption of the independence of irrelevant alternatives, which is the key assumption of the RUM. Estimated probabilities will be used to construct the inclusive-values index of the underlying utility associated with various choice occasions and value the willingness to pay for the option to take a trip to any given site (Signorello, 1994).

Whatever the models used, it is important to consider that the consumer of cultural assets very often engages in a multipurpose trip. If the trip is both cultural and recreational, as happens in a heritage city, it could be difficult to estimate how many visitors are interested in historical buildings and how many are interested in all the other opportunities the city offers (shopping, performing arts events, and suchlike). In such a case, the total price should be divided into the different characteristics' price levels.

Finally, the most important weakness of TCMs is that they can only measure the direct recreational benefits. TCMs cannot be used to estimate either the option or existence value. TCMs also suffer a truncation bias because the category of households which have to pay high travel costs to visit the site and therefore prefer not to make any visit, cannot be taken in account.

5. STATED PREFERENCE METHODS

Stated preference methods recur in surveys based on specifically structured questionnaires submitted to a significant sample of individuals to describe the individual behaviour in a 'hypothetical market' where a non-marketed asset is traded. We distinguish indirect and direct stated preference methods.

In the indirect stated preference methods, people are asked to respond to hypothetical markets but their responses can only indirectly allow valuing the asset of interest.

Conjoint analysis (CA) is the generic term for a class of survey-based methods particularly used in market research to test the introduction of new or modified products. It follows an approach *à la* Lancaster because goods are considered as a bundle of attributes. Respondents are asked to choose between two or more alternative options. Each option consists of a different combination of two or more attributes of the asset and a trade-off exists between the attributes considered. One of the attributes is a price or cost variable, through which we can indirectly infer the marginal value of the other attributes and the economic value of the public asset.

Respondents can simply be asked to choose the most favoured combination of goods (and/or its attributes) and the associated price variable (this is why it is also called conjoint analysis); or they can be asked to rank a given set of options in a decreasing preference order (this is the contingent ranking method (CR)). The CR is one of four different kinds of elicitation formats (the others are the rating, graded pair comparison, and the dichotomous choice) used in conjoint analysis.

Both methods are based on stochastic approaches and are modelled on a random utility model. The estimated WTP of each attribute and of the public asset is, therefore, expressed in stochastic terms and their reliability depends on the statistical significance of the indirect utility function adopted. They are accomplished by considering the total differential of the estimated random utility function with respect to the price variable and the attribute observed, and by computing the price change which would be equivalent to any attribute change.

On the one side, CR can be considered an evolution of contingent valuation because it allows for more information to be had: not only the indirect inferring of the use and non-use value of the public asset but also the rate of substitution between each attribute and the WTP. In the CR approach we can also have the rank-order preferences for a set of alternative dimensions and levels of the public asset. It is particularly suitable for deals with multidimensional commodities where there are relevant trade-offs among the commodity attributes and multilevel solutions. For instance, this method has been adopted to investigate the significant choice variables of museums' consumers. It allows for the determination of how consumers trade off between ticket price and opening hours of the museum (Herrmann et al., 1999). Moreover, respondents might be more willing to rank their preferences than to explicitly announce their WTP for a public asset. The awareness of the trade-off between the price and welfare change should reduce the incidence of strategic behaviour.

On the other side, the reliability of estimates of the indirect utility function require higher costs than CV estimates because the ordinal measures of WTP obtained must be conducted on a larger sample and more sophisticated statistical techniques must be used. The right number of alternatives to be considered may be questionable: too many options could make respondents confused and could reduce the value of information gained. Usually, no more than three or four options are considered and the range over which the price is specified has to be limited.

5.1 The Contingent Valuation Method

Contingent valuation (CV) is a direct stated preference method. It basically consists of asking individuals, in surveys or experimental settings, to reveal their personal valuation of a non-priced asset or increments (or reductions) in non-priced assets, by using contingent markets (Randall et al., 1983).

The main steps of CV analysis are the sample selection, the description of the contingent market and the choice of technique for eliciting willingness to pay.

Under its apparently simple structure, many problems drawing on aspects of economics, psychology and political theory must be solved to obtain reliable information on the individual WTP and/or the individual WTA.

The first problem concerns what has to be measured. The choice between WTA and WTP could be relevant and WTA exceeds WTP the more the income elasticity of demand for the asset increases and the more the elasticity of substitution between the public and private goods decreases. In the case of a unique cultural asset, WTP would be the individual's entire income and the WTA would be infinite.

There are several reasons for the different measures between WTA and WTP (O'Doherty, 1998). Ethical reasons can lead to the compensation of the present generation for the next generation's benefits being considered as immoral and can therefore result either in a refusal to answer the WTA question or in inflated responses. Psychological reasons proposed by the 'prospect theory' developed by Kahnemann and Tversky (1979) provide an explanation for the divergence between WTP and WTA. They show that the value function for losses is steeper than that for gains and this justifies the difference between the two measures. In CV studies, however, the WTP estimate is usually preferred, as it is easier to quantify.

Other psychological aspects which influence the responses of individuals can bias the validity and reliability of the CV. The revealed willingness to pay shows the intention to perform specific behaviour but specific behaviour rarely actually occurs.

The second critical point of CVM concerns sample selection. The population whose WTP is to be measured is determined by the nature and location of the asset to be valued. This might not be an easy task in the case of well-known cultural assets around the world. Probability sampling procedures are usually used to select the sample which will receive the CV questionnaire. Cost considerations have sometimes led to the use of convenience samples but the WTP values obtained cannot be generalised in a larger population (Cropper and Alberini, 1997).

The increasing use of CV studies to estimate public goods and the use of these estimates in policy decision-making and litigation (natural resource damage assessment) make the definition of a common design questionnaire inevitable. The NOOA panel[2] suggests a large number of stringent requirements for CV studies.

The third key point of the CV method is the design of the questionnaire. The three main elements of the questionnaire to elicit a valid and reliable WTP are:

1. a plausible description must be provided of the scenario in which the public asset changes. This aims to improve individuals' familiarity with

the problem to be analysed (Cummings et al., 1986);
2. the type of WTP question adopted; and
3. the choice of payment vehicle to make individuals aware of the budget constraint.

Some questions regarding the socio-economic characteristics of the respondents (age, income, profession, education) are also required at the end of the interview. The choice of a common structure has been readily accepted.

The choice of question format for eliciting WTP is much more controversial. We can face different biases depending on the WTP elicitation question adopted. The simple question 'What is the most you would pay ...?' for the asset (open-ended format) could prove to be a difficult one. Respondents have no reference amount and may prefer not to answer the question or offer such diverse amounts as to produce a high dispersion in the answers. To avoid these problems, a payment card format which lists different monetary values can be offered to the respondents. The card can show point values or intervals of values from among which the respondents can choose.

In most recent CV surveys, the most commonly used elicitation technique is the closed-ended format (dichotomous choice) which requires only a yes–no answer from the respondent on a stated amount for the item. This format reproduces the situation consumers face everyday in the market and in a referendum setting and has been shown to be incentive compatible, that is, it allows for the reduction of the free-rider problem. This is also the reason why the NOOA panel suggests a referendum format. The main weakness in this elicitation format, however, is statistical inefficiency. An affirmative answer means that the respondent's WTP is at least equal to the sum proposed in the questionnaire but it could be higher. On the contrary, people who answer 'no' to the WTP stated in the questionnaire could be more or less distant from the stated WTP.

This technique is also called single-bounded as the stated WTP is the boundary of two intervals: the interval where respondents' WTP goes from the stated WTP to infinity (or their budget constraint) and the interval where respondents' WTP goes from zero to the stated WTP. To avoid this drawback, follow-up questions have been proposed which try to find out in which interval the WTP of each respondent lies (double-bounded format) (Hanemann et al., 1991). After the 'yes' answer, a follow-up question with a higher bid (usually double the earlier WTP) is asked; after the 'no' answer, a follow-up question with a lower bid (usually half of the earlier WTP) is asked. Using the double-bounded format, the latent WTP amount is limited to a narrower interval than the single binary choice question and a higher statistical efficiency is thereby achieved. A key point in this format is how they define the bid vector from which to choose the bid to insert in the questionnaire at random. An open-ended CV survey is usually used as a pre-test to determine the possible distribution of WTP. The double-bounded format allows us to avoid the starting-point bias which was the main reason for abandoning the iterative bidding game.[3] This bias is strictly connected to respondent weariness, anchoring and yea-saying. In the case of a double-bounded approach we do not have respondent weariness because there is only a single follow-up bid. Nor do we have an anchoring factor because the second bid is very different from the first. The yea-saying in the second bid is less likely because the respondents in the second bid are a censored sample with a WTP equal to or higher than the first bid.

Even if the CV method is the one most commonly used to estimate public goods, some technical aspects must be improved to increase the reliability of the estimates. Implausibly large values (a closed-ended approach can avoid this problem) and zero WTP values have to be minimised due to strategic behaviour or to protest bids. The validity of the results obtained through a CV survey has to be tested in different ways: by comparing CV estimates with the results of actual or simulated market transactions and with estimates produced by indirect methods, such as TCM, which infer WTP from actual behaviour.

Even though the CV method is the one most commonly used to estimate public goods, the validity of this method is controversial. The debate is still alive and is based on technical and theoretical reasons.

5.2 Theoretical Debate on CV Method

The main positive aspects of the CV method, as already mentioned, are the excellent opportunity to recover existing or non-use values and the ability to estimate option value and its flexibility, which allow for the analysis of new policy options for which there are no data available (Hanemann, 1994).

The negative aspects of the CV method are the credibility and reliability of responses and the consistency in responses with the economic theory (Diamond and Hausman, 1994). All the elements commonly required to design a reliable survey mentioned above try to increase the content validity of CV estimates.

There are two main theoretical criticisms which make decision-makers uncertain about the use of the outcome of this method. The first criticism is that asking for a hypothetical payment is different from asking for a real payment and respondents can act strategically. The second criticism is that CV results could be inconsistent with economic theory (Hoevenagel, 1996). The WTP value for some specific goods is found to be similar to the WTP value for more inclusive goods, that is, the WTP to restore a single monument could be found to be roughly equal to the WTP for restoring two or more monuments (perfect embedding). In this case, the normal economic assumption 'more will always be better' is not applicable. The hypothetical character of the CV could be one of the causes of the embedding effect. In CV studies, respondents, when asked to value a specific private or public good, will show their mental accounts or good causes account irrespective of the description of the particular item examined and use CV responses to get moral satisfaction rather than to assign an economic value. The misperception hypothesis can be another cause of embedding but can be overcome with a careful design of the survey, which includes the use of focus groups and pre-testing. Substitution effects can produce different WTP values for embedded goods and their independently valued equivalents (regular embedding). The same item is assigned a lower WTP value if the WTP is inferred from the WTP value for a more inclusive item rather than if that item is valued on its own. The problem, therefore, is what is the appropriate context in which the goods have to be valued. This, however, is not inconsistent with economic theory and can be explained in terms of substitution effects.

The other criticisms CV researchers have to face are the following:

1. how stable preferences are. A number of test and re-test studies aim to show consistency in value over time (reliability);
2. what is expressed in the WTP value and what is a permissible argument in the utility function on which it is based; and
3. how WTP varies with factors like income which usually influence it (what is income elasticity).

Even the most optimistic experts on CV studies advocate caution in the adoption of the outcomes obtained in them and suggest checking the quality (peer review) of the specific CV study (the review process must focus each step of the study, from the design of the questionnaire to analysis of data and presentation of results) before using the results obtained. To test CV results, we can turn to other behavioural estimation criteria such as simulated markets and referenda. In the absence of a real reference point (the price of the good), a general criterion which can be used in assessing the quality of the CV estimate is the 'preponderance of evidence' criterion. As pointed out by Hanemann (1994) 'when the public valuation is the object of measurement, a well-designed contingent valuation survey is one way of consulting the relevant experts – the public itself' (Hanemann, 1994, p. 38).

A referendum has recently been proposed as a good alternative to CV (Frey, 1997). As the NOOA panel suggests, a referendum CV format, which is a dichotomous choice, should be favoured in eliciting WTP. The main question Frey formulates, therefore, is why we do not turn directly to a referendum. The adoption of popular referenda for cultural policy could have the important advantage of managing to 'avoid the principal–agent problem and constitute an effective barrier against the *classe politique*' (Frey, 1997, p. 241).

The strength of an institutional referendum is the combination of evaluation and decision-making. Referenda can also avoid the implementation problems typical of WTP studies. The weakness is that from a referendum, we only obtain 'yes or no' information, while in CV studies, the estimate of the WTP allows us to collect more information on the sample. Knowing the main correlation in the sample between the WTP and the socio-economic characteristics of population provides us with a lot more information than a referendum can. This information could allow for a better design of cultural policy.

The main difference between these two instruments is that they have different aims. Referenda allow us to overcome the obstacles inside the politico-economic process. CV studies can be used in different cases: litigation, introduction of new cultural services and planning a more efficient cultural policy design based on information about the consumers' surplus of different classes of respondents.

5.3 CV Surveys in the Arts Sector

The CV is potentially capable of capturing all the economic values of non-marketed goods. This feature makes it particularly suited to estimate CH where non-use values often represent a significant part of the total economic value.

The strength of CV is stressed by empirical studies estimating the total social welfare provided by CH or by changes in CH which have yet to be carried out. Most of them prefer to adopt CV instead of the other methods mentioned above.[4] However, compared to the large amount of literature which has been published about the evaluation of environmental goods and the damage they suffer from pollution, relatively few empirical studies on the valuation of cultural assets have been carried out yet. These studies concern a wide range of CH and situations which make it difficult to classify them and compare the findings obtained.

We can distinguish CV studies by the type of benefit estimated and the type of cultural good or service observed. The valuation of the individuals' WTP concerns the following benefits for CH: protection from air pollution, protection from abandonment/neglect, protection from urban development/ infrastructure, gaining access and maintaining the present level. The objects of CV studies on CH are single goods (for example, a cathedral) or multiple goods and services (for example, a group of monuments, a group of buildings, an archaeological site and the arts). The studies on multiple cultural goods should minimise the part–whole bias, that is, the overestimation of the WTP for a single good which also includes the preferences for CH in general. Despite this classification, it is difficult to compare the findings obtained because in each combination of benefits and type of good, only a few studies have been done. Moreover, the findings can differ because of the different format of the elicitation question (payment card, double- or single-bounded dichotomous choice, open-ended) and the instrument of payment chosen (tax, entry fee, donations, and so on).

Nevertheless, some interesting observations emerge from the literature review reported in Table 9.2.

Each study attests the significantly positive value of the individual's WTP for the conservation or restoration of CH. The value of the single item seems to be larger than the value of multiple goods. This could be due either to the uniqueness of the single item evaluated or to the part–whole bias. Nevertheless, the values on CH indirectly result from the estimation of the WTP for benefits from different types of conservation which can contrast other individual interests. The value of Lincoln Cathedral, for example, which is inferred from the WTP for protection against specific damage (air pollution) can only be approximately compared with the value of Durham Cathedral estimated by the WTP for gaining access (Pearce and Mourato, 1998). The latter is more concerned with the use of the cultural asset. The former concerns more the long-running value and preservation of cultural assets from irreversible damage caused by air pollution which threatens future generations more than the present one. Therefore, even if the percentage of the WTP in per capita GNP is almost the same, the meaning could be different.

For the same reason, different WTPs as a percentage of the per capita GNP cannot be used to rate cultural sites and define priorities for conserving CH.

Most of the CV studies present a large proportion of respondents declaring a zero WTP (about 30 per cent on average for users and about 60 per cent for non-users). This can be partially explained as a protest or lack of interest in the survey. Part of them, however, could reflect the true preferences of the individuals. Only a minority of well-educated individuals appreciate CH. This minority has a high level of consumption of CH and often has an economic rent because it might be willing to pay over and above the asking price in order to access cultural sites. The recreational and educational aspects of CH are always appreciated (the values expressed by users are higher than those expressed by non-users).

Table 9.2 Classification of cultural heritage CV studies

Type of Benefit / Type of good	Single item		Multiple goods			
	Cathedral	Other	Group of monuments	Group of buildings	Archaeological site	Arts
Protection from air pollution	Lincoln Cathedral, UK (Pollicino and Maddison, 2001) Nidaros Cathedral, Norway. (Navrud et al., 1992)		Washington, DC, USA (Morey et al, 1997)	Neuchatel, Switzerland (Grosclaude and Soguel, 1994)		
Protection from abandonment		Nicastro Castle, Italy (Mazza, 1999) Northern Hotel in Fort Collins, USA (Kling et al, 2000)	Bulgarian monasteries, Bulgaria. (Mourato and Danchev, 1997) Historic Core of Split, Croatia (Pagiola, 1999)	Fes Medina, Morocco. (Carson et al., 1997) Grainger City, Newcastle, UK (Garrod et al., 1996) Noto, Italy. (Cuccia and Signorello, Chapter 10, this book)	Machu Picchu, Peru (Hett and Mourato, 2000)	
Protection from urban development/ infrastructure		Ste. Genevieve, Missouri, USA (Chambers et al., 1998)			Stonehenge, UK (Maddison and Mourato, 1998) Campi Flegrei, Italy (Riganti and Willis, 1998)	
Gain access	Durham Cathedral, UK (Willis, 1994)	Rivoli Castle, Italy (Scarpa et al., 1998) Warkworth Castle, UK (Powe and Willis, 1996)			Canadian rock paintings, Nopiming Park, Canada (Boxall et al., 1998) Greek Theatre Palazzolo Acreide, Italy (Signorello, 1998a)	
Maintain at present level		Colon Theatre, Buenos Aires, Argentina History (recorded heritage) centre, UK (Ozdemiroglu and Mourato, 2000) Musée de la civilisation in Quebec, Canada (Martin, 1994) Royal Theatre Copenhagen, Denmark (Hansen, 1997)	Napoli Musei Aperti, Italy (Santagata and Signorello, 2000)			Arts in Sydney (Throsby and Withers, 1986)

Note: This table is an expanded and updated version of Table 6 from Pearce and Mourato (1998).

The non-use benefits produce smaller but nevertheless positive values. In cases of unique CH, even if the value is small but those who benefit are many, the total aggregated benefit value can be significant. All these aspects can have economic policy implications. 'Using general taxation could be inequitable unless the tax system is sharply progressive' (Pearce et al., 2001, p. 12). A central cultural policy based on general taxation collects funds from everyone but gives benefits to a very limited segment of the population which can personally sustain the burden of cultural expenditure. A pricing mechanism, where it is technically possible, can be a more equitable funding scheme: the price can be differentiated to get the consumers' surplus and protect society's weaker segments (the young, senior citizens, students, teachers and so on). It is disputable whether foreigners, national visitors and residents have the same WTP for the conservation of the cultural item observed. The geographical limits of CV studies have to be further looked into.

5.4 Further Developments on CV in the Arts Sector

Further developments on CV studies should follow two different aspects: an empirical aspect and a theoretical one.

The empirical aspect concerns the design of the CV studies and the elaboration of data. Both survey design and statistical tests contribute to better assessing the validity and reliability of the estimates produced by CV studies.

As we mentioned above, CV studies in the arts sector are just at the beginning: they vary widely in the key question format and payment method (tax, entry fee or voluntary funding). The question about the role of experts in the valuation of CH is still open. The individualistic approach shared by all the economic evaluation methods must be combined with expert judgement. The peculiar attributes of CH can accommodate expert opinions. However, to avoid a paternalistic approach, the role of experts could be limited, for example, to the piloting stages of the CV studies on the potential range of values to submit to the full sample selected for the survey. Most CV studies overcome this problem by interviewing focus groups of experts from different backgrounds or by other forms of interview (Delphi technique). A common procedure, which adopts the NOAA guidelines to the peculiar aspects of CH, should be developed to go over the specificity of estimates produced and try to get some results which could also be generalised and transferred to other similar sites for which little or no data exist. The benefit transfer, however, seems to be more difficult in CH than in environmental goods because of the high degree of uniqueness which characterises so many cultural assets. Benefit transfers are possible only for cultural sites which are similar in size, style, external conditions, construction material and state of conservation. Moreover, the estimates of transfers must be valid and reliable.

A larger number of CV studies on CH is also expected to contribute to improving the validity of estimates. The large number of CV studies on environmental goods already allows some meta-analysis to be carried out to test the convergent validity of the CV results. Comparisons between the estimates on an environmental good obtained by a CV study and estimates on the same good obtained by other stated or revealed preference methods confirm that CV estimates can be very similar and somewhat smaller than revealed preference estimates (Carson et al., 1996). Similar studies should be done for CV studies on CH when the number increases. The validity of CV studies could be checked by experiments in a laboratory setting to simulate a real market transaction on a selected sample.

Research is also involved in improving the reliability of the data obtained, stability and reproducibility of a measure with repeated statistical tests over different periods of time.

The main weakness of a CV survey is the radical choice it imposes (all or nothing). Fortunately, there are other stated preference methods (conjoint analysis and contingent ranking) which can be considered an evolution of CV simply because they simulate the actual process of formation of individual preferences, which usually compare different goods and levels of consumption. This is particularly relevant in CV studies which aim to investigate the WTP for different combinations of price and levels of output (for example, more or less congested museums) or price and type of conservation of cultural goods (for example, different preservation options or different cleaning cycles).

The theoretical development concerns both positive and normative aspects.

From the positive point of view, the CV method of estimating demand for public and partially public goods can be a useful instrument for testing what psychological findings can be relevant to economics. Recently, increasing interest has been shown in economic literature towards psychological findings relevant to economics (Rabin, 1998). Some aspects of the non-use values of CH can easily be reduced to psychological foundations (sense of identity and cultural memories). CV and other stated preference methods and experiments obviously come from this direction and can more realistically explain the formation of preferences, the change of tastes and how the preferences change according to the different degree of knowledge of the cultural good (Paradiso and Trisorio, 2001).

CV surveys can also help to explain the motivations on which social preferences are based. It has been demonstrated that self-interested behaviour may not be the only determinant of individual preferences for the provision of public goods (Throsby and Withers, 1986). Rational free-rider behaviour is frequently contradicted by empirical research. If we compare the WTP elicited using a compulsory method of payment and the WTP elicited asking for voluntary contributions, we can argue if and when there are other rational motivations to induce individuals to express a positive WTP for a public asset. 'Guilt, sympathy, an ethic for duty, a taste for fairness, or a desire for recognition may all influence an individual's contribution to charity' (Andreoni, 1988, p. 57). The role of social preferences and altruistic behaviour has been tested in some studies on CH. A pioneering CV study on the assessment of the access value to Durham Cathedral (Willis, 1994) shows that 'the current policy of voluntary contributions results (statistically) in the same revenue as that which would be generated under a compulsory entrance charge' (Willis and Garrod, 1998, p. 4).

Santagata and Signorello (2000) reiterate the interesting findings of Willis (1994) and show in the case study on the Naples *Musei Aperti* scheme that 'the amount of voluntary contributions is greater than the maximum total revenue we could get from the market system' (Santagata and Signorello, 2000, p. 196). This interesting outcome can have useful policy implications. It allows the role that the voluntary contribution schemes can play in the provision of public cultural assets to be taken into account.

From the normative point of view, the positive findings mentioned above can be useful for policy indications. Cultural policies based on general taxation that benefits a very limited niche group of consumers who, in most of the surveys conducted show a WTP or willingness to donate higher than the access price or tax they pay, have inequitable distribution effects. Where it is technically possible, pricing schemes should be designed to apply the efficient rule that the marginal cost has to be paid by those who really benefit from the cultural goods. The risk is that only a few people show their preference for cultural values and assets because CH is only appreciated by those with a certain degree of knowledge and education. The public authority, in this approach, should not take the place of individuals and decide how and how much to invest in the conservation of CH. The public authority should limit itself to giving individuals the instruments to express their own preferences for the arts and heritage.

6. CONCLUSIONS

In this chapter we have explained the economic reasons for estimating the demand for CH. The approach proposed is an individualistic one based on the estimation of WTP for the conservation and/or exploitation of cultural assets. The optimal level of CH conservation is determined by individual preferences and not by the paternalistic decisions of a public authority. This democratic approach, however, cannot easily be applied, especially in the particular area of CH.

We have described the elements of the economic value of CH which make CH difficult to be appreciated by everyone. The artistic and historic value of a cultural asset can be understood only by a very limited group of experts, usually jealous of their knowledge. There is an identity and social value of the cultural asset which can be appreciated by everyone and has also to be taken into account when policy-makers have to programme a conservation plan and decide on priorities for conservation.

A brief description of the main methods for measuring the demand and value of CH has been carried out. A distinction between the two classes of the revealed preference and stated preference methods has been shown. The weakness and strength of each method, especially in the evaluation of CH, have been described.

The description of valuation methods has particularly focused on CV because it is the most suitable method for valuing the total economic value of any work carried out on CH. The CV studies on CH have been summarised and classified by type of item and kind of benefit whose WTP has to be estimated. Despite the widespread use of CV studies on environmental goods, only a small number of CV studies in the arts and heritage have been carried out so far. The lack of CV studies on CH threatens the validity of the estimates proposed.

Further developments in the quantity and quality of the results obtained are expected. As their validity increases, the political acceptability of the results can also be put to good use for policy indications. The positive and normative aspects of these studies should go together. Unfortunately, at present, research seems to proceed independently of what the policy implications might be. The effect of such behaviour could reduce this line of research to a theoretical exercise totally separated from the empirical examples on which it is based.

NOTES

*   The authors wish to thank participants at the workshop on economics of cultural heritage held at the University of Catania in November 1999 for useful comments on an earlier version of the chapter. While the chapter is the result of common reflections, Cuccia has written sections 1, 2, 3, 5.3 and 5.4 and

Signorello has written sections 4, 5, 5.1, 5.2 and 6.

1.   To combine the merit good characteristic of the CH with the economic rationality principle we have to assume that individuals have an imperfect rationality (Elster, 1979) and/or that in the case of CH they act on grounds of community preference (Musgrave, 1987).
2.   The special panel of economists appointed by the US National Oceanic and Atmospheric Administration in 1993 following the *Exxon Valdez* oil spill in Alaska in 1989 (Arrow et al., 1993).
3.   The bidding game can be considered as an extreme case of dichotomous choice questions: the respondent is asked a series of dichotomous choice questions until some point estimate of WTP is reached (Hanemann et al., 1991).
4.   At present, few non-market valuation studies on CH apply indirect revealed preference methods (Allison et al., 1996).

REFERENCES

Allison, G., Ball, S., Cheshire, P., Evans, A. and Stabler, M. (1996), *The Value of Conservation: A Literature Review of the Economic and Social Value of the Cultural Built Heritage*, London: Department of National Heritage, English Heritage and Royal Institution of Chartered Surveyors.

Andreoni, J. (1988), 'Privately Provided Public Goods in a Large Economy: The Limits of Altruism', *Journal of Public Economics*, **35**, 57–73.

Arrow, K., Solow, R., Portney, P, Leamer, E., Radner, R. and Schuman, H. (1993), *Report of the NOOA Panel on Contingent Valuation*, Washington, DC: Federal Register, pp. 4602–14.

Bockstael, N., McConnel, K. and Strand, I. (1991), 'Recreation', in Braden, J. and Kolstad, C. (eds), *Measuring the Demand for Environmental Quality*, Amsterdam: Elsevier.

Boxall, P., Englin, J. and Adamowicz, W. (1998), 'Valuing Undiscovered Attributes: A Combined Revealed-stated Preference Analysis of North American Aboriginal Artefacts', paper presented at the World Congress of Environmental and Resource Economists, Venice.

Brown, G.M. Jr and Mendelsohn, R. (1984), 'The Hedonic Travel Cost Method', *Review of Economics and Statistics*, **66**, 427–33.

Carson, R., Flores, N., Martin, K. and Wright, J. (1996), 'Contingent Valuation and Revealed Preference Methodologies: Comparing the Estimates for Quasi-public Goods', *Land Economics*, **72**, 80–99.

Carson, R.T., Mitchell, R.T., Conaway, M.B. and Navrud, S. (1997), *Contingent Valuation of the Benefits of Conserving the Fez Medina, Quantification of Non-Moroccans' Willingness to Pay*, Cambridge, MA: Harvard University of

Graduate School of Design, Unit of Housing and Urbanization.

Chambers, C.M., Chambers, P.E. and Whitehead, J.C. (1998), 'Contingent Valuation of Quasi-public Goods: Validity, Reliability, and Application to Valuing a Historic Site', *Public Finance Review*, **26** (2), 137–54.

Clawson, M. and Knetsch, J. (1966), *The Economics of Outdoor Recreation*, Baltimore, MD: Johns Hopkins University Press.

Cropper, M.L. and Alberini, A. (1997), 'Contingent Valuation', in J. Eatwell, M. Milgate and P. Newman (eds), *The New Palgrave: A Dictionary of Economics*, London: Macmillan, pp. 420–4

Cummings, R.G., Brookshire, D.S. and Schulze, W.D. (1986), *Valuing Environmental Goods: A State of the Arts Assessment of the Contingent Method*, Totowa, NJ: Rowman & Allanheld.

Diamond, P.A. and Hausman, J.A. (1994), 'Contingent Valuation: Is Some Number Better than No Number?', *Journal of Economic Perspectives*, **8** (4), 45–64.

Elster, J. (1979), *Ulysses and the Sirens*, Cambridge, UK: Cambridge University Press.

Freeman, M.A. (1993), *The Measurement of Environmental and Resource Values: Theory and Methods*, Baltimore, MD: Resources for the Future.

Frey, B.S. (1997), 'Evaluating Cultural Property: The Economic Approach', *International Journal of Cultural Property*, **6**, 224–31.

Garrod, G.D., Willis, K.G., Bjarnadottir H. and Cockbain, P. (1996), 'The Non-priced Benefits of Renovating Historic Buildings: A Case Study of Newcastle's Grainger Town', *Cities*, **13**, 423–30.

Grosclaude, P. and Soguel, N.C. (1994), 'Valuing Damage to Historic Buildings Using a Contingent Market: A Case Study of Road Traffic Externalities', *Journal of Environmental Planning and Management*, **3**, 279–87.

Hanemann, M.W. (1994), 'Valuing the Environment Through Contingent Valuation', *Journal of Economic Perspectives*, **8**, 19–43.

Hanemann, M.W., Loomis, J. and Kanninen, B. (1991), 'Statistical Efficiency of Double-bounded Dichotomous Choice Contingent Valuation', *American Journal of Agricultural Economics*, **73**, 1255–63.

Hanley, N. and Spash, C.L. (1993), *Cost–benefit Analysis and the Environment*, Aldershot, UK and Brookfield, USA: Edward Elgar.

Hansen, B.T. (1997), 'The Willingness-to-pay for the Royal Theater in Copenhagen', *Journal of Cultural Economics*, **21**, 1–28.

Herrmann, A., Franken, B., Frank, H., Ohlwein, M. and Schellhase, R. (1999), 'The Conjoint Analysis as an Instrument for Marketing Controlling, Taking a Public Theatre as an Example', *International Journal of Arts Management*, **1** (3), 59–69.

Hett, T. and Mourato, S. (2000), 'Sustainable Management of Machu Picchu: A Stated Preference Approach', paper submitted to Conference on Sustainability,

Tourism and the Environment, Dublin.

Hoevenagel, R. (1996), 'The Validity of the Contingent Valuation Method: Perfect and Regular Embedding', *Environmental and Resource Economics*, **7** (1), 57–77.

Kahnemann, D. and Tversky, A. (1979), 'Prospect Theory: An Analysis of Decision Under Risk', *Econometrica*, **47** (2), 263–91.

Kling, R., Revier, C. and Sable, K. (2000), 'Estimating the Public Good Value of Preserving a Local Historic Landmark: The Role of Non-substitutability and Information in Contingent Valuation', paper presented at the XI Association for Cultural Economics Conference in Minneapolis.

Krutilla, J.V. (1967), 'Conservation Reconsidered', *American Economic Review*, **57**, 787–96.

Maddison, D. and Mourato, S. (1998), 'Valuing Different Road Options for Stonehenge', Report for English Heritage, UK.

Martin, F. (1994), 'Determining the Size of Museum Subsidies', *Journal of Cultural Economics*, **18**, 255–70.

Mazza, F.M. (1999), 'Un'Applicazione della Contingent Valuation al Castello di Nicastro', unpublished PhD dissertation, University of Reggio Calabria.

Mitchell, R.C. and Carson, R.T. (1990), *Using Surveys to Value Public Goods: The Contingent Valuation Method*, Washington, DC: Resources for the Future (2nd printing).

Morey, E., Rossmann, K., Chestnut, L. and Ragland, S. (1997), 'Valuing Acid Deposition Injuries to Cultural Resources', Center for Economic Analysis, Boulder, University of Colorado.

Mourato, S. and Danchev, A. (1997), 'Preserving Cultural Heritage in Transition Economies: A Contingent Valuation Study of Bulgarian Monasteries', Report to DGXII, European Commission, Brussels.

Mourato, S. and Pearce, D. (1999), *Dealing with Low Willingness to Pay for Cultural Heritage: Statistical and Policy Implications*, London: CSERGE.

Musgrave, R.A. (1987), 'Merit Goods', in J. Eatwell, M. Milgate and P. Newman (eds), *The New Palgrave: A Dictionary of Economics*, London: Macmillan, pp. 452–3.

Navrud, S., Pederson, P.E. and Strand, J. (1992), 'Valuing Our Cultural Heritage: A Contingent Valuation Survey', Center for Research in Economics and Business Administration, University of Oslo, Norway.

O'Doherty, R. (1998), 'The Theory of the Contingent Valuation Method', in 'Heritage, the Arts and the Environment: Pricing the Priceless', *Hume Papers on Public Policy*, **6** (3), 67–83.

Ozdemiroglu, E. and Mourato, S. (2000), 'Valuing our Recorded Heritage', Report to the Museums and Galleries Commission, London.

Pagiola, S. (1999), 'Valuing the Benefits of Investments in Cultural Heritage: The Historic Core of Split', World Bank Economists' Forum, Alexandria.

Paradiso, M. and Trisorio, A. (2001), 'The Effects of Knowledge on the Disparity Between Hypothetical and Real Willingness To Pay', *Applied Economics*, **33**, 1359–64.

Pearce, D., Maddison, D. and Pollicino, M. (2001), 'Economics and Cultural Heritage', University College London: Centre for Cultural Economics and Management (CCEM), mimeo.

Pearce, D. and Mourato, S. (1998), *The Economics of Cultural Heritage*, London: Centre for Social and Economic Research on the Global Environment (CSERGE).

Pollicino, M. and Maddison, D. (2001), 'Valuing the Benefits of Cleaning Lincoln Cathedral', *Journal of Culture Economics*, **25**, 131–48.

Powe, N. and Willis, K. (1996), 'Benefits Received by Visitors to Heritage Sites: A Case Study of Warkworth Castle', *Leisure Studies*, **15**, 259–75.

Rabin, M. (1998), 'Psychology and Economics', *Journal of Economic Literature*, **36**, 11–46.

Randall, A. (1991), 'Total and Nonuse Values', in Braden, J.B. and Kolstad, C.D. (eds), *Measuring the Demand for Environmental Quality*, New York: Elsevier Science, pp. 303–21.

Randall, A., Hoehn, J. and Brookshire, D.S. (1983), 'Contingent Valuation Surveys for Evaluating Environmental Assets', *Natural Resources Journal*, 635–48.

Riganti, P. and Willis, K. (1998), 'Categorical Nesting and Temporal Reliability of Estimates for Complex Historic Goods', paper presented at the European Association of Environmental and Resource Economists (EAERE) World Congress, Venice.

Rosen, S. (1974), 'Hedonic Prices and Implicit Markets: Product Differentiation in Pure Competition', *Journal of Political Economy*, **82**, 34–55.

Santagata, W. and Signorello, G. (2000), 'Contingent Valuation and Cultural Policy: The Case of "Napoli Musei Aperti"', *Journal of Cultural Economics*, **24**, 181–204.

Scarpa, R., Sirchia, G. and Bravi, M. (1998), 'Kernel vs. Logit Modeling of Single Bounded CV Responses: Valuing Access to Architectural and Visual Arts Heritage in Italy', in Bishop, Richard C. and Romano, D. (eds), *Environmental Resource Valuation: Applications of the Contingent Valuation Method in Italy*, Dordrecht: Kluwer Academic Publishers, pp. 233–44.

Signorello, G. (1994), 'La Contingent Ranking e la Stima dei Beni Pubblici', in Atti del Convegno Ce.S.E.T., Naples.

Signorello, G. (1998a), 'Il Valore di Fruizione di un Bene Archeologico', mimeo, University of Catania.

Signorello, G. (1998b), 'Valuing Birdwatching in a Mediterranean Wetland', in Bishop, R.C. and Romano, D. (eds), *Environmental Resource Valuation: Applications of the Contingent Valuation Method in Italy*, London, UK: Kluwer Academic Publishers, pp. 173–91.

Smith, V.K. (1991), 'Household Production Functions and Environmental Benefit Estimation', in Braden, J. and Kolstad, C. (eds), *Measuring the Demand for Environmental Quality*, Amsterdam: Elsevier, pp. 210–32.

Throsby, C.D. and Withers, G.A. (1986), 'Strategic Bias and Demand for Public Goods', *Journal of Public Economics*, **31**, 307–27.

Towse, R. (1994), 'Achieving Public Policy Objectives in the Arts and Heritage', in Peacock, A. and Rizzo, I. (eds), *Cultural Economics and Cultural Policies*, Dordrecht: Kluwer Academic Publishers, pp. 143–65.

Willis, K.G. (1994), 'Paying for Heritage: What Price for Durham Cathedral', *Journal of Environmental Planning and Management*, **3**, 267–78.

Willis, K.G. and Garrod, G.D. (1998), 'Estimating the Demand for Cultural Heritage: Artefacts of Historical and Architectural Interest', in 'Heritage, the Arts and the Environment: Pricing the Priceless', *Hume Papers on Public Policy*, **6** (3), 1–16.

10. A Contingent Valuation Study of Willingness to Pay for Heritage Visits: Case Study of Noto[*]

Tiziana Cuccia and Giovanni Signorello

1. INTRODUCTION

Faced with shrinking general public financial resources, public administrators of heritage cities are looking for other financial sources to preserve their monuments and historical buildings and also to ensure adequate facilities for a growing number of tourists. A suitable solution might be to charge tourists a user fee. At a time when reducing taxes is a primary political issue, financing restoration projects in part from user revenues seems to be a very attractive political proposition.

Pricing access to cultural goods raises many important issues and the extent to which users should pay directly for the visit is controversial. Such payments, however, are probably more widely accepted today than in the past. Empirical evidence, coming from the performing arts (Kirchberg, 1998) and principally from related sectors (for example, outdoor recreation in parks and other leisure activities) generally indicates that the full potential of revenues from user pricing is not being achieved. Many studies reveal a positive attitude towards payment and that people generally accept user fees as a reasonable method of paying for leisure activities (Heritage Conservation and Recreation Service, 1976; Mourato and Pearce, 1999).

There are various approaches to establishing a user price. Some of these approaches are based on costs, others base their access price either on the comparable prices charged by other managers for equivalent services (going-rate approach) or on the benefits accruing to users (demand-oriented approach). This latter approach, which is based on the beneficiaries-pay principle, requires the knowledge of what the users are willing to pay.

In the previous chapter we provided a general overview of non-market valuation tools that can be employed for estimating the demand and value of heritage assets. In this chapter we report on the results of an empirical case study where the contingent valuation method (CVM)[1] is used to estimate the demand curve and consumer surplus accruing to visitors to Noto, an Italian heritage city well known for its Baroque style of historical monuments and buildings, and to convert users' willingness to pay to revenue-capture potential.

Our CVM application intercepts, on site, a random sample of national and foreign tourists. In the questionnaire, the valuation question is posed according to the double-bounded dichotomous choice format and the econometric analysis of data sets is based on a linear logit model. Estimates of survivor functions, which show how demand varies with access price, are used to identify the charge that would raise maximum revenue-capture potential.

2. METHOD: THE DOUBLE-BOUNDED DICHOTOMOUS CHOICE CVM

The contingent valuation method is a survey-based tool. A group of representative people are asked to reveal their willingness to pay by making hypothetical choices within a carefully constructed market scenario. A CVM survey must be viewed as a communication device. Since details always matter when communicating, a considerable effort must be devoted to the design of the scenario, and especially to the valuation question. The goal is to create a virtual setting capable of producing satisfactory hypothetical transactions and incentive (and a less cognitive burden) behaviour in the respondents (Bishop and Heberlein, 1979). The format for eliciting the respondents' choice is one of the essential components of the scenario. Dichotomous choice single-bounded and double-bounded formats are now dominating the applied literature. In the single-bounded format, respondents are asked whether or not they would pay a specified price, which varies according to the individual. This format offers several advantages over other continuous elicitation formats such as open-ended, iterative-bidding games and payment cards. It appears to be incentive compatible and, in particular, it mimics daily marketplace transactions where people decide to take or leave a specific good for a given price and do not engage in price negotiations. Further, it allows for the framing of the valuation question in terms of a referendum, that is, the typical delivery mechanism of many public goods. However, a number of drawbacks arise with a single-bounded elicitation mode. This format requires a relatively large sample size since the information on value that can be collected is widely distributed from a statistical point of view. A larger sample size means higher survey costs so, in order to avoid these additional costs and obtain more information about preferences, it has been proposed that the first single-bounded CV question be followed up with a second question, of the same format, involving a different bid, higher or lower depending on the individual's reaction to the first bid. This questioning mode is referred to as the double-bounded dichotomous choice format (Hanemann et al., 1991) and since it is an extension of the single-bounded format, it is convenient to initially illustrate its basic structure.

Let us assume that the preferences of a generic tourist in an art heritage city are represented by an indirect utility function $V(Z,Y)$, where Z is a binary variable which takes a value of one if access to the historical site is possible and zero if it is not, and Y is net income. If the state of the world is free access to the city, the Hicksian equivalent surplus WTP for the individual is the amount that satisfies the equation:

$$V(P, 1, Y - WTP) + \varepsilon_0 = V(P, 0, Y) + \varepsilon_1.$$

This WTP associated with each observed choice is not completely known to the external observer who can only observe the deterministic component V and not the stochastic component ε, which is known only to the tourist. Hence, WTP is itself a random variable from the point of view of the analyst.

In a typical single-bounded CV survey, the tourist is asked to state whether he/she is willing to pay a specified ticket A_0 to have access to the heritage city. According to the random utility framework developed by Hanemann (1984), the probability of obtaining a 'yes' answer is formally represented by:

$$\text{Prob (yes} \mid A_0) = \text{Prob}(A_f \le WTP) = 1 - G_{WTP}(A_0; \theta) = F_\eta(\Delta V)$$

where:

$G_{WTP}(A_0; \theta) = \text{Prob}(WTP \le A_0)$ is the cumulative distribution function (c.d.f.) of the random variable WTP^2
θ is a vector of parameters to be estimated
F_η is the c.d.f. of the random error $\eta = \varepsilon_0 - \varepsilon_1$
$\Delta V = V(1, Y - A_0) - V(0,Y)$ is the utility change.

The above expression ties together a probability defined over WTP space with a probability defined over utility space. Then, by assuming the distribution for η is the same as assigning a distribution for $G_{WTP}(A_0; \theta)$, this also means that the distribution of responses is entirely determined by the distribution specified for the *WTP*.

With the single-bounded format, the answer given by each respondent reveals that the exact numerical *WTP* is replaced by a much less informative notion: the *WTP* amount lies above the price offered in the survey if the respondent agreed to pay that bid or below if he/she declined. In other words, the observed response determined by the relationship between the latent *WTP* and the bid A_0 establishes a single-bounded interval data on *WTP*. If the individual's choice is for a 'yes', the *WTP* is bounded from below by A_0 (that is, the respondent is willing to pay at least the A_0 amount). How much more the individual might be willing to pay is not expressed because it has not been requested. We know only that the individual *WTP* lies in the interval between A_0 on the left side and infinity (or income or fraction of income) on the right side. If the choice of respondent is for a 'no', the *WTP* is bounded from above by A_0; the individual may be willing to pay some price below A_0 or may not be willing to pay anything at all. That is, the respondent's *WTP* lies in the interval bounded by zero on the left side and by A_0 on the right side.

The double-bounded format allows for the collection of more information about underlying *WTP* while at the same time preserving the positive features of the single-bounded dichotomous choice format. After the first question has been answered, it is followed by a second one with a higher bid A_u in response to a 'yes' answer or with a lower bid A_d in response to a 'no' answer. In this way, the latent *WTP* amount is limited to a narrower interval than the single binary choice question and thereby a higher statistical efficiency, is achieved. Following Hanemann et al. (1991), the four different outcomes are:[3]

Prob (yes, yes $| A_0, A_u$) = Prob ($A_0 \leq WTP$ and $A_u \leq WTP$)
= Prob ($A_0 \leq WTP | A_u \leq WTP$)*Prob ($A_u \leq WTP$)
= Prob ($A_u \leq WTP$) = $1 - G(A_u)$ $\qquad\qquad$ [$A_u - \infty$]

Prob (no, no $| A_0, A_d$) = Prob ($A_0 > WTP$ and $A_d > WTP$) = $G(A_d)$ $\quad$ [$0 - A_d$]
Prob (yes, no $| A_0, A_u$) = Prob ($A_0 \leq WTP < A_u$) = $G(A_u) - G(A_0)$ $\quad$ [$A_0 - A_u$]
Prob (no, yes $| A_0, A_d$) = Prob ($A_0 > WTP \geq A_d$) = $G(A_0) - G(A_d)$ $\quad$ [$A_d - A_0$]

Actually, the double-bounded format allows for the definition of three possible interval estimates of *WTP*: *WTP* is either less than the low amount asked, or between the two amounts, or larger than the high amount. The log-likelihood function for the standard double-bounded interval-data model from all sample observations is (Alberini, 1994):

$$\ln L(A_0, A_u, A_d) = \Sigma\{[y_1 y_2] \ln [1 - G_{WTP}(A_u)]$$
$$+ [y_1(1 - y_2)] \ln [G_{WTP}(A_u) - G_{WTP}(A_0)]$$
$$+ (1 - y_1) y_2 \ln [G_{WTP}(A_0) - G_{WTP}(A_d)]$$
$$+ [(1 - y_1)(1 - y_2)]\ln G_{WTP}(A_d)]\}$$

where y_1 takes on a value of one if the answer to the first question is a 'yes', and zero otherwise, and y_2 is also a dummy variable that takes on a value of one if the response to the second question is 'yes' and zero otherwise.

3.   MATERIALS

3.1   Description of the Site

Noto is a small heritage city in the South of Sicily, 33 km from Syracuse and one of the most attractive tourist sites in Sicily, built on a hill 6 km from the coast. The location is quite important for the study: Noto is a city where tourists go for the uniqueness of its built cultural heritage and not for other kinds of attractions, such as beaches. Therefore, the results obtained by the sample of tourists are not biased by the presence of other attractions in and around the city but only express the willingness to pay (WTP) for visiting the historical centre of Noto.

The main feature of Noto is the Baroque style of its numerous churches, monasteries and noble palaces all built in the same kind of white limestone after the earthquake of 1693. The harmony of the whole heritage area, mainly concentrated in the two main streets which divide the historical centre, shows the noble and rich past of this city which for a long time was the capital of the area called Val di Noto from 878, during the Arab domination, right up to 1817, when Syracuse became the capital of the province.[4] This information is necessary for understanding the problem investigated in this research.   Indeed, the historical buildings are concentrated in only two streets that no longer represent the centre of daily life. This makes the possibility of asking for a payment to access the most significant part of the historical walk at least technically feasible. At present, access to the most significant part of the historical streets is limited to pedestrians. Therefore, it is easy to imagine the possibility of buying a ticket for access.

Moreover, the past economic welfare represented by the monuments contrasts strongly with present economic conditions. In the past, the main source of income for the higher social classes came from a flourishing agricultural activity which has been declining over the last few centuries. This caused a slow but continuous migration of owners of the historical buildings – and particularly the new generations of noble families – towards other economic interests and other urban centres. Only a few old members of the noble families still live in Noto. Most of their private residences have been abandoned or have been partially sold to public authorities (essentially the Municipality).

The ecclesiastical diocese does not participate in the revitalisation of the city because of financial constraints: only four of its twelve churches can be visited at the moment and after many years, the restoration of the Cathedral, whose dome collapsed because of seismic activity and lack of maintenance work, has still not been completed.

The public authorities bought or rented some historical buildings for use mainly as schools (especially the monasteries) or as the civic museum and library. On one hand, the public use of the historical buildings helps to preserve them; on the other, the present uses of these buildings does not contribute to promoting tourism.

At present, visitors cannot enjoy their trip to Noto to the same extent as they would if so much work in progress were not blocking the exterior view of many historical buildings. A great number of restoration projects will soon be under way thanks to financial support from international organisations (UNESCO, EU).

Following the taxonomy of the historical evolution models of cities of art suggested by Mossetto (1992a),[5] Noto is a typical example of a 'residual model', a city where art is a by product that emerges because the city has lost all its traditional, historical roles. The city is an 'open museum' that can survive only if it is able to promote a highly specialised tourist image.

3.2 Tourism Flows

In a recent survey on tourism demand for Italy (Touring Club Italiano, 1999), conducted at international level, Sicily is ranked fourth among the known Italian sites (after Rome, Venice and Milan) and sixth among the most desired tourist destinations; however, it is ranked only tenth among the actually visited Italian sites. Apart from the structural and social reasons which can justify this difference between the potential and actual tourism demand for Sicily, this evidence can be interpreted in a positive way. Tourism is a potential resource for Sicily that has not yet been exploited as it could.

The most recent official data on the trend of tourism arrivals and presence on the island show that, from the 1995–98 period, there was a 26.58 per cent increase in the total arrivals and a 16.66 per cent increase in the total time spent. In the same period, tourist arrivals in the administrative Province of Syracuse, whichincludes the Municipality of

Noto, increased more than the regional tourist arrivals (+39.66 per cent). The trend of time spent is also positive (+15.42 per cent) even if it is below the regional value. In particular, the Municipality of Noto, which represented only 16 per cent of tourism flow in the province in 1998, increased its tourism flow markedly: +74.39 per cent for arrivals and +48.17 per cent for time spent in the 1995–98 period. National arrivals have risen more than foreign arrivals: +88.24 compared to +15.32. The domestic time spent increases (+80.62) while the foreign time spent decreases significantly (–50.21 per cent): this means that the national tourists' average length of stay is on the increase and the foreign tourists' average length of stay is decreasing.[6]

3.3 Survey Instrument

The data were collected through a face-to-face survey of 560 tourists visiting Noto during Spring 2000. Respondents were selected using a stratified random sample of adult tourists. Stratification was done according to a nationality criterion. A quota (50 per cent) design was used to ensure the inclusion of both Italian and foreign tourists. This quota design, which contrasts with the geographical composition of the tourist flow observed in the previous year, was adopted to split the overall sample into two groups in order to implement a test of statistical equivalence in the behaviour between Italian and foreign tourists.

The payment vehicle used was an entrance fee for each visit to the historical centre of the heritage city. Non-price differentiation was assumed and all the data were collected by personal interviews conducted by trained local interviewers. Tourists were intercepted, after the visit, near the main gate to the city and in hotels; they were well informed about the goal of the survey and were also asked not to register protest against the payment scheme. The trained interviewers felt that almost all of the respondents fully comprehended the motivations of the survey, took the issue seriously, enjoyed being asked and answered to the best of their ability.

The questionnaire included three sections. In the first section we asked questions about nationality, residence and the visit to Noto. In the second section we included all the questions concerning the WTP.[7] The first discrete choice valuation question was worded as follows:

The entrance to Noto's historical centre is presently free. Let us assume that, as already happens in many other arts cities, each adult tourist is required to pay an entrance ticket to visit the historical centre of Noto and this revenue would go towards covering the maintenance and conservation cost of the cultural assets. Let us assume that the price of the entrance ticket is ... lire. If this were to be the case would you be willing to pay ... lire for the entrance ticket to visit the historical centre of Noto? (before answering, please take into account what you have already spent to visit Noto. We emphasise that the payment of the ticket would only allow entrance to the historical centre. All other services, such as tourist guides and so on would not be included).

This first question was followed up by a similar second payment question replacing the first amount A_0 by a second amount, A_d smaller if the first response was 'no' or A_u bigger if it was 'yes'. In the questionnaire we introduced a third valuation question: the double-bounded discrete choice question was followed up by an open-ended (or continuous valuation) question. Respondents, depending on the pattern of their answers, were asked to specify the maximum amount they would be willing to pay in order to gain access to the city contingent upon the scenario. Respondents were made aware of the consistency of their answers with the choices made in the previous discrete choice stages. This open-ended format was intended to discover those individuals with no positive valuation (protest bidders) as well as the ones declaring unrealistic bids (outliers). In order to identify protest behaviour, those subjects with zero WTP were asked for the reason for this answer. It is clear that this combination of valuation questions provides more statistical information to the analyst. The open-ended non-zero bidder values of WTP give useful insights. They allow for the exploration of possible errors in value formation and test for eventual yea-saying bias by analysing self-contradicting respondents. However, the open-ended WTP data set has a drawback: the potential anchoring effect of the proposed prices to the open-ended WTP statement.

As usual, in the final section of the survey we asked questions to identify the socio-economic profile of the respondent.[8]

3.4 Experimental Design

The double-bounded dichotomous choice format requires the determination of the three prices (A_0, A_u, A_d) to be used in the valuation questions and the allocation of the total sample size among bids. These statistical design choices have raised a great deal of attention since they could influence the magnitude and the efficiency of WTP estimates. The literature offers several optimal criteria (Alberini, 1994). However, in this CVM study we adopt a criterion based on quite a long bid vector and on an equal allotment of the whole sample among bids. These solutions were favoured because they allow for analysis of the data set using either parametric or non-parametric models. A vector of seven prices was chosen according to the evidence on WTP displayed by a previous payment card CVM survey carried out on a sample of 200 tourists by using the same stratification criterion.[9] The amounts for the first bid vector were 2,000, 3,000, 5,000, 6,000, 8,000, 10,000 and 15,000 lire.[10] Each price has been posed to a sub-sample of 80 individuals chosen at random according to the above general stratification criterion. If the answer to the first question was affirmative, then the following second higher bid vector was 3,000, 5,000, 6,000, 8,000, 10,000, 15,000 and 20,000 lire. If the answer to the first discrete choice question was negative, then the second lower bid vector was 1,000, 2,000, 3,000, 5,000, 6,000, 8,000 and 10,000 lire.

3.5 The Data

Implementation of the survey revealed that 90 tourists (16 per cent of 560 respondents) answered with a zero open-ended WTP for the entrance fee. These respondents were asked why they gave that negative reaction to pricing access to the historical centre. The reasons given for this choice are displayed in Table 10.1. Almost all of the respondents engaged in protest behaviour against the scenario. They believed that pricing access is illegal and that funds for restoration projects of cultural heritage must come from general taxation or from the owners of the private historical buildings. These 90 respondents were dropped from the analysis because they reacted negatively to the hypothetical situation posed to them through the questionnaire.

Table 10.1 Reasons for a zero open-ended WTP answer

Reasons	Frequency	%
I have the right to get in to the historical centre free.	42	46.7
The maintenance and conservation costs must be paid by the public local authority and by the owners of cultural assets.	37	41.1
If I had to pay, I would prefer to go to some other place.	5	5.6
I think that it is not worth paying to get in to this historical centre.	6	6.7
Total zero bidders	90	100

Sample statistics for selected variables of respondents are presented in Table 10.2. The two groups of tourists are statistically different only for the variable *FVIS*, which measures whether the respondent is visiting Noto for the first time, and for the variable *VISMUS* which indicates the number of visits to museums and other cultural heritage assets over the last twelve months.

Demand for Heritage

Table 10.2 Summary of characteristics of tourists in the surveys

Characteristic	Legend	Mean whole	Mean Italian	Mean foreign	t statistic
FVIS	First visit (0,1)	0.86	0.81	0.91	−3.28
AGE	Age	44.21	44.58	43.86	0.59
GENDER	Sex (1 M, 0 F)	0.52	0.53	0.49	0.76
EDUC	Education level (1–4)	3.23	3.18	3.27	−1.26
ASS	Membership of assocn	0.18	0.18	0.17	0.22
VISMUS	(1,0)	9.2	7.42	10.88	−3.87
N	Visits	470	227	243	

Table 10.3 displays the double-bounded discrete choice data set giving the joint frequencies of the four possible pairs of responses in the sample, and a full breakdown of the answers given by the 470 respondents. The pattern of yes–yes pairs is regular except in the upper tail of distribution where there is a violator in the sequence.

Table 10.3 Summary of the double-bounded discrete choice answers

First price (second price)	yes–yes (%)	yes–no (%)	no–yes (%)	no–no (%)	N
2,000 (3,000, 1,000)	61 (86)	7 (10)	3 (4)	0	71
3,000 (5,000, 2,000)	62 (91)	5 (7)	1 (1)	0	68
5,000 (6,000, 3,000)	47 (69)	14 (21)	7 (10)	0	68
6,000 (8,000, 5,000)	38 (57)	19 (28)	6 (9)	4 (6)	67
8,000 (10,000, 15,000)	34 (50)	21 (31)	5 (7)	8 (12)	68
10,000 (15,000, 8,000)	11 (17)	33 (52)	11 (17)	9 (14)	64
15,000 (20,000, 10,000)	20 (31)	10 (16)	22 (34)	12 (19)	64
Overall	273 (58)	109 (23)	55 (12)	33 (7)	470

4.   ESTIMATE OF DEMAND CURVE AND CONSUMER SURPLUS.

The econometric estimate of demand function $1 - G_{WTP}$ and the calculation of summary statistics (mean and median) for the willingness to pay have been made by using the standard interval data logit model[11] and a linear index function (Green, 2000):[12]

$$1 - G_{WTP} = 1/ [1 - \exp - (\beta X)]$$

Tables 10.4–6 give the maximum likelihood estimated coefficients for logit models,[13] and also report point and interval estimates of the non-negative mean WTP[14] calculated analytically by using the formula $1/\beta$ [1 +

exp(α)] provided by Hanemann (1984), where β is the coefficient of the price and α is the augmented intercept.[15]   Confidence intervals are calculated by applying the bootstrapping Krinsky and Robb simulation procedure (see Park et al., 1991).

Table 10.4 The double-bounded discrete choice answers: econometric results

Variable	Coefficient	Standard error	*t* - statistic
Constant	1.9345	0.6728	2.87
BID	−0.000326	2.303E–05	−14.16
FVIS	0.762729	0.3002	2.54
AGE	0.001839	0.0083	0.22
GENDER	−0.364683	0.2194	−1.66
EDUC	0.365270	0.1387	2.63
ASS	0.311143	0.2906	1.07
Number of yes–yes cases	273		
Number of yes–no cases	109		
Number of no–yes cases	55		
Number of no–no cases	33		
Log likelihood	−496.06		
Sample size	470		
Restricted WTP point estimates (Lit)	11,506		
Krinsky and Robb confidence intervals	99%	95%	90%
(Lire)	10,560–12,519	10,814–12,287	10,933–12,156

Table 10.5 Multivariate logit model (Italian sample)

Variable	Coefficient	Standard error	*t* - statistic
Constant	−0.55971	0.9315	−0.60
BID	−0.003049	3.201E–05	−9.53
FVIS	1.159057	0.3840	3.02
AGE	0.018912	0.01194	1.58
GENDER	−0106553	0.3121	−0.34
EDUC	0.7159849	0.2080	3.44
ASS	−0.165053	0.4190	−0.39
Number of yes–yes cases	134		
Number of yes–no cases	38		
Number of no–yes cases	31		
Number of no–no cases	24		
Log likelihood	−237.54		
Sample size	227		
Restricted WTP point estimates Lit	11,309		
Krinsky and Robb confidence intervals	99%	95%	90%
(Lire)	10,012–13,024	10,274–12,529	10,449–12,304

Table 10.6 Multivariate logit model (foreign sample)

Variable	Coefficient	Standard error	t - statistic
Constant	5.13269	1.119	4.59
BID	−0.0003712	3.499E−05	−10.61
FVIS	−0.25692	0.549	−0.47
AGE	−0.01455	0.012	−1.19
GENDER	−0.60466	0.317	−1.91
EDUC	0.08906	0.204	0.44
ASS	0.35576	0.423	0.84
Number of yes–yes cases	139		
Number of yes–no cases	71		
Number of no–yes cases	24		
Number of no–no cases	9		
Log likelihood	−248.20		
Sample size	243		
Restricted WTP point estimates Lit	11309		
Krinsky and Robb confidence intervals	99%	95%	90%
(Lire)	10,586–12,945	10,777–12,638	10,873–12,469

In all the estimated logit models, the bid variable is highly significant and has the expected sign. Among the other socio-demographic variables, the level of *EDUC* (education) is significant in the overall sample and in the case of the Italian tourist subsample. Willingness to pay a fee also increases with Italian people visiting the city for the first time. In relation to the subsample of foreign tourists, all variables, except the bid, are insignificant. The variable *AGE* produces the opposite effect on the willingness to pay a fee. The positive sign of the *AGE* coefficient in the Italian sample provides somewhat counterintuitive results. Typically, the WTP decreases with age.

Figure 10.1 Estimated logit demand functions

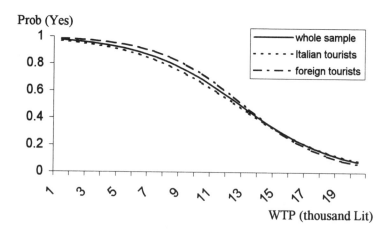

The estimated conditional mean values are of a reasonable size and are statistically equivalent between groups (see also Figure 10.1). This is an important result and contrasts with the commonly-held view that Italians are unsympathetic towards private contribution to the supply of public goods.

5. ESTIMATING REVENUE-CAPTURE POTENTIAL

The estimated demand functions were then used to assess total revenue-capture potential. To reach this goal, the logit functions were employed to identify the levels of participation reported in Table 10.7. The constant term inserted in the logit equation to produce the percentages of acceptance to pay each fee is the augment intercept.

Table 10.7 Estimated revenue-capture potential

Fee (lire)	Rate of acceptance	Number of tourists	Annual revenue (lire)
1,000	0.98	45,298	44,222,341
2,000	0.97	45,298	87,642,556
3,000	0.96	45,298	129,832,527
4,000	0.94	45,298	170,184,335
5,000	0.92	45,298	207,863,360
6,000	0.89	45,298	241,772,571
7,000	0.85	45,298	270,552,106
8,000	0.81	45,298	292,649,563
9,000	0.75	45,298	306,498,671
10,000	**0.69**	45,298	**310,821,604**
11,000	0.61	45,298	305,010,984
12,000	0.53	45,298	289,466,307
13,000	0.45	45,298	265,713,665
14,000	0.37	45,298	236,195,740
15,000	0.30	45,298	203,778,821
16,000	0.24	45,298	171,175,979
17,000	0.18	45,298	140,509,784
18,000	0.14	45,298	113,128,916
19,000	0.10	45,298	89,653,883
20,000	0.078	45,298	70,151,356

The total revenue-capture potential is calculated using the following equation:

$$REVENUE = FEE * (A * V)$$

where *FEE* is the proposed user fee, A is the level of acceptance (Prob(yes)), and V is the estimated number of visitors. The results in Table 10.7 and in Figure 10.2 show that the revenue would be maximised by setting the price of access to the heritage city at 10,000 lire. This charge is very close to estimated mean WTP values, and higher than fees usually paid in the region to gain access to other cultural goods. This would raise 310 million lire in revenues.

Figure 10.2 Estimated revenue-capture potential

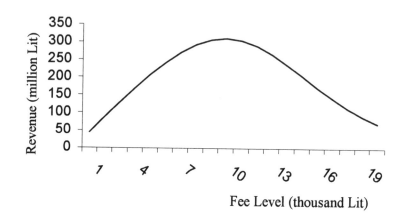

Fee Level (thousand Lit)

6.   CONCLUSIONS

Public authorities of heritage cities are looking for alternative sources of funding to restore and maintain their built cultural heritage. Tourist fees are given serious consideration although their implementation presents many practical problems. An important issue that must be investigated is how visitors respond to this specific policy instrument. This study was implemented to provide economic information for this policy debate. A contingent valuation method was used to elicit visitor WTP estimates and to generate economic information to assess participation rates and revenue-capture potential.

Results show that CVM is a powerful tool, especially when information on willingness to pay is gathered through the discrete choice format. The resulting econometric equation readily allows estimates of demand function, consumer surplus, participation rates and revenue-capture potential. The experiment reveals that there is a general support for fees. We interviewed 560 tourists and only 16 per cent of the whole sample refused to pay any fee to enter the historical core of the city. Analysis of the data indicates that tourists are willing to pay more than what is currently charged for visiting other cultural sites in the region where Noto is located and indicates that the demand function and the expected WTP do not vary according to the nationality of visitors.

NOTES

*   The authors wish to thank David Throsby and Ruth Towse for their useful comments on an earlier version of this chapter presented at the 11th International Biennial Conference of the Association for Cultural Economics International, Minneapolis, USA, 28–31 May 2000. Partial support was provided by the Consiglio Nazionale delle Ricerche, Research Grant 9603902PS15 (Research Co-ordinator: Walter Santagata, University of Turin). Cuccia wrote section 3, Signorello the remaining portion of the chapter.

1. A valid substitute or complement to CVM is the travel cost method. However, the practical implementation of this method can be very hard when many substitute sites are present in the market area and visitors engage in a multipurpose trip.

2. The function $1 - G_{WTP}(A_0; \theta)$ is the inverse of the cumulative probability function. It is called the survival function and in economic terms represents a demand function.

3. On the right-hand side, in brackets, the four double-bounded intervals where WTP is assumed to fall are indicated.

4. Touring Club Italiano (1969), pp. 649–56.

5. Mossetto (1992a, 1992b) distinguishes three main historical evolution models of 'cities of art'. In the first model, 'economic dependent', the trend in the investments in arts strictly depends on the economic cycle. In the second model, 'culture dependent', the economy of the cities is based on arts and culture, with pros and cons. In the third model, corresponding to the case in hand, culture and arts are byproducts that come either from political decisions or from the natural evolution of a city that has lost all its other roles; in this case, tourism can cause either stagnation (the degradation of cultural heritage) or stability, if tourism specialisation is well managed.

6. As for the geographical composition of the tourist flow, domestic tourists account for 87.44 per cent, while foreign tourists make up the remaining 12.56 per cent. Among the foreign tourists, languages spoken are 41 per cent French, 26 per cent German, 8 per cent English and 2 per cent Spanish.

7. The survey was also designed to collect voluntary contributions to a special fund for the preservation of cultural heritage assets in Noto. The analysis of this data set will be presented in a future paper.

8. In the survey of foreign tourists, we used questionnaires translated into English, German, French and Spanish. A copy of the full questionnaire is available

from the authors, upon request.

9. In a follow-up paper we will compare PC and DC estimates. Preliminary results show that PC estimates of WTP are, as expected, lower than the DC value.

10. Prices were given in Italian lire. At the time of the survey, 1,000 lire was approximately equal to $0.5.

11. In an earlier version of this chapter, we also report non-parametric analysis carried out by using the Turnbull estimator. Demand curves and mean WTP are almost identical to logit estimates (Cuccia and Signorello, 2000).

12. The index function is the difference in the utility function, and is denoted as the summed product of the parameter estimates and the explanatory variable, βX.

13. Parameters and summary statistics were estimated by using *ad hoc* Gauss programmes developed by J. Cooper.

14. The mean WTP is the area under the survivor function.

15. The augmented intercept is the original intercept plus the rest of the $n - 1$ parameters other than the bid parameter estimate multiplied by the respective means of the explanatory variable X.

REFERENCES

Alberini, A. (1994), *Efficiency v. Bias of Willingness-to-pay Estimates: Bivariate and Interval Data Models*, Washington, DC: Resources for the Future.

Bishop, R.C. and Heberlein, T.A. (1979), 'Measuring Values of Extra-market Goods: Are Indirect Measures Biased?', *American Journal of Agricultural Economics*, **61**, 926–930.

Cuccia, T. and Signorello, G. (2000), 'A Contingent Valuation Study of Willingness to Pay for Visiting a City of Art: The Case Study of Noto', paper presented at the 11th International Biennial Conference of the Association for Cultural Economics International, Minneapolis, USA, 28–31 May.

Green, W.H. (2000), *Econometric Analysis*, Upper Saddle River, NJ: Prentice-Hall.

Hanemann, W.M. (1984), 'Welfare Evaluations in Contingent Valuation Experiments with Discrete Responses', *American Journal of Agricultural Economics*, **66**, 332–41.

Hanemann, W.M., Loomis, J. and Kanninen, B. (1991), 'Estimation Efficiency of Double Bounded Dichotomous Choice Contingent Valuation', *American Journal of Agricultural Economics*, **73**, 1255–63.

Heritage Conservation and Recreation Service (1976), *Evaluation of Public Willingness to Pay User Charges for Use of Outdoor Recreation Areas and Facilities*, Superintendent of Documents, Washington, DC.

Kirchberg, V. (1998), 'Entrance Fees as a Subjective Barrier to Visiting Museums', *Journal of Cultural Economics*, vol. 22 (1), 1–13.

Mossetto, G. (1992a), *L'Economia delle Città d'Arte*, Milan: Etas Libri.

Mossetto, G. (1992b), 'The Economics of the Cities of Art: The Tale of Two Cities', in *Ricerche Economiche*, vol. XLVI (1–2).

Mourato, S. and Pearce, D. (1999), *Dealing with Low Willingness to Pay for Cultural Heritage: Statistical and Policy Implications*, London: Centre for Social and Economic Research on the Global Environment (CSERGE).

Park, T., Loomis, J.B. and Creel, M. (1991), 'Confidence Intervals for Evaluating Benefits from Dichotomous Choice Contingent Valuation Studies', *Land Economics*, **67**, 64–73.

Touring Club Italiano (1969), *Sicilia*, Milan: TCI.

Touring Club Italiano (1999), *La Marca Italia*, Milan: TCI.

11. Organised Art Consumption

Maurizio Caserta

---

1. INTRODUCTION

Enjoying the arts is a time-consuming activity and one that requires input of human capital. In some cases it might even require the services of a consultant or adviser. As a result, various organisational forms are possible in art consumption. At one extreme, households get from the market (or public sector) the work of art and produce 'at home' together with anything else required to appreciate that work of art. At the other extreme, households get everything from the market (or the public sector) required for a proper appreciation of the work of art and add to it only the time they spend on the art. The actual organisational form which prevails in any given circumstance depends on the relative efficiency of one form as opposed to another. This chapter addresses the general question of the organisation of art consumption and focuses on the consumption of museum services in Sicily.

The general question of the organisation of art consumption is addressed by looking at the consumer as endowed with entrepreneurial abilities. Within this general approach, the neoclassical theory of the active consumer is more extensively reviewed: its structure is illustrated and its limits discussed.

Particular attention is then devoted to a specific organisational form of art consumption, consisting in the creation of museum societies which are interpreted here in the light of the economic theory of clubs. Sicily is looked at with reference to ten important museums. An attempt is made to represent the particular organisational form associated with the consumption of the services of these museums. Finally, a few suggestions are given as to the possible interpretation, in the light of the theory reviewed, of the picture that emerges from this representation.

2.   THE ORGANISATION OF CONSUMPTION

Consumption implies the satisfaction of needs. However, for needs to be satisfied, the objects of consumption must be appropriately designed. What makes a design appropriate is not only that the object of consumption be theoretically appropriate but also that consumers be provided with or possess the appropriate capabilities for that kind of consumption. If the need is the need for food, not only must the object of consumption be capable of satisfying that need but consumers must also know what the nutritional values of that particular food are and how to eat it. If the need is the need for arts, not only must the object of consumption be a work of art but consumers must also possess some knowledge of that kind of art and 'speak' its basic language.   Unless such capabilities are available, no match is possible between needs and products and consumption becomes impossible. Different organisational solutions are possible according to whether capabilities are developed and acquired by consumers or whether it is producers who design them or whether some intermediate body develops the necessary language to make the consumer 'speak' to the producer. Each individual solution will imply a different set of boundaries between producers and consumers, with the consumers playing an increasingly active role as a larger set of capabilities is developed within the household.

Such an active consumer has not been ignored in related literature. Bianchi (1998), for instance, has recently collected a number of essays on the entrepreneurial role of consumers. In these essays, consumers are viewed as constantly combining own time, market goods and services and other inputs into ultimate objects of consumption. In doing so, however, consumers do not move from a given technology, thus combining inputs to minimise costs.

They are viewed instead as constantly engaged in a process of discovery of new and better ways of combining those inputs. Such ways of combining inputs are defined as capabilities by Langlois and Cosgel (1998) in one of the essays in the volume. In their essay they look at the question of how far consumers go to develop capabilities for consumption, that is, to what extent consumers act as consultants for themselves. In some cases consumers may be forced to internalise the consultant function because no adequate consultant service is available from the market or because producers do not fix standards for consumption. In other cases such services may be available in the market or may be provided more cheaply and directly by the producer. The actual organisation of consumption that eventually prevails will depend, according to Langlois and Cosgel, not so much on the production and transaction costs, but more significantly on the 'changing distribution of capabilities in the economy'. This means that a deeper understanding of the organisation of consumption is possible by looking at the reasons why, at a given historical time, consumers rather than producers, or consumers rather than consultants, find themselves better equipped to develop and fix standards for consumption.

This approach is quite different from that developed by Becker, Stigler and Lancaster.[1] There consumers are assumed to play an active role in consumption too, as they face and solve a choice of technique problems, combining market goods and services, own time and input of human capital into final objects of consumption. However, they are assumed to select the preferred technique from a given technology, whose process of development is not discussed. This means that a number of interesting questions cannot even be asked. It cannot be asked, for example, why consumers at a given point in time find themselves endowed with specific capabilities. It cannot be asked why, at some other point in time, they have to accept the standards for consumption fixed by producers. What can be asked is a limited number of questions concerning the circumstances under which the provision of consumption capabilities shifts from consumers to producers or vice versa.

The circumstances referred to here are the various configurations of the price system: a change in the price system might shift the boundaries between consumers and producers and lead to a different organisation of consumption.

For these questions to be significant, however, both consumers and producers should be in a position to provide such capabilities. If the distribution of capabilities is very asymmetrical, even a small change in prices can lead to a different organisation of consumption. A different approach will be required in this case to explain the actual boundaries between consumers and producers.

3. ART CONSUMPTION

Art and the consumption of arts and culture require the input of time and human capital. Furthermore, it is not a destructive activity, but one that creates human capital. In his 1994 survey of cultural economics, David Throsby stresses precisely this point: 'In contrast to ordinary goods, the current consumption of cultural goods can be seen as adding to, rather than subtracting from, the process of capital accumulation over time' (Throsby, 1994, p. 3). In the case of live arts, he adds that their consumption 'is highly time-intensive, indicating that the price of leisure time is likely to be more influential in determining demand than the ticket price itself' (p. 7). This means that the paradigm of the active consumer is quite appropriate for the art consumer: art consumption requires that the consumer be endowed with specific capabilities that enable him/her to combine his/her time and market goods and services into final objects of consumption. In the field of art consumption, therefore, just like in most other fields, a problem arises as to the best organisation of consumption, that is, as to the right position of the boundaries between consumers and producers. The solution to the problem might imply, for instance, an organisation where the consumer plays the least active role, thus leaving to the producer the fixing of standards for consumption. Alternatively, the art consumer might become engaged in a process of search and development eventually leading to the acquisition of the necessary capabilities for consumption. In a case like this, it is the art consumer who sets the standards for consumption.

Consumers might also share capabilities among themselves. Capabilities have the nature of non-rival goods, so they can be shared without reducing the benefits of individual consumers. In that case, consumers will specialise in a subset of the whole array of capabilities necessary for art consumption and share that subset with other consumers. To do so, consumers will set up a club where information circulates freely and where they can teach one another.

A club will emerge as the natural organisational solution when non-rival goods such as knowledge and information cannot be easily provided in the marketplace. A very good example of such clubs in the fields of arts is provided by the 'museum societies'. Think of the British Museum Society or the Friends of the Royal Academy in London. Their purpose is not only to support the museum or gallery but also to enable members to enjoy and appreciate them too.

The main question to be addressed in this chapter is what explains, at a given time and in a particular place, the actual organisation of art consumption. What is at issue is whether it is consumers who search for and develop the necessary capabilities, or whether they are provided directly by the producer, or whether an external consultant provides those services, or, finally, whether consumers group together in clubs for the provision of those services. The solution which prevails depends on production and transaction costs but also on the changing distribution of capabilities in the economy. The capabilities in question are not only those required to combine one's time and the art goods and services provided by the market or other institutions, but also those intermediate ones required to successfully search for and develop what can be called the final capabilities.

As pointed out in the general case, the neoclassical approach to the active consumer, that advocated by Becker, Stigler and Lancaster, can significantly answer only a limited number of questions. In some cases, the distribution of capabilities is so asymmetrical that even considerable changes in relative prices, the main determinant in the organisation of consumption in the neoclassical approach, will have no effect on the actual boundaries between consumers and producers. In these cases, a historical analysis of the distribution of capabilities in the economy will shed more light on the actual organisation of consumption. If an art gallery opens in an industrial town, it is very unlikely that consumers will fix standards for art consumption and this will be true no matter how low the price of consultant services or how easy it is to set up a museum society. The standards for consumption will certainly be fixed by the art gallery. However, there are circumstances where significant questions can be asked within the neoclassical approach and where significant answers can be provided. Such circumstances are those where the distribution of capabilities is not so asymmetrical that, if we consider the previous example, it makes sense to ask whether, in order to benefit fully from the art gallery, it is better to read a book, or join the art gallery Friends Society, or follow the gallery guide.

The actual circumstances in which the question regarding the organisation of art consumption is addressed are those found in Sicily. The particular art consumption referred to is the consumption of regional museum services. It is a fact that there is no existing museum society attached to any of these museums, although national-based multipurpose art associations operate in Sicily. In the following, an attempt will be made to explain why this is the case. The explanation will be given within the neoclassical approach. Although the approach has its limits, it seems to provide a sensible answer in the given circumstances. Before turning our attention to Sicily, the 'household production theory', that is, the neoclassical theory of consumption mainly associated with Gary Becker, will be briefly sketched with a view to providing a framework in which to ask the question about Sicily.

4.   THE NEOCLASSICAL ACTIVE CONSUMER

Art consumption can be studied with the aid of 'household production theory'.[2] In such an approach, consumers are supposed to run a production process combining market goods and services, own time and other inputs and yielding commodities for the final consumption. As Becker put it: 'These commodities include children, prestige and esteem, health, altruism, envy and pleasures of the senses, and are much smaller in number than the goods consumed' (Becker, 1991, p. 24). Other examples exist of such commodities. One can think of a meal made through combining market purchases, own time and the ability to cook. In fact, very few commodities are produced just by means of market goods and nothing else; this approach is therefore quite general. It appears obvious in all these cases that changes in the pattern of demand of market goods may not necessarily be due to changes in preferences or in market prices, but might be due to changes in the household production technology or in the input available for production.[3]

Within this approach, consumers maximise the utility function subject to the constraint placed upon them by their money income, to the time constraint and to a production function. The solution to this problem consists in an allocation of time among consumption and work and an allocation of earnings among the various market goods. Changes in market prices and wage rates and thus, changes in the shadow prices of the commodities, will give rise to a different allocation of time and earnings. However, changes in shadow prices might also result from reasons other than changes in market prices or wage rates. In particular, consumption is not just a destructive activity; at times it can create human capital. If this is the case, the cost of production and hence the shadow prices of the various commodities might be reduced as a result of this capital accumulation.

Household production theory appears appropriate for the analysis of art consumption. As pointed out earlier, art consumption almost never results from the use of market goods or services and nothing else. It is one of those 'pleasures of the senses' which, to be pursued, requires one's own time and other inputs as well as market goods or services. Goods and services like CDs, musical instruments, concerts, plays, picture galleries, archaeological collections and archaeological sites cannot be consumed without spending a certain amount of time on them or without the aid of some previous knowledge, both general and specific. What is actually consumed, then, is the outcome of a production process that uses market goods and services, own time and human capital as input. This means that consumers face a choice-of-technique problem in that they have to determine the most efficient combination of those inputs. Stated formally, a household seeks to maximise

$$U = U(Z_1, \ldots, Z_m)$$

where Z_i represents the final commodities consumed by the household, subject to a production function f_i for each commodity

$$Z_i = f_i(x_{1i}, x_{2i}, \ldots, t_{1i}, t_{2i}, \ldots, S_1, S_2, \ldots)$$

where x_{ji} represents the market goods and services; t_{ji} the time devoted by the jth person in the household to the production of the ith commodity and S_j the human capital of the jth person.

It is reasonable to assume that, in order to produce the same commodity, different techniques are available, so that households become engaged in a cost minimisation problem. To solve the problem, the prices of market goods and those of individuals' own time must be given. As to the input of human capital, this can be taken as given or resulting from earlier consumption or investment. The solution to the problem might imply, for example, that to produce a given amount of Z_i, a combination using a few market goods and a large amount of own time is superior to another one using more goods and less time. When it comes to art commodities, it might be the case that a given amount of one of those commodities can be obtained by means of only a few market services and a large amount of time. Think of a visit to a picture gallery; given the price structure, it might be better to buy just the ticket and spend more time visiting the collection, rather than hiring a guide as well as buying the ticket and completing the visit more quickly. Although both combinations provide the same amount of the art commodity, one implies a lower cost than the other.

A change in the price structure could lead to a reversal of the technique, that is, less time and more market goods. What actually happens in this case, is that something that was previously produced 'at home' is bought from the market. While the first option implies that the household creates the information required to produce the commodity 'picture gallery appreciation', the second option implies that the same kind of information comes from the market. What is at issue here is whether the shadow price of the information produced 'at home' is higher or lower than the price of the same piece of information produced outside the household. In this case, information is an intermediate product that is bought from wherever it is cheapest.

In fact, information is not the only intermediate product required for producing the art commodity to be consumed. Comfort is another one. An exhibition can be visited at a convenient hour in an overcrowded gallery or at an unsociable hour in an empty gallery. If comfort is a priority, a visit at an unsociable hour must be arranged, at some cost. Alternatively, one can subscribe to the museum society and get special previews, reserved for members of the society. In this case, comfort will no longer be produced by the household but will be received from outside the household as an intermediate product, designed to be used as input in the production of the 'museum appreciation' commodity. The requirement for this external purchase to occur is that the shadow price of comfort, when produced at home, is higher than the corresponding price (subscription fee) charged by the museum society.

Consumption is not just a destructive activity; at times it can create human capital. If this is the case, the cost of production and, hence, the shadow price of the various commodities might be reduced as a result of capital accumulation through earlier consumption. The more time I devote to arts consumption, the more knowledgeable and perceptive I become, and the more productive I will be the next time I consume arts. Thus, when consumers solve their optimisation problem, they will have to take into account the effects of earlier consumption of arts on subsequent arts capital. Such effects will reduce the shadow price of arts consumption, making such a commodity more attractive than other commodities. Once new human capital is in place, the productivity of the time input is increased. In general, this means that the shadow price of arts will tend to fall over time and the consumption of arts will tend to rise.[4]

The human capital created by households, while consuming, is not a rival good. I can always tell somebody else what the best way to look at a painting is without necessarily depriving myself of the benefit of that piece of information. This means that it is possible to benefit from other people consuming arts. Arts consumption, therefore, produces positive externalities. An interesting question arises as to whether individual households perceive the social advantage of their consumption. Generally speaking, the answer is no.

However, within a museum society, if a suitable context is provided where information can be exchanged, individual subscribers could benefit from the knowledge acquired by other subscribers. When such a context exists, individual subscribers could specialise in the production of specific knowledge and exchange it in the particular context provided. In that case, the human capital produced while consuming is partly used as an input in subsequent consumption and partly exchanged for similar inputs produced by other households. Such inputs will then be used in the household production process yielding arts appreciation. Thus, the household production function will include as inputs, not only the knowledge acquired through their own consumption, but also that acquired by other households.

Following this line of reasoning, different organisational structures of arts consumption become possible. Art commodities may be produced chiefly 'at home' or may result from a production process which takes place almost entirely at the production site. Furthermore, the provision of capabilities necessary for arts consumption could come from a 'museum society' whose main purpose is to circulate information among subscribers. Which structure emerges in the end depends on the preference structure, the consumer income and production and transaction costs. The better equipped the consumer in the capabilities for consumption, the more likely it is that the boundary will be shifted towards the producer. The higher the consumer income, the more costly leisure is, the more likely it is that the boundary will be shifted towards the consumer. The more interested the consumer is in a multiform approach to arts or in building up an identity as an arts consumer, the more likely it is that he/she will join a museum society.

Drawing on the household production approach, a model could be set up to answer all these questions. In the remainder of this chapter a more limited question will be raised and discussed concerning the decision to join a museum society. On the basis of this discussion, a tentative answer will be given to the question of why no such society exists in Sicily.

5.   MUSEUM SOCIETIES AS CLUBS

Museum societies can be looked at as clubs providing non-rival and excludable goods. The economic theory of clubs[5] shows that there is a particular number of subscribers and a particular dimension of the club that maximise the net benefit for individual subscribers. Given the dimension of the club, the higher the number of subscribers, the lower the individual benefit and individual cost. Given the number of subscribers, the higher the dimension of the club, the higher the individual benefit and individual cost. In both cases, the highest net benefit will be found where the distance between the two curves is maximised. When the number of subscribers and the dimension of the club are both variable, an equilibrium combination of the two variables can be determined where the net benefit is fully maximised. Assuming that the individual cost is an opportunity cost, and not just a subscription fee, the club will be joined as long as the net benefit is positive.

As Buchanan shows, given the dimension of the club, it is very unlikely that the net benefit will be positive with a low number of subscribers. For the club to get started, a certain number of subscribers is required so that total cost can be shared. Subscribers could also decide to turn down new subscriptions once the highest net benefit is reached. In the case of a museum society, the good provided by the club is an intermediate good used in the final consumption of museum services. The museum society will be joined, therefore, if the benefit granted by the subscription is higher than the benefit provided by the same intermediate good produced 'at home'. Quite clearly, in this decision, it is the expected number of subscribers that plays the crucial role. What is true for a low number of subscribers, is not necessarily true for a higher number. The benefit provided by the intermediate good produced at home may be higher than the benefit provided by the same good produced by the club when the number of subscribers is low and lower when the number of subscribers is high.

If the same intermediate good can also be bought from the market, the benefit from joining the museum society must be set against the benefit from that purchase as well as against the benefit from home production. It might be that the decision not to join a museum society stems not from the higher productivity of the home production process but from the higher productivity of the market production process. In this case, the intermediate good will be bought from the market and the production of the art commodity will be less time intensive.

Neoclassical consumer theory, therefore, is perfectly well equipped to explain why, at a given time and under certain circumstances, the organisation of arts consumption or, in particular, of museum consumption, is more home based, club based or market based. If households' own time and inputs of human capital figure prominently in the production of the art commodity, the organisation of arts consumption will definitely be home based. If that human capital, or the associated capabilities, are too costly to develop or employ in that process of consumption, households will get the necessary capabilities from the market in the guise of consulting services or similar aids (books, electronic guides, CDs, web sites and so on.). Finally, arts consumption will be club based if sharing capabilities turn out to be the most efficient way of organising consumption. The solution that prevails in any given circumstance will depend on the market price system and on the shadow price system.

However, for this approach to be of any significance, households should be able to move easily from one organisational solution to another. This means, for example, that households can have recourse to their capabilities when there is an increase in the price of books or the subscription fee for the museum society. In formal terms, this means that the isoquants of the household production function show a low degree of curvature. A small change in prices will give rise to a consistent change in the chosen technique. Otherwise, in the case of a high degree of curvature, a given change in prices will not produce a significant change in the chosen technique and, hence, in the organisation of museum consumption. Similarly, firms should be able to provide the necessary consulting services when the opportunity cost of time for households goes up and home production ceases to be efficient. Again, this means that the firm production possibility curve tends to be flat with a slowly decreasing marginal rate of transformation. A small change in prices will make it worthwhile for a number of firms to provide those consulting services.

The possession of a particular capability deserves attention. When deciding whether to join a museum society, households have to form an expectation on the number of subscribers. A high number of expected subscribers may make the subscription worthwhile but a low number may not. In the formation of this kind of expectation, one particular point must be noted: the expectation of a single household depends on the expectations of other households.

Households will therefore have to form expectations of expectations: they will join the club if other households do so; but the other households will do so if they expect the first ones to join the club, which in turn again depends on an expectation. This means, for example, that two households may end up not joining a club despite the fact that, if they co-ordinated their actions and joined the club, they would both benefit from it. What is missing, therefore, is the capability to perceive that there is a general tendency towards a certain behaviour, namely, the tendency to subscribe to a club. If households perceived that the benefits from joining the club are generally taken for granted, they would join the club and find that a high number of people are, in actual fact, subscribing to the club.

Thus a given reduction in the subscription fee will not render the action of subscribing to a museum society necessarily superior to buying consulting services from the market or to producing those services 'at home'. Therefore, the price system alone cannot explain why the particular organisation of museum consumption excludes museum societies. A more significant analysis is one which tries to identify the reasons why households do not possess the capability mentioned earlier. In the case of Sicily, this may be the relevant analysis to conduct.

6. THE ORGANISATION OF ARTS CONSUMPTION IN SICILY

At first glance, it looks as if arts consumption in Sicily tends to be home based. This means that in the consumption of art commodities, it is households rather than producers who fix the standards for consumption. In particular, households produce at home what could be provided by clubs or by the market. In the case of museum services, the market is usually replaced by the public sector, as museums are mostly owned by the public sector. Consulting services, therefore, can be offered both by the market and by the public sector.

Quite clearly, this circumstance is of significant importance. However, in the following, it will be assumed that whenever consulting services are offered by the public sector, they are offered at the same conditions as the market.

The evidence in favour of the previous argument comes from ten important Sicilian museums. They are archaeological museums and art galleries. Nine of them are regional museums, one is a national museum. The archaeological museums are: the Agrigento National Archaeological Museum; the Paolo Orsi Regional Archaeological Museum in Syracuse; the Antonio Salinas Regional Archaeological Museum in Palermo; the Aeolian

Regional Archaeological Museum in Lipari; and the Regional Archaeological Museum in Camarina. The art galleries are: the Regional Museum of Pottery in Caltagirone; the Messina Regional Museum; the Palazzo Abatellis Regional Gallery in Palermo; the Agostino Pepoli Regional Museum in Trapani; and the Palazzo Bellomo Regional Gallery in Syracuse.

Evidence shows that no museum society is attached to any of these museums. When it comes to consultant services, various forms are possible. Museums can aid consumption by providing libraries and bookshops. They can also offer photographic and historical archives. Finally, they can offer lectures and guided tours. The evidence[6] shows that only two museums offer lectures on a regular basis. Six out of ten offer guided tours. Only two have historical archives while five have photographic archives. Finally, seven have a library but only three have a bookshop. It looks then as if the consultant function in the consumption of museum services in Sicily is, in most cases, internalised by households. This means that it is households who fix the standards for consumption and use their own capabilities to produce what would otherwise be bought from the market or received from the public sector or a club.

One possible explanation for this state of affairs lies in the relatively higher efficiency of households in the production of the goods or services required for the consumption of museum services, an explanation perfectly in line with the neoclassical approach to art consumption. To support it, one could say, for example, that museums find it difficult to have regular lectures on issues regarding the exhibits because the expected low rate of attendance does not allow covering costs. Similarly, one could say that the expected low number of subscribers does not justify subscribing to a museum society as the benefits associated with that subscription are smaller than the benefits of home production. In this chapter, particular attention has been focused on the role of museum societies and on the fact that hardly any society of this kind exists in Sicily.

When we look at countries like the USA or Britain, the popularity of museum societies stands out quite clearly.[7] Italian museum societies do not enjoy the same degree of popularity. According to FIDAM,[8] the national association of museum societies, 87 museum societies exist in Italy. Of these, only one is based in Sicily, the *Amici dei Musei, dei Monumenti e dei siti di Sicilia*, in Enna. It is, therefore, quite clear that arts consumption in Sicily is not organised around museum societies. Earlier it was suggested, as a tentative explanation for this particular organisation of arts consumption, that the cause was the expected general low interest in setting up a museum society. Such an expectation, due to the expected low benefits, makes subscribing to museum societies hardly worthwhile. The result of all this is that very few societies are established.

The next question to address is what explains the expected general low interest in setting up a museum society. It must be pointed out that this is an expectation of an expectation, which means that once a conviction is established it is very difficult to eradicate it, as expectations are constantly fulfilled. If I do not do something in the expectation that somebody else will not do it in the expectation that I will not do it, I create the conditions for expectations to be constantly fulfilled. The conviction that museum societies are useless will genuinely make museum societies useless, as hardly anybody will join them. But where did this conviction originate from in the first place?

Many tentative answers could be given here. One could look at the role played in Sicily by public authorities, which might have made private provision of public goods redundant in some cases. Alternatively, one could look at the preference for informal groups as opposed to formal groups: why should I join a club when I can do basically the same things a club does with my own circle of friends? In fact, the origin of that conviction may even be a matter of chance: this would not make the persistence of that conviction less understandable.   Once it is established, the conviction is capable of reinforcing itself through time.

7.   CONCLUDING REMARKS

The purpose of this chapter was to provide an explanation of an aspect of the organisation of arts consumption in Sicily. This aspect concerns the role of bodies known as museum societies. The central observation of this chapter was that in Sicily, these societies, unlike the rest of Italy, and especially unlike other countries, are virtually non-existent. This state of affairs was interpreted in the light of the neoclassical consumption theory, stressing the role of household production. The argument put forward was that museum societies prove inefficient compared to home production. The consequence of this relative inefficiency is that households produce 'at home' what they could otherwise receive from a club like a museum society. The reason for this inefficiency lies in the low number of expected subscribers. Such a low number prevents the club from providing high benefits to its subscribers and makes home production superior to club production. Changes in prices will alter the incentives faced by households and might change the organisation of consumption.   However, changes in prices sometimes produce little change in the organisation of consumption.   A reduction in subscription fees, for example, may not make museum societies any more popular than they were before the reduction.   What might be required instead, is a consistent increase in the expected number of subscribers. This means that in some cases, the analysis of the reasons why such low expectations are entertained by households is of greater relevance than the analysis of the effects of changes in prices. This is why a few suggestions were made about the reasons for such low expectations.

NOTES

1. See Becker (1965), Stigler and Becker (1977), Lancaster (1971).
2. The main references for the 'household production theory' are Becker (1965, 1996); Stigler and Becker (1977).
3. Caserta and Cuccia (2001) discuss an application of household production theory in the case of the supply of arts labour.
4. These effects are described in Stigler and Becker (1977).
5. See Buchanan (1965).
6. The main source of information is the museum web sites.
7. To give just a few numbers concerning London museums, Friends of the Royal Academy has 83,000 subscribers, Friends of the Tate 26,000, the British Museum Society 12,000 and Friends of the V&A 12,000.
8. *Federazione Italiana degli Amici dei Musei.*

REFERENCES

Becker, G.S. (1965), 'A Theory of the Allocation of Time', *Economic Journal*, **75**, 493–517.

Becker, G.S. (1991), *A Treatise on the Family*, Cambridge, MA: Harvard University Press.

Becker, G.S. (1996), *Accounting for Tastes*, Cambridge, MA: Harvard University Press.

Bianchi, M. (ed.) (1998), *The Active Consumer*, London: Routledge.

Buchanan, J.M. (1965), 'An Economic Theory of Clubs', *Economica*, 32, 1–14.

Caserta, M. and Cuccia, T. (2001), 'The Supply of Arts Labour: Towards a Dynamic Approach', *Journal of Cultural Economics*, (25), 3.

Lancaster, K. (1971), *Consumer Demand: A New Approach*, New York: Columbia University Press.

Langlois, R.N. and Cosgel, M.M. (1998), 'The Organisation of Consumption', in M. Bianchi (ed.) (1998), *The Active Consumer*, London: Routledge, pp. 78–90.

Stigler, G. and Becker, G.S. (1977), 'De Gustibus non est Disputandum', *American Economic Review*, **67** (2), 76–90.

Throsby, D. (1994), 'The Production and Consumption of the Arts: A View of Cultural Economics', *Journal of Economic Literature*, March, vol. XXXII, 1–29.

PART IV

Comparative Perspectives

12. Constrained Choice and Heritage Designation: Its Application in France

Françoise Benhamou

1. A THEORETICAL FRAMEWORK

Property rights consist of the right to use, obtain income from and sell an asset. In the case of a house or château, these rights consist of living in the building or renting it, and they allow the owner to change the façade, build a new wing or additional square metres, and so on. Restrictions occasionally may occur, for example, when the changes affect the rights of neighbours.

If the house or château is listed, the case is different. The owner meets a panoply of obligations whose purpose is preservation. The Chief Architect for Historic Monuments verifies the compatibility of the work with the original building; he oversees the work, and chooses the companies to be hired.

These restrictions to property rights result from the nature of historical monuments as assets. They are privately owned assets with a public dimension resulting from their cultural and historical value. In other words, one can consider that they constitute a legacy to be passed on to future generations. They are a part of the nation's artistic heritage. This twofold nature (private and collective) implies a specific definition of property rights.

Barzel (1997) provides a stimulating framework for understanding the nature of property rights. An asset has multiple attributes. From an economic point of view, property rights are not related to the whole asset but to their various attributes.[1]

As commodities have many attributes,[2] including the set of services that they provide, the full knowledge of attributes and ownership is costly. Thus, property rights are never fully delineated, and a rise in transaction costs may result from incomplete information. These costs include the cost of defining and protecting property rights.

Moreover, Barzel shows that 'two or more individuals may own distinct attributes of the same commodity' (Barzel, 1997, p. 4). In such a case, restrictions on the owner's behaviour should be imposed in order to protect the rights of the other owner(s). These restrictions are costly and they imply implicit or explicit contracts which involve the possibility of pursuing the other owner in order to protect one's rights.

Historical buildings are multi-attributed assets. Some attributes belong clearly to the private owner but others have to be shared out among different owners. They concern the historical quality of the asset and its cultural characteristics. In other words, some attributes belong to the nation and the state or local authorities have a right to capture a part of the property rights linked to the historical or cultural dimension of the property.

In such a situation, a separation has to be imposed on property rights of the same commodity. This separation presents two characteristics. Firstly, it is costly. Costs increase in order to delimit the respective rights and duties of each owner. In some cases, the separation is even impossible. Secondly, it introduces a diminution in the individual well-being of the owner, which then has to be compensated for.

2. PUBLIC OWNERSHIP VS. COMPENSATION FOR SHARED OWNERSHIP

If we accept the economic justifications for the government's power over cultural or historical private properties, two alternative arrangements are possible. Let us examine in which cases it is legitimate to take private property for public use. In other cases, a compensation payment is submitted to the appliance of a set of obligations for the private owner.

2.1 The Case for Public Domain

If an individual owns some attributes and the rest of society the others, separation implies that the individual owner transfers a subset of the commodities' attributes and retains the rest. As Barzel notes in a very different field from cultural heritage, 'restrictions on the owner's behaviour may be imposed in order to enhance the separation of their individual rights' (1997, p. 4). The complete separation prevents the owner from carrying out an inaccurate restoration; it defines the rights and limits of the rights of the private owner. It also prevents the private owner from prohibiting the use of the asset by other agents. This use is strictly limited to two different elements:

1. a right to visit; and
2. a right to control the cultural and architectural qualities of the property.

If the separation is not clear or if it is impossible, free-riding occurs: nobody is ready to pay for the upkeep and restoration of the building. A solution is the transfer of the commodity into the public domain. The state or public authorities can acquire ownership of the building, in special cases specified by law: in France, in the case of an emergency, when the survival of the building is threatened by its bad state of repair, a decree can lead to such an acquisition. This decree is submitted to a decision by the *Conseil d'Etat*, the Court of Appeal for administrative litigation. This power to acquire property from private individuals may occur through a non-consensual transfer.[3]

A non-consensual transfer implies opportunity costs. Costs are linked to the time required to arbitrate in the case of a dispute concerning ownership. They include a sum to be paid to the owner in the form of indemnities for the loss of a part of his/her property rights.

2.2 The Case for Compensation

According to Miceli, government regulation of private property does not generally require compensation 'it is viewed as a legitimate exercise of the government's police power' (Miceli, 1997, p. 137).

On the contrary, when ownership is shared, two arguments for compensation apply:

1. First of all, the owner's rights are limited by the regulations. As seen above, he/she cannot hire the repair companies he/she wishes, and has to take orders from an expert when he/she undertakes restoration work. These restrictions imply an increase in the cost of the work: the cost of restoring listed monuments is generally higher than for unlisted monuments (Leniaud, 1992), since restoration implies both the hiring of skilled labour and the use of specialised and hence expensive building materials.
2. Secondly, the income flow generated by the asset may be limited by those restrictions. For example, the impossibility of altering a building in order to locate a McDonald's restaurant generates a loss for the owner. The rights to receive the income flow from the asset are restricted by listing.

Thus we can hypothesise that listing affects the market value of the asset.

Moreover, as Creigh-Tyte (2000) notes, the owner of a normal building which is newly listed will face limitations which did not apply before the listing decision and which have not already been discounted in the pre-listing decision. The greater the limits of any transformation of the building for commercial purposes, the lower the value of the asset. This is the implicit origin of compensation.

3.   THE LEVEL OF COMPENSATION

In France, 39 per cent of listed buildings are houses, castles and manors (Table 12.1). Private owners own 33 per cent of listed buildings, whatever their function, and 47 per cent of listed or registered buildings (Table 12.2). The cost of collecting information and the cost of implementation and enforcement of law and regulations are probably high, for different reasons, including the uniqueness of cultural commodities.   Unfortunately, these transaction costs have never been seriously evaluated. This could be due to a kind of collusion between owners and governments. These costs grow with the number of regulations and laws defined by heritage policies.

Table 12.1 Types of listed or registered buildings in 1994

	Listed or registered	Listed
Religious buildings	41	57
Military buildings	4	4
Public service buildings	6	5
Castles and manors	15	11
Houses	26	18
Economic or industrial buildings	3	2
Others	5	3
Total	100	100

Source: Cardona and Lacroix (1998).

Table 12.2 Ownership of listed or registered monuments in 1994

	Listed or registered	Listed
State	4	7
Department	1	2
City	44	56
Non-profit institution	1	-
Private owner	47	33
Other	3	2
Total	100	100

Source: Cardona and Lacroix (1998).

In order to adopt a policy in this field, these costs should be compared with the individual or collective costs generated by free markets.

In France, as in most European countries (except in the Low Countries), compensation is organised through subsidisation. In France, the law stipulates that the state may finance 50 per cent of restoration work on historic monuments (these subsidies can reach 100 per cent if local authorities also provide subsidies) and between 20 and 40 per cent of restoration work for registered monuments. Protection also offers tax deductions for building or repair work and for management or caretaker fees, and relief from inheritance tax.[4]

The loss for the private owner should be less than the increase in the collective well-being, even when taking into account the transaction costs resulting from the application of heritage policies and the compensation for the disadvantage paid to the owner. A difficulty arises from inaccurate information on the value of the asset. Compensation should result from an evaluation of heritage and especially from the loss in value of an asset resulting from listing. As Allison et al. (1996), Frey (1997) and Frey and Oberholzer-Gee (1998) show, the evaluation of heritage is not easy.

The only existing survey on the effects of listing on the value of buildings is provided by the UK Department of National Heritage (1994), analysed further in Creigh-Tyte (2000). Creigh-Tyte compares returns of listed and unlisted office properties in the UK since 1980. According to this survey, 'over the period 1980–1995, listed properties built before 1974 match or exceed their unlisted equivalents of the same vintage. Moreover, the percentage of annual return for the oldest (pre-1945) listed properties exceeds the return for all properties by 0.8 of a percentage point' (p. 225). This issue can be interpreted as an argument against compensation: if the value of a commodity is not affected by regulations, why should governments consider listing as a source of prejudice to the owner? But data collected in this survey only concerns offices; analysis of data on residential buildings could throw additional light on the question of value.

Such a survey is not possible in France, since there are no data available. Nevertheless, the permanent growth in the number of listed (and registered) buildings may be viewed as a sign of a weak decrease in the value of an asset due to listing. Tables 12.3 and 12.4 show this growth.

Therefore two hypotheses are possible:

1. Listing is a mark of architectural quality (which determines the market value of the goods): one can reasonably suppose that the title of 'historical monument' increase the value of the asset, since it is an indication of quality. But the degree of improvement depends on different environmental factors[5] and collective tastes.

2. The amount of subsidies overcompensates the loss due to listing.

Table 12.3 Total number of historical monuments listed

Year	1849	1859	1869	1879	1889	1899
Total	759	797	1,354	1,523	2,133	2,337
Year	1909	1919	1929	1939	1949	1959
Total	3,426	4,929	6,847	7,907	8,797	9,340
Year	1969	1970–79	1980–89	1993		
Total	10,128	11,267	13,393	14,529		

Sources: Agnus and Zadora, 1987 and Cardona and Lacroix, 1999.

Table 12.4 Total registrations in the additional inventory of historical monuments since 1962 (thousands)

Year	1962	1963	1964	1965	1966	1967	1968	1969
Total	14.8	15.0	15.3	15.6	15.7	15.8	16.0	16.3
Year	1970	1971	1972	1973	1974	1975	1976	1977
Total	16.5	16.8	17.2	17.6	17.9	18.4	19.0	19.3
Year	1978	1979	1980	1981	1982	1983	1984	1985
Total	19.7	20.1	20.4	20.7	21.0	21.2	22.1	22.4
Year	1986	1987	1988	1989	1990	1991	1992	1993
Total	23.1	23.9	24.7	25.3	26.1	26.8	27.6	28.2
Year	1994	1995	1996	1997				
Total	28.8	29.4	30.0	30.5				

Sources: Agnus and Zadora (1987), Cardona and Lacroix (1999).

Therefore listing is costly, and its impact on collective well-being is ambiguous. Moreover, the costs resulting from listing imply that governments should make choices from among the set of commodities that could be expected to be preserved by listing. According to Peacock (1998), governments have accelerated the process of accretion with various measures. Nevertheless, public decisions are constrained by:

1. uncertainty linked to changes in collective tastes and knowledge; and
2. cost of obtaining sufficient information.

Individuals who perceive that the value of their assets or commodities will increase with listing, are encouraged to apply for listing; formal or informal contracts should restrain undesirable behaviour, especially moral hazard positions on preservation.

4. CONCLUDING REMARKS

A complementary hypothesis concerning subsidies and tax deductions concerns their restrictive function: they create a regulation cost, and thus tend to limit the propensity of the legislator to list new buildings. They also limit the losses due to the potential capture of the regulator by the owners who wish to increase rents as a result of the certification of quality due to listing.

NOTES

1. Barzel introduces a categorical distinction between legal and economic notions of ownership (Foss and Foss, 2000).
2. For a definition of the notion of characteristics, see Lancaster (1979).
3. We can consider such a case as a compulsory purchase.
4. For more details, see Benhamou (1996).
5. Lichfield (1998) brings an indirect contribution to this question.

REFERENCES

Agnus, J. and Zadora, E. (1987), *Repères sur les Monuments Historiques*, Paris: La Documentation Française.

Allison, G., Ball, S., Cheshire, P., Evans, A. and Stabler, M. (1996), *The Value of Conservation*, London: English Heritage.

Balsamo, I. (1997), 'André Chastel et l'Aventure de l'Inventaire', in Nora, P. (ed.), *Science et Conscience du Patrimoine*, Paris: Fayard, pp. 257–67.

Barzel, Y. (1997), *Economic Analysis of Property Rights*, 2nd edn, Cambridge: Cambridge University Press.

Benhamou, F. (1996), 'Is Increased Public Spending for the Preservation of Historic Monuments Inevitable? The French Case', *Journal of Cultural Economics*, **20** (2), 115–32.

Cardona, J. and Lacroix, C. (1999), 'Statistiques de la Culture. Chiffres Clés', La Documentation Française, Paris.

Creigh-Tyte, S.W. (2000), 'The Built Heritage: Some British Experiences', *Recherches Economiques de Louvain*, **66** (2), 213–30.

Department of National Heritage (1994), *What Listing Means: A Guide for Owners and Occupiers*, London: DNH.

Foss, K. and Foss, N. (2000), 'Assets, Attributes and Ownership', *International Journal of Economics of Business*, forthcoming.

Frey, B.S. (1997), 'The Evaluation of Cultural Heritage. Some Critical Issues' , in M. Hutter and I. Rizzo (eds), *Economic Perspectives on Cultural Heritage*, Basingstoke: Macmillan, pp. 31-49.

Frey, B.S. and Oberholzer-Gee, F. (1998), 'Public Choice, Cost–Benefit Analysis, and the Evaluation of Cultural Heritage', in A. Peacock (ed.), *Does the Past Have a Future? The Political Economy of Heritage*, London: Institute of Economic Affairs, pp. 27-54.

Lancaster, K. (1979), *Variety, Equity and Efficiency*, Oxford: Basil Blackwell.

Leniaud, J.M. (1992), *L'Utopie Française. Essai sur le Patrimoine*, Paris: Mengès.

Lichfield, N. (1988), *Economics in Urban Conservation*, Cambridge: Cambridge University Press.

Miceli, T.J. (1997), *Economics of the Law. Torts, Contracts and Property Litigation*, Oxford: Oxford University Press.

Peacock, A. (1998), 'The Economist and Heritage Policy: A Review of the Issues', in A. Peacock (ed.), *Does the Past Have a Future? The Political Economy of Heritage*, London: Institute of Economic Affairs, pp. 1-26.

13. Funding Heritage: The Scottish Experience

Gerald Elliot

Scotland, like Sicily, is a significant region with a devolved administration within a unitary nation state, the United Kingdom. Recently, the degree of devolution to Scotland was extended; for the past two years there has been a parliament with a Scottish Executive which independently determines arts and heritage expenditure in Scotland, though this is within a total block grant agreed by the UK national parliament in London.

Sources of funding for arts and conservation in Scotland are varied (see Appendix Tables 13.1–2 and Figure 13A.1). Performing arts – theatre, music, literature, fine arts and crafts, all come within the compass of the Scottish Arts Council (SAC). The Arts Councils in the UK are parastatal bodies (QUANGOs).[1] SAC gets a yearly grant from the UK government, at present about £30 million, which it allocates at its discretion. Its clients range from Scottish Opera, which takes £8m. of the total, to individuals receiving a few hundred pounds.

The Scottish Arts Council has its critics, who resent that an unelected QUANGO should decide the allocation of public funds. However, the Council, appointed by government, is broadly based and consists of people carefully selected for their interest and expertise in the arts. The alternative, giving the responsibility to the civil service administration, with the sporadic intervention of parliamentary committees, is much less attractive in the UK, where 'arm's-length' bodies that distance government from direct control are a preferred model of administration.

Museums and galleries have their own annual grant, most of which goes to the National Museum and the national galleries in Edinburgh. Local authorities also play an important part in covering the running costs of their museums and art galleries. Glasgow, a city larger than Edinburgh but without its national status, finances its own considerable galleries and museums. Where new buildings are required, central government steps in.

In recent years the British government has been increasingly ready to provide money for improvement and expansion, and the new devolved government in Scotland will bring even greater pressure in this direction.

There has been much government activity over the past twenty years to renew the fabric of larger cities. This is seen as contributing directly to the welfare of the people living there; but also, more broadly, as restoring the self-respect of the community, providing employment and encouraging new industries to develop there. In Scotland, Glasgow has been the prime example, a city rich in fine buildings but hit hard by the decline of its traditional shipbuilding and engineering. Edinburgh has been less in need of large-scale restoration but the elegant terraces and crescents of its early nineteenth-century New Town have benefited from schemes to encourage owners with grants to renew their houses. Some of these projects have come through local government, others from central government. Scotland has also had, for many years, a development body (currently named Scottish Enterprise) with funds to promote employment and new industry. Some of those funds have passed into conservation of buildings whose activities will generate employment. The recently built Festival Theatre in Edinburgh had Scottish Enterprise among its funders.

There are other direct sources for conservation money. Historic Scotland, and its counterpart in England, English Heritage, are government agencies which have developed from the civil service departments which looked after ancient monuments. Historic Scotland exhibits and markets its sites and buildings. Ruined castles and abbeys are prominent in its range, a reminder of Scotland's earlier turbulent history. The agency also conducts archaeological work and provides grants for restoration of historic buildings outside its stewardship.

The National Heritage Memorial Fund (NHMF) came into being from money set aside by the British government for a scheme to buy out private land development rights, which was dropped. It provides money principally to conserve old buildings but its support now extends to many other aspects of historic conservation, including landscape, museums, education and conservation trusts. Its activities have been immensely strengthened by the arrival of the National Lottery. When this was founded in 1993, the government decided to earmark a proportion of the proceeds to arts and heritage. Through it, large sums of money have been made available of which Scotland has had an appropriate share. The arts share from the National Lottery, amounting to £20 million or so a year, is administered by the Scottish Arts Council, and the heritage share, of similar size, by the NHMF. There have recently been changes in government lottery policy and the level may be reduced somewhat but the contribution will still be weighty.

The new lottery money has helped with the continuing problem common to all countries of getting hold of enough money to preserve buildings and objects of historic value, particularly acute in places like Sicily, where heritage is rich and income below the European average. For many years, British government policy has been that public expenditure in this area should be matched by private money. Apart from making projects possible which government could not contemplate on its own, this enlists the active interest of people outside the narrow circle of administrators and professionals and helps to build an organisation more enterprising and more responsive to public needs. When the building of a new Museum of Scotland was finally approved by government after years of pressure from its board of trustees,[2] this was only on the basis that a large proportion of the cost should be met by private funds to be raised from charitable trusts, companies and individuals.

That was triumphantly achieved. Substantial money came from the USA, with the Royal Yacht *Britannia* berthed in New York to attract wealthy contributors.

Private benefactors have always been central to arts funding in the USA. Some have extended their interest to Europe. Names like Sackler and Beinz appear on many of the public galleries. The UK has benefited from similar home-grown 'Mycenases', though not to the same extent. There is a drive in the UK to endow private patrons with social prestige similar to that which they enjoy in the USA, while providing tax breaks to make their generosity less painful.

It is as important to bring private responsibility into heritage projects as it is to get private money. When the Heritage Lottery Fund supports, say, the restoration of a disused church in a Highland village, it is concerned to establish that the church will have a good future use and that there is an organisation in being to run it properly. It may eventually have to be the local government council which takes responsibility, but a private body is thought to be preferable.

A few years ago, the NHMF acquired and endowed a small country house, Paxton, of historic interest, in the Scottish Borders. It put it in the hands of a trust board which administers the endowment income but also works to supplement it by admission charges and the development of other activities which would attract visitors. It now has children's playgrounds, a music festival, a restored salmon house on the banks of the river Tweed and art exhibitions, all in conjunction with its original purpose as a country house museum. It also has a support circle of Friends of Paxton House. It is unlikely that a government organisation could have had the flexibility or imagination to achieve so much.

Friends' societies have become increasingly popular in Britain. They are open clubs formed by individuals and bodies who are ready to make an annual subscription to support an activity in which they believe, be it an opera company, museum, gallery or festival. They get some privileges from this, most directly in reduced entrance charges. The financial benefit that their subscriptions bring to the organisation is not large but they form a core of enthusiasts who help to promote interest. They provide volunteer help in running the organisation and in fund raising. Perhaps most important of all they can be called on to champion the organisation if it comes under threat, perhaps from a government unsympathetic to its financial needs. The Scottish National Gallery is funded almost entirely by direct government grant. It has so far managed to finance its ambitions by the clever wooing of rich donors. Unfortunately, it is precluded by government from charging entrance fees (an ancient British tradition which dies amazingly hard). It has recently set up a Friends' body which, if properly cultivated, will give added political and possibly financial strength.

Nearly all the bodies in Scotland which distribute heritage funds, and the larger of the organisations which receive them, have their own independent boards. These may be appointed by government, as with the Scottish Arts Council, or in the case of private organisations, by their members (this amounting often to self-election). These boards are, as would be expected, of varying competence but they do understand their responsibilities and try to carry them out conscientiously. As well as bringing their own skills and experience to the service of the organisations, public board members provide a conduit between the organisations and the public they are intended to serve much more directly than could come through a government department and a minister. When, a few years ago, there was considerable conflict in Scotland over a proposal by the national galleries to move the Portrait Gallery from Edinburgh to Glasgow and to set up a larger, new gallery there, the battle was fought, not with the Minister and his department, but with and through the individual trustees. The increasing role of private support in public bodies broadens the responsibilities of trustees. Friends' bodies give support, but will also develop their own views on the organisation, not always welcomed by its boards and director. The time may come soon for Friends to have a nominee on government appointed boards.

Much of the large sums needed for conservation of buildings can only be found through government and its agencies but there is plenty of room for private local conservation trusts, which can at least provide the initiative which will later attract money from public or substantial private sources. In Edinburgh, there is the Cockburn Association, a local civic trust named after an outspoken conservationist judge of the nineteenth century. Through much of its history it has been mainly engaged in fighting the wholesale demolition policy of the City Council. In these more enlightened times it has set up its own conservation trusts encouraged by the Council and restored and sold a number of old houses which private developers found too risky.

The leading private conservation body in Scotland is the National Trust. It was set up to take into care and conserve historic buildings which otherwise could have fallen into ruin. It has a membership of over 230,000, but their yearly subscriptions cover only a small part of its annual costs. Much of the rest comes from donations, legacies, and the income from a large endowment which it has built up. It is also greatly dependent on grants from the public sources already mentioned. Initially, its field was castles and country houses whose owners could no longer afford to maintain them but it has extended to urban houses both grand and humble, gardens, stretches of coastline, offshore islands, and even a large Highland estate, with its full sporting and agricultural management. It relies greatly in the running of its properties on voluntary help. Visitors to its domains number over 1,700,000 per annum. The National Trust in Scotland, which has developed in parallel with its much larger counterpart in England, is always being pressed to extend its scope but must restrain itself to within prudent financial limits. For many years now it has refused to take on new properties offered unless they are fully endowed by the donors and it strives to make its properties pay for their costs through entrance charges and services such as shops and holiday cottages.

It is appropriate, lastly, to mention the help provided by European funds, notably the European Regional Development Fund, in the conservation of Scottish heritage buildings. Access to these monies is of course through the British government. The administration in Scotland works closely with its counterpart in London to take the maximum advantage of what is on offer from Brussels. I have no doubt that Sicily is just as skilful in getting these benefits.

I hope that this survey of the institutions for heritage conservation in Scotland may be of some help to Sicilians in considering new ways of conserving their own heritage. Italy and Sicily have their own institutions, some of them similar to those in Scotland but there may be dark places where the practice of other countries could throw some light. It seems to me particularly, that Sicilians should turn some attention to the potential of private initiative and funding and a higher degree of private interest, with strong boards of management, the enlistment of personal wealth in the conservation cause and the vigorous encouragement of support through Friends' and members' bodies.

APPENDIX: FINANCE OF THE ARTS AND HERITAGE IN SCOTLAND*

Table 13A.1 Expenditures on the arts and heritage in Scotland [a] *(£ m.)*

Funding allocator	1999–2000	2000–2001
Historic Scotland	32.2	32.3
National Museums	15.3	14.4
National Galleries	10.6	11.6
Scottish Arts Council	29.6	30.9
Lottery fund	21.8	19.7
Museums and galleries	34.4	34.8
Local government[b]	37.2	34.8
Business sponsorship	11.9	16.0
National Trust for Scotland	(1998) 22.2	(1999) 20.4

Notes:

a. Double counting may be present in these figures.

b. Estimated figures.

Sources: Peacock et al. (2001); Historic Scotland (1998–1999; 1999–2000); The
          National Trust for Scotland (1998–1999).

Table 13A.2 European funding for the arts and heritage in Scotland (£ m.)

Total amount	11,359
Historic Scotland	69
National Trust for Scotland	727

Sources: The Arts Council of England (1986–1987; 1997–98); Historic Scotland
          (1998–1999); The National Trust for Scotland (1998–99).

---

* Data assembled by Anna Mignosa.

Figure 13A.1 Arts and heritage funding in Scotland (£ m.), 1997–2000

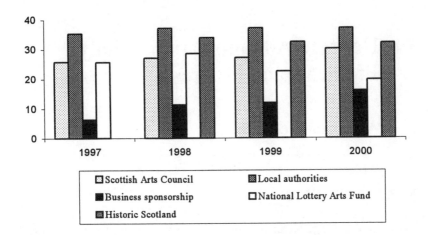

Sources: Peacock et al. (2001); Historic Scotland (1998–99; 1999–2000).

NOTES

1. QUANGO stands for quasi-autonomous non-governmental organisation and is a body favoured in the UK for distributing funding from government sources to grant recipients in several areas, the arts, heritage, sport and so on. Universities are also funded that way.
2. Arts and heritage organisations in the UK are typically non-profit companies with charitable status. The Board of Trustees has legal responsibility for ensuring sound management and financial probity.

REFERENCES

Arts Council of England (The) (1986–87; 1997–98), *Artstat – Digest of Arts Statistics and Trends in the UK*, London, UK: Arts Council of England.

Historic Scotland (1998–99; 1999–2000), *Annual Report and Accounts*, Edinburgh, UK: Historic Scotland.

National Trust for Scotland (The) (1998–99), *Annual Report and Accounts*, Edinburgh, UK: National Trust for Scotland.

Peacock, A., Baird, G., Elliot, G., Havergal, G., Macdonald, D., Massie, A. and Murray-Watson, A. (2001), *Calling the Tune – A Critique of Arts Funding in Scotland*, Policy Institute, Edinburgh.

14. Heritage Administration in Italy: Problems and Progress

Annalisa Cicerchia

---

1. INTRODUCTION

The cultural heritage sector in Italy, after a long period of stasis, in recent years has experienced a number of important legislative innovations and new policy orientations. The main developments are:

1. a shift, albeit tentative and slow, from a piecemeal emergency situation to a planning–programming approach;
2. an increased role for cultural policies within the general framework of public policy;
3. enhancement and diversification of financial resources for protection and conservation;
4. simplification of administrative procedures;
5. a new impulse to heritage reconstruction and restoration aimed at public use;
6. increased awareness of the economic and occupational dimension of heritage, once uniquely seen as a source of expenditure; and
7. a general government reform in terms of easing control and decentralisation.

Italian heritage policies are, however, subject to considerable elements of conflict, which mainly concern the use made of cultural built heritage and central–local government dynamics.

The way these conflicts are dealt with, and hopefully solved, will significantly affect the future of a promising sector for Italy.

2. CONSERVATION AS A MISSION: THE STATE'S CENTRALISED ROLE IN HERITAGE CONSERVATION

In a country like Italy, where an overabundant production of rules and regulations is the norm, cultural heritage is relatively Spartan. The basic text (the Bottai Law) dates back to 1939.[1] Its main aim is protection and conservation and it is still a fundamental reference for at least two major questions:

1. definition of which goods are to be intended as cultural and therefore what has to be protected; and
2. definition of general government mandates and missions, that is, who is to provide protection and how.

Only in late 1999 was there a reorganisation into a *Testo Unico*, which by nature is systematic rather than innovative, of accumulated legislative changes in this sector over time, which are often contradictory and even difficult to interpret.[2]

The overriding feature in the basic legislation was identifying the essential state mission towards heritage, namely protection and conservation, where 'protection meant exclusion from the interaction with work other than protection itself, by subjects other than the state centre' (Barbati, 2000). It is possible that on this same legal basis, which is the mandate for that mission, and certainly in the interpretations which prevailed up until quite recently, protection and conservation were conceived almost exclusively for the benefit of future generations, while the interests of the present generation were paradoxically considered less important. Protection could possibly consist of a number of merely conservative provisions, that is, the introduction of restrictions on use and other forms of limitation. Owing to a lack of adequate financial resources, little else followed. For a long time, according to the prevailing idea on conservation in that period, stacking and storing masterpieces and antiques of great value in museum warehouses and basements was considered reasonable, albeit extreme, behaviour from the state mission in this area.

3. RAISING MONEY FROM HERITAGE: RENTABILITY AND OTHER USES

One of the key problems in strategic public planning is co-ordination between all those involved who are in a position to affect its success in design planning and implementation, for many reasons and in different roles. Its co-ordination often seems Utopian, particularly in Italy. At a closer glance, the problem of disorganisation, which periodically returns at the expense of effectiveness when dealing with direct and indirect heritage policies, rather than due to a lack of co-ordination, seems to be the result of a conflict between different objective functions. Although this problem deserves closer examination it is however not possible here, as only a few, sketchy examples can be provided.

If, on the one hand, since 1939, the objective function has seen the state administration mission on cultural heritage as one of protection, on the other hand, the objective function which inspired the so-called 'cultural mines' operation by the Ministry of Labour in the mid-1980s[3] or other extraordinary heritage-centred initiatives to create new jobs, was aimed at reducing unemployment or promoting economic development in areas lagging behind (an analogous, European-scale approach can be found in Jacques Delors' White Paper). In the former case, heritage is the object and main target of the policy; in the latter, it is the means to a different end.

Since the mid-1990s, many other objective functions have been increasingly aimed at heritage, namely the generating of public funds, whereby heritage is considered a stock requiring careful administration. In this perspective, the latest Italian economic and financial planning documents often submit ideas on the possible use of cultural heritage to raise money. Further objective functions inspire policies which somehow involve heritage at different territorial levels of government.

Obviously, the whole question may become extreme and may be seen as the potentially irresolvable conflict between an interpretation of cultural heritage as an instrument to attain a vast array of economic policy goals and a vision which highlights its belonging to the world of ends. A clear analysis of this dispute, in terms of public choice, and its underlying rationale may be found in Causi (1999). The first point raised by Causi is how to create a balance between goals which are right for cultural policies and which place heritage in the category of ends, and other economic policy goals, which consider heritage an instrument for the attainment of other ends. In his opinion, heritage policies should never superimpose other economic policy goals with their own goals and the main aim of public heritage policies should be to maximise the different kinds of benefits which can be derived from the very existence of cultural heritage, rather than other goals, such as enhancing employment (Causi, 1999). Once it has been established that cultural policy goals cannot be subordinated to other goals, it is possible, or rather necessary, to lead those responsible for such policies to plan and implement their actions taking into account their effects on other economic variables, to control and orient them.

If the entire question is formulated within the framework of an organic and taxonomic system of relationships among general strategic objectives and means to attain them,[4] there is little doubt that the cultural use and enhancement of the cultural and symbolic value of heritage, belong to the category of ends.[5]   This does not mean that economically sound and employment-generating policies are not as desirable as they used to be, more or less deliberately and intentionally, when that was the main practice prevailing in Italy prior to the 1970s.   On the contrary, those policies represent fundamental action programmes for the attainment of strategic and cultural objectives and may sometimes even be viewed as built-in constraints on the programme of action.

It would be a serious (logical and hence political) mistake, however, to confuse ends and means and to propose heritage policies solely aimed at increasing employment and local economic development, rather than at widening and deepening cultural heritage uses for present and future generations.

Within a programmatic framework, increasingly stimulated by EU initiatives,[6] which is intended to give the different heritage management strategies their right place, the intermediate-instrumental objectives of protection, conservation, restoration and sound management of economic and employment variables could be integrated into a co-ordinated and comprehensive system, capable of rationally handling the unavoidable trade-offs and drastically reducing conflict among the different stakeholders.

Admittedly, once means and ends are put in their proper place, not only do production of public value and employment necessarily belong to means, but so do heritage protection and conservation, thus completely reversing the long-standing practice of heritage administration in Italy.

4.   HERITAGE FOR SALE: A CURRENT DILEMMA

After decades of jealous love, in the 1990s, the Italian state has come to the conclusion that part of its cultural built heritage should be sold.   This turning point was reached after a long, slow and halting process, arising from two converging, albeit distinct, lines of political action:

1. the need to restore public finances, and therefore include that particular form of stock represented by the public cultural built heritage in the accounts; and
2. the need to economically rationalise the whole management of public properties, getting rid of all unnecessary forms of non-profit-making public property through privatisation.

Vaciago (1999) has discussed this controversial process, which led to the recent implementation of this principle.[7] The application of market principles to cultural built heritage nonetheless raises two objections. The first is based on a vast literature ascertaining that the promotion of heritage cultural value is, and remains, an eminently public task. The second, in the traditional line of cultural economics and heritage studies, states that heritage-generated 'profit' is far more complex and multifaceted than a financial one. If, however, the question of privatisation has finally taken root in Italy, even if in a strongly conditional way, this is due to the fact that the very definition of cultural heritage is still too vague and comprehensive to represent a clear selection of what deserves protection and should by no means be subjected to public control.

In Italy, the tendency to enlarge the concept of heritage and cultural goods, also common in other countries, is spreading, possibly as a reaction to an old, exclusive, classical tradition to label only 'antiques and works of art' as 'cultural'.[8] The current trend is to make heritage coincide with material culture. If, in principle, this stance can be agreed upon on an intellectual and even cultural–political level, in strictly technical terms, it produces more problems than it solves. Considering the widening gap between the amount of heritage to be protected and the public resources to provide such protection, there is a serious need to define heritage on a planning–programming level strongly enough to make it unique. This definition of cultural heritage/goods would never claim to be universally accepted. On the contrary, it should merely have an operational and programming sense. It would be unique in the sense of 'being capable of discriminating' what is to be protected because of its excellence (for historical or artistic merits or because it was, so to speak, 'culturally selected' by the razor of time) and must therefore be enhanced and optimally managed while what is not excellent must therefore settle for a back seat in the rush for the allocation of scarce resources.[9]

In other words, what is suggested here is the adoption of a programming concept of cultural goods/heritage, to be applied solely in a planning framework, in support of public decision-making.[10]

In this way, we touch on the delicate question of heritage evaluation, a problem which Italian authorities have typically tried to evade through the uncontrolled broadening of the heritage category. There are currently some 500,000 listed buildings, 17,700 scheduled monuments and 8,500 conservation areas in England. In Italy, apart from some unofficial attempts,[11] we have no idea of what we have. What we do know, is that there are many sundry items in built heritage – buildings, archaeological areas, not to mention mobile goods – to be protected. There is not even a complete list of *vincolato*, that is, buildings whose cultural interest has been officially recorded and are therefore restricted in use and ownership. The 'Risk Map' has so far located 51,000 monuments, including 17,000 churches, 8,200 villas and palaces and 2,000 museums and libraries (Bodo and Cicerchia, 2000).

Even today, if we could find a number of possible theoretical and technical solutions to the problem of evaluation and selection,[12] especially in the field of multi-criteria analysis, in political terms, a satisfactory resolution is still a long way off. Marco Causi (1999) has described in detail the never-ending struggle of the so-called technical staff (that is art historians and archaeologists) at the Heritage Ministry against more selective approaches.

There is, however, an important change in this field, brought about by the Economic and Financial Planning Document for 2000, which compelled the Heritage Ministry to establish a set of rules to select culturally important public buildings which will be put up for sale from time to time.[13] The Ministry now has a deadline to declare whether a building is culturally important or not, so that the sale can proceed, or otherwise to state why it cannot be privatised. On the one hand, this change may be considered as a first step towards a process of evaluation along the above-suggested paths. On the other hand, the process sounds dangerously akin to the old Italian tradition of opting for day-to-day solutions to problems, rather than a planning-oriented and consistent management style.

5. HOW IS THE TERRITORIAL DIMENSION OF HERITAGE BEST ANALYSED AND MANAGED?

Cultural built heritage, like natural heritage, is intrinsically territorial. Manmade landscapes and regions, especially in Europe and in Italy, are built around monuments, historical cities and archaeological sites. Nonetheless, over the past fifty years, cultural heritage policies in Italy have failed to include coherent, territory-based strategies. Despite a lively debate on decentralisation, 'territory' is still seen in mere juridical and administrative terms, which is tantamount to not being perceived at all. Current approaches waver between very detailed and singular views of the individual 'cultural good' and (though less frequently) macro, statistical, quantitative analysis that does not identify local and territorial peculiarities.[14]

On the contrary, policies for a valuation and cost-effective management of cultural heritage basically require an appropriate territorial dimension. Defining such a dimension is no easy task, on institutional, conceptual and theoretical levels. This would imply investigating the relationship between cultural heritage value and its territorial environment, developing variables or indicators to express this relationship, the impact of land-use planning on cultural heritage conservation and valuation policies and the different impacts of these policies on different categories of cultural goods.

Whatever the outcome of such complex investigations, there can be little doubt that cultural built heritage certainly has a strong local nature and may have, depending on what Lichfield (1988) calls cultural quality or on its tourist appeal, historical meaning or a mix of other factors of regional, national or international importance.

Similarly, for impacts, local ones are obviously strong, from the environmental, economic and employment point of view. Measuring them, however, is still difficult, despite recent (and less recent) interesting efforts (see Lemaire and Ost, 1984, and Ost, 1999).

How do those different impacts affect the political process and decision-making policy? As regards the present state of heritage policies in Italy, the state retains its key role in protection and conservation, despite a general orientation towards decentralisation, while making institutional room for regional and local government in the field of management and valuation (an ambiguous concept, whose meaning ranges from restoration to increased access).

Carla Barbati (2000) notes that the centre, in any case, struggles to cover every requirement; it intervenes everywhere and resists being side-lined. The risk in considering local government as simple counterparts is real: the new regulation establishes a number of negotiating venues between state and regional government, laid down in the recent constitutional reform which increased its strength and power.

The protective role of the state remains the most important function concerning heritage. Critics observe that protection neither exhausts nor solves the entire range of possible public interventions in the field of cultural heritage. They believe that proper heritage protection cannot be identified by a set of purely conservation measures, again through the application of restrictions and constraints. Barbati, on the other hand, remarks that protection must be compatible with other functions: heritage valuation, enhancement, use and management, carried out in such a way as to acknowledge that cultural goods are a resource in themselves and help to find resources for their conservation.

The concept of protection itself, however, should be discussed in more detail. Recent research carried out in Italy thanks to EU Structural Funds,[15] has been aimed at building a network of information and data management at local (municipal) level to minimise natural and manmade risks to cultural built heritage (seismic, hydro-geological, pollution, anthropological and so on), based on the assumption that local authorities are better qualified for accurate diagnosis, tailored prevention and timely alert. This aspect of protection is important in Italy, a country generously endowed with both monuments and every kind of risk, of which Pompeii, destroyed by the eruption of Vesuvius in AD 79 is symbolic as is the Basilica of St. Francis of Assisi, devastated by an earthquake in 1997.

Probably, a desirable scenario for the future might lie in a new concept of protection and conservation by the state, which should carry on with its recently acquired role of both financing body and major fundraiser for heritage; co-ordinating policies at national and community levels; providing the general framework for a full development of local potential; and setting nation-wide strategic objectives and performance measures for the public sector.

6.   CONCLUDING REMARKS: IN FROM THE MARGINS

Among the pictorial themes dear to young artists from foreign academies who spent a year or two of their training in Rome in the eighteenth century and who were often great painters, was the rural landscape with ruins as a recurring theme. Wild countryside, where Roman monuments are depicted in a state of decay, covered with ivy, amidst grazing sheep. Although this familiar picture may have been a little extreme, it manages to capture what used to be the fate of a large part of cultural built heritage in Italy. The last few years have witnessed a dramatic change in state heritage policy: a real march in from the margins of the institutional scene, towards its decisional and strategic core.

Not only has the Heritage Ministry been constantly increasing its budget (by more than 40 per cent between 1996 and 2000), thanks also to a new possibility of diversifying its sources of income (such as the lottery) but, and more importantly, in 1999 it was included in the selected group of ministries which decide national economic policy choices and the allocation of state resources.

The development of new relationships between the public and private sectors (new fiscal provisions, cultural foundations, and so on) is also seen as important progress. There is also a promising role for the so-called Third Sector, which is still being investigated.

In this march in from the margins, the Italian state probably still defends its role as 'Guardian of the Treasure' with a certain amount of jealousy. Many observers criticise this attitude but the state is no longer a 'sleeping guardian', and there are signs, such as a set of programming agreements between state and regional government, which in time may help the Guardian to learn how to share its burden for the benefit of all.

NOTES

1. In that same year, Law no. 1497 was enforced: it is equally fundamental for the way landscape is conceived as a public asset.
2. See Cammelli (2000).
3. 'Cultural mines' refers to an initiative sponsored during the 1980s by the Italian Ministry for Labour, aimed at temporarily employing young people (it was hoped that there would be no less than 10,000), especially in southern Italy, in cataloguing cultural heritage. The entire operation took place without substantial guidance and planning by the Heritage Ministry, and, despite huge extraordinary investments – about \$300 million, slightly more than the entire expenditure of the Heritage Ministry at the time – its actual results were disappointing: an average cost of \$7.5 million for each of the 39 projects which were approved (with a maximum peak of about \$22,000,000 and a minimum of \$2,000); the total number of new job positions created was way below expectations (3,800) and ephemeral. As far as cataloguing itself went, the result of 'cultural mines' was modest. Institutional and organisational conflicts, as well as scientific problems (the activity did not comply with national standards established by the *Istituto Centrale per il Catalogo e la Documentazione*) resulted in an almost complete failure of the entire enterprise.
4. See Cicerchia (1998).
5. In 1993, Di Palma, Bianchini and Marchesi developed a hypothetical programme structure for a possible budget reform in the Italian Heritage Ministry. It was based on the Ministry statute and regulations, and itt identified four general goals for the Ministry's activity: 1. basic knowledge of heritage; 2. heritage protection and maintenance; 3. increased access to and evaluation of heritage; and 4. enhanced innovative research. These general goals were subdivided into specific first- and second-rate goals. Policies and actions, measured through goal and outcome indicators, were then attached to second-rate goals. Finally, the experiment proposed an *ad hoc* budget for the Ministry, related to the suggested programme structure (Di Palma et al., 1993).
6. See, for instance, the increased role of cultural resources in the 2000–2006 Community Support Framework.
7. Still a principle, however: a few buildings (less than 50, compared to an estimated patrimony of over 40,000 between state and municipal properties), upon authorisation by the Heritage Ministry, have indeed been put up for sale, but the process is only just beginning.
8. This is the definition contained in the 1939 law.
9. Which, to be true, since 1996 are increasingly more scarce in Italy, thanks to a markedly innovative policy of resource diversification, to be dealt with in the

concluding section of this chapter.

10. Benhamou has recently suggested seriously considering the hypothesis of de-listing cultural built heritage. The idea is enticing, but hardly applicable to Italy, because it assumes that there is an actual list to cut. Such a list does not exist in Italy.

11. Like 'The Risk Map of the Cultural Heritage in Italy' (1996), where a tentative census of the existing heritage was attempted on a bibliographic basis.

12. For a synthetic review of the outstanding valuation methods, see Cicerchia (1998).

13. See Cicerchia (2001) for a more detailed discussion on this *Regolamento*.

14. In Italy, the sole noteworthy exception is the Heritage Ministry's Risk Map Project, where a quantitative approach to cultural heritage merges with the perception of local differentiation on the matter of vulnerability of goods and the natural or man made hazards, on a scale reaching municipal data desegregation (Bodo and Cicerchia, 2000).

15. I am referring to the two Risk Map projects carried out within the framework of the ARCHIMED and INTERREG programmes, both started in 2000. They both reproduce the centrally applied methodology of 1996 to create local systems of civil protection for cultural heritage.

REFERENCES

Barbati, C. (2000), 'Nuova Disciplina dei Beni Culturali e Ruolo delle Autonomie', *Aedon*, **2**.

Bodo, C. and Cicerchia, A. (2000), 'The Risk Map of the Cultural Heritage in Italy', *World Culture Report 2000*, Paris: Unesco.

Cammelli, M. (2000), 'Il Testo Unico, il Commento e . . . Ciò che Resta da Fare', *Aedon*, **2**.

Causi, M. (1999), 'Riforma della Pubblica Amministrazione e Modelli di Intervento sui Beni Culturali', *Documenti di Lavoro ISAE*, **3**, 7–18.

Cicerchia, A. (1998), 'Una Struttura di Programma per i Beni Culturali', *Economia della Cultura*, **3** (8), 295–313.

Cicerchia, A. (2001), 'Il Progetto OIKIA. Una Banca Dati a Supporto della Decisionalità Pubblica in Materia di Patrimonio Culturale', *Aedon*, **1**.

Di Palma, M., Bianchini and Marchesi (1993), *I Beni Culturali. Linee Guida di Programmazione e Valutazione dei Progetti*, Naples: Formez.

Lemaire, R.M. and Ost, C. (1984), 'Evaluation Economique du Patrimoine Monumental. Presentation d'une Méthode d'Analyse', CEE, SG/CULTURE/22/85/FR, November, Brussels.

Lichfield, N. (1988), *Economics in Urban Conservation.*, Cambridge, UK:

Cambridge University Press.

Ost, C. (1999), 'Spatial Indicators for the Economic Valuation of the Cultural Heritage', paper presented at the international seminar on 'Regional Planning Requirements of Cultural Heritage Conservation', DGX – CE Raphael programme, 26 and 27 January.

Vaciago, G. (1999), 'Il Futuro degli Immobili Pubblici', *Documenti di Lavoro ISAE*, Rome, **1**, 7–24.

Postscript

Since this book was written, there has been a reorganisation of public administration in Sicily introducing new managerial rules. At the time of going into print, these rules had not been fully implemented and authors were not able to take them into account in their analysis.

Index

'active' conservation 38, 39, 40–41
admission charges 8, 103–4, 140, 147
   see also Noto case study (contingent
      valuation study, willingness to
      pay); willingness to pay (WTP)
advertising costs, and valuation of
    cultural heritage 127
aesthetic value 122
Alberini, A. 131, 150, 154
Allison, G. 99, 185
Ames, P.J. 66
Andreoni, J. 140
Anheier, H. 88
archaeological discoveries, and
    information technology 106
archaeological sector, favouring of 81,
    84–85
archaeological sites, Sicily 102
art consumption
    clubs 172–74, 175–77, 191–92
    neoclassical approach 167–72, 173
    organisation of 164, 166–68, 171, 173
    Sicily 174–77
arts, economic study of 48
Assessorato Regionale dei Beni Culturali
    Ambientali (Regional Office for
    Culture, Sicily) 21–22, 53
    bureaucracy, problems caused by
      28–29
    funding/expenditure 23–24, 27
associations, nature of 95
asymmetric information 50–51, 54, 123

Bank of Sicily, Foundation of 96–99
banking foundations 96–99
Banks, J.S. 52, 55
Barbati, C. 197, 202
Barbetta, G.P. 88, 92
Barzel, Y. 181–82
Becker, G.S. 166, 168
Benhamou, F. 9

best practice frontiers 66–67
Bianchi, M. 165
Binni, L. 112
Bishop, R.C. 148
Blaug, M. 48
Bobbio, L. 48
Boccacin, L. 94
Bockstael, N. 128
Bodo, C. 201
Borzaga, C. 93
Breton, A. 55, 56
Brosio, G. 48
Brown, G.M. Jr 128
Buchanan, J.M. 172
built heritage 4
    definition 3
    as public goods 11
    territorial dimension of 201–2
bureaucracy
    monitoring/control of 52, 54–55,
      56–58
    problems caused by 28–29
bureaucrats, and policy-making process
    50–51, 54–55

capabilities, and consumption 165–68,
    171, 173
capital accumulation, and art
    consumption 166, 169, 170–71
Carson, R.T. 125, 139
Causi, M. 198, 201
Cicerchia, A. 201
'cities of art' 152
Clawson, M. 127
clubs 167, 172–74
    friends' societies (UK) 191–92
    museum societies 167, 168, 171–74,
      175–77
co-operatives 95
Cockburn Association 192–93
Colonna, C. 16